Lola's War

Olivera Simic

Lola's War

Rape Without Punishment

Olivera Simic
Griffith Law School
Griffith University
Nathan, QLD, Australia

ISBN 978-981-99-1941-3   ISBN 978-981-99-1942-0 (eBook)
https://doi.org/10.1007/978-981-99-1942-0

© The Editor(s) (if applicable) and The Author(s), under exclusive license to Springer Nature Singapore Pte Ltd. 2023
This work is subject to copyright. All rights are solely and exclusively licensed by the Publisher, whether the whole or part of the material is concerned, specifically the rights of translation, reprinting, reuse of illustrations, recitation, broadcasting, reproduction on microfilms or in any other physical way, and transmission or information storage and retrieval, electronic adaptation, computer software, or by similar or dissimilar methodology now known or hereafter developed.
The use of general descriptive names, registered names, trademarks, service marks, etc. in this publication does not imply, even in the absence of a specific statement, that such names are exempt from the relevant protective laws and regulations and therefore free for general use.
The publisher, the authors, and the editors are safe to assume that the advice and information in this book are believed to be true and accurate at the date of publication. Neither the publisher nor the authors or the editors give a warranty, expressed or implied, with respect to the material contained herein or for any errors or omissions that may have been made. The publisher remains neutral with regard to jurisdictional claims in published maps and institutional affiliations.

Cover photo by Una Škandro, reproduced with permission of DAH Theater, Belgrade, Serbia. Performance "For Your Own Good" by DAH Theatre.

This Palgrave Macmillan imprint is published by the registered company Springer Nature Singapore Pte Ltd.
The registered company address is: 152 Beach Road, #21-01/04 Gateway East, Singapore 189721, Singapore

*There are some who are in darkness
And the others are in light
And you see the ones in brightness
Those in darkness drop from sight.*
—*Bertolt Brecht*, The Threepenny Opera *(1928)*

*Dedicated to Lola and all women survivors of wartime rapes
who did not receive the justice they deserved.
Their courage and resilience remains a powerful reminder
of the importance of placing women's narratives of war and its aftermath
in the literature on armed conflicts and mass atrocities.*

Acknowledgments

I would like to thank Associate Professor Barbora Hola, Professor Heather Douglas, Zoe Rathus AM, Dr. Victor Igreja, Professor Elisabeth Porter and three anonymous reviewers for their valuable comments on previous drafts of this book. I would also like to thank Ellie Conroy and Elizabeth Englezos who provided much needed research support. Thank you to Dr. Tanya Lyons for her expert knowledge and keen editorial skills that greatly improved the final manuscript.

The Law Futures Centre together with the Griffith Law School organised a seminar at which I presented some ideas from this book. I thank all those who listened, questioned and provided critical comments that helped me find new ways of grappling with some of the ideas. I would also like to thank all of my interlocutors in Bosnia and Herzegovina, from whom I have learnt the meaning of justice and care in times of transition over many years.

Thank you to Palgrave Macmillan for showing interest in my project and providing ongoing support throughout writing this manuscript. Griffith University provided the funds and allowed me the much needed time to complete the numerous fieldtrips, the research and writing.

Finally, I express my deepest gratitude and respect to Lola, who has entrusted me with her story and without whom this book would not have come into existence.

Contents

1	Introduction	1
2	War and Rape	11
3	Lola's War	35
4	Becoming a Victim in the Eyes of the Law	67
5	Crime with No Punishment	101
6	Women Living in 'Not-War Not-Peace' Time	127
Epilogue		149
Bibliography		157

CHAPTER 1

Introduction

At the time of writing this introduction I came across a new book by African-American feminist philosopher Myisha Cherry who claims that 'rage' can be a useful emotion in our struggles against injustices.[1] Cherry joins other feminists who argue that women should be entitled to unleash their anger in the same way that men do.[2] 'Feminist rage' and 'feminist curiosity'[3] are emotions that I channel into my own work. I lean on my rage against misogyny to produce writing that I hope will serve as a catalyst for societal change.

Listening to and learning from women survivors of mass atrocities has been my preoccupation for the past twenty years. I have documented women's stories of suffering and resilience during armed conflicts and their aftermaths. Learning about women's violation at the hands of men

---

[1] Myisha Cherry, *The Case for Rage: Why anger is essential to anti-racist struggle* (Oxford University Press, 2021).

[2] Soraya Chemaly, *Rage Becomes Her: Power of Women's Anger* (Atria Books, 2018).

[3] Cynthia Enloe, *The Curious Feminist: Searching for Women in a New Age of Empire* (University of California Press, 2004).

leaves me with overwhelming feelings of incomprehensibility and bewilderment, and I am torn between feeling 'terror as usual'[4] and 'shock'.[5] Time after time, each story enrages me anew. These emotions serve as the impetus for my writing and have prompted the writing of this book.

I come from a country ravaged by war. I was nineteen when the war started in Bosnia and Herzegovina (BiH). My brother was twenty-two when drafted into the army and expected to shoot at his compatriots. The 1992–1995 war was fought between former friends and neighbours and resulted in more than 100,000 deaths. Some 2.5 million people were displaced, 20,000 women were raped,[6] 800,000 homes were destroyed and there was widespread abuse of human rights.[7] In July 1995 the first genocide in Europe since World War Two was committed in Srebrenica, when 8000 Bosniak men and boys[8] were systematically murdered by the Serb armed forces in the span of a few days.[9] BiH is a land in which a total of 750 mass graves were uncovered after the war, and

---

[4] Michael Taussig, *The Nervous System* (Routledge, 1992) 17–18.

[5] Ivana Maček, *Sarajevo Under Siege: Anthropology in Wartime* (University of Pennsylvania Press, 2011) 3.

[6] This is the number that is widely used in the literature and it represents an estimation. The real number of women victims of wartime rape during the war in BiH has never been confirmed. On the critical analysis and discussion around the number of victims of wartime rape in BiH which has 'a thin evidentiary basis', see Janine Natalya Clark, *Resilience, Conflict-Related Sexual Violence and Transitional Justice: A social-ecological framing* (Routledge, 2022), 297.

[7] Edina Becirevic, *Genocide on the River Drina* (Yale University Press, 2014).

[8] Bosniaks are the ethnic group of native Bosnian Muslims against whom genocide was committed in Srebrenica in 1995. I use the term interchangeably with Bosnian Muslims.

[9] On 26 February 2007, the International Court of Justice (ICJ) issued its opinion in *Application of the Convention on the Prevention and Punishment of the Crime of Genocide (Bosnia and Herzegovina v. Serbia and Montenegro) (Judgment)* [2007] ICJ Rep 43. In its first judgement interpreting the 1948 *Convention on the Prevention and Punishment of the Crime of Genocide*, opened for signature 9 December 1948, UN DOC A/RES/3/260 (entered into force 12 January 1951), the ICJ held that the massacre of Bosnian Muslims at Srebrenica in July 1995 amounted to genocide.

with some 7000 people still missing.[10] It is the post-conflict and post-genocide nation state in which survivors live together with perpetrators and bystanders—all burdened with the trauma of war and unresolved past grievances.

In this complex socio-legal environment I undertook a longitudinal, in-depth case study of a Bosnian Serb woman wartime rape survivor with the aim of exploring her encounters with the transitional justice mechanisms, particularly the war crimes trials and reparation programmes implemented in BiH. The case study discusses three interrelated aspects: a quest for justice of a woman rape survivor; her experience as a trial witness; and the personal and judicial legacies of surviving wartime sexual violence.

To explore these phenomena I use the case of Lola, a woman who was gang raped during the war in BiH in the spring of 1992 while she was detained in a Croatian detention camp with her three young children. Lola is not the real name of the woman survivor whose story this book is based on. Although she wanted to be identified with her full name, in accordance with the ethics approval gained from Griffith University Human Research Ethics Committee (GU Ref No: 2022/339) a pseudonym is used in order to protect her identity. Names and other identifying details of people who feature in this book (including acquitted war criminals) and Lola's family members and acquaintances have also been changed or simply not used to protect their privacy. The names of prosecuted war criminals have not been changed. No facts have been altered. Using Lola's case as an illustration, this book aims to disclose and reflect on the broader socio-legal issues related to the relevance and consequences of the systemic failures experienced in a post-conflict context. This book explores the meanings of justice by using the in-depth narrative of a woman wartime rape survivor who has come out the other side of a legal trial but remains empty handed and with no justice in sight.

Lola's life serves as an illustration that enables me to shine a spotlight on BiH's institutional failures and demonstrate how laws that should

---

[10] 'Bosnia-Herzegovina: 25 years after the end of the conflict COVID-19 brings additional uncertainty for the families of the missing', *International Committee of the Red Cross* (Web Page, 18 January 2021) https://www.icrc.org/en/document/missing-persons-bosnia-herzegovina-25-years-after; Faruk Zorlu, 'Over 7000 Victims of Bosnian War Still Missing', *Anadolu Agency* (Web Page, 21 July 2018) <https://www.aa.com.tr/en/europe/over-7-000-victims-of-bosnian-war-still-missing/1210377>.

be working for those most vulnerable and endangered, did not work for Lola, and instead they let her down at each point of her journey. Her case enables me to delve into the nuances and dangers of institutional deficiency and the effects and impacts of this on Lola's life. If the system has failed once as it has in Lola's case, my concern is that it can fail again. In that sense, Lola's case may serve as a cautionary tale that invites more nuanced and empirically based investigations into women's experiences with the transitional justice mechanisms.

In the literature, scholars refer to those who have experienced wartime sexual abuse as 'victims' and/or 'survivors'. I acknowledge that women who have experienced wartime rape may prefer one identity over the other and some use either term, to describe their experiences at different times. Lola however, never called herself 'survivor' and I wanted to honour her choice when talking about her experiences. In our many conversations she always referred to herself as 'victim' of the crimes she experienced. It is common for women who experience wartime rape to use the term 'victim' because the word is used by police and in criminal proceedings to denote that the person who has experienced an offence is not responsible for the offence. In this study, I use the terms 'victim' and 'survivor' interchangeably because Lola is a victim but she is also a survivor; a resilient and brave woman who keeps struggling for justice and truth against all odds. Furthermore, the terms 'wartime rape', 'sexual abuse in war' and 'sexual violence in war' are also used interchangeably throughout the study as they all refer to the rape and other forms of sexual violence committed during the war in BiH.

This book is a micro-level, individual-focused study based on repeated interviews that bring to the fore Lola's 'justice lenses' and her 'justice narrative' to demonstrate how transitional justice mechanisms—notably criminal trials and reparation—are lived through and embodied 'on the ground'. This is a qualitative study and a thorough investigation of the ways justice is experienced by a woman survivor in a particular post-conflict context. It is an intimate and close-up examination of one woman's 'justice journey' and the reader will be taken on this journey in order to gain a deeper insight into the everyday life of a survivor of wartime sexual abuse. Through listening to the voice of Lola the reader will gain a deeper understanding of the BiH war and its multigenerational consequences.

Lola is a rural Bosnian Serb woman who in the first two months of the war became a widow, displaced, unemployed, homeless and disabled. She was the sole caretaker of her nine-month-old baby, four-year-old daughter and six-year-old son. They were all forcibly taken from their family home and sent to the detention and rape camp. In the span of just a few weeks, Lola's whole life was torn into pieces and turned into a nightmare. Lola was twenty-nine years old at the time. Her husband was thirty-two years old when he was drafted by the Serb armed forces. He was killed in the first few days of the war.

My study draws on multiple interviews with Lola and dozens of court and other records of her case. Lola gave me access to numerous documents that she had preserved over the years, such as copies of original documents, including doctors certificates, court decisions, audio and video material, administrative paperwork, transcripts, appeals and other materials, all of which amplified her story. I also drew on semi-structured online correspondence and face-to-face interviews with the representatives of local non-governmental organisations (NGOs) and state institutions, all of whom have come into contact with survivors of wartime rape in BiH. This variety of sources has helped me to understand the physical and psychological costs associated with the practice of transitional justice mechanisms which have inadvertently further exacerbated the trauma, poverty and discrimination that women such as Lola have experienced.

My study focuses on women and their lived experiences, yet it moves beyond abstract notions of 'women victims of wartime rape'. The reader is immersed into the life of one woman. Lola's narrative provides a vivid insight into what it is like to live through—and try to make sense of—transitional justice and its mechanisms.

RAPE WITHOUT PUNISHMENT AND THE EVASION OF JUSTICE

Scholars of transitional justice have seldom paid attention to the lives of women survivors following criminal trials for wartime rape. This book addressed this gap in the literature and argues that the case study of a woman wartime rape survivor *living through* and *practising* transitional justice mechanisms provides original insight into the legacies of wartime rapes. The book incorporates the local expertise gleaned by a survivor who has struggled to rebuild her social and inner worlds and sustain hope for the future by depicting what (in)justice in transition may look like. The study here aims to provide a rich, empirically based and reflective account of what I call 'the transitional justice life trajectory' of a survivor, and offers a critical perspective on the (in)justices of transitional justice projects. This book illustrates the reality of 'doing transitional justice' and engages the reader with the real-life impacts of the otherwise well-intentioned transitional justice mechanisms. With this study I seek to understand how women, such as Lola, articulate their traumatic life experiences (filled with destruction, loss of loved ones and the enormous physical and mental pain associated with this) and discern the intersection of the realm of the everyday and the realm of transitional justice processes.

The study exposes the manifold struggles a woman survivor has to go through in order to achieve some form of justice from state authorities in post-war BiH. It reflects on Lola's lived experiences and the consequences of practising justice, which can be unpredictable, even accidental. In Lola's case, only one of the eight wartime rapists was found guilty. He was sentenced to six years imprisonment in September 2016, yet the BiH judiciary never executed his sentence. Six years has since passed (at the time of writing), and all the while Lola's fear has not diminished. She fears that her wartime rapist will track her or her children down to seek revenge for testifying against him. At the time of publishing this book, Lola's rapist is still at large and inaccessible to justice authorities.

I still vividly remember the moment when Lola told me that her wartime rapist was not in jail. I had phoned Lola to tell her how all the challenges that she faced during the trial had paid off by seeing her rapist prosecuted and sentenced. I cheerfully said, 'Finally, he is prosecuted. Twenty-five years later, but still there is a justice and he is in jail now'. I expected Lola to share my sentiment but instead a silence stretched between us. I waited. I realised something was not right but never expected to hear what I heard that day.

'But, he is not in jail. He is free', Lola said carefully, almost whispering as if I was a child needing to be protected from bad news.

I was confused. I grimaced my face and felt numb with awfulness. 'But, he was sentenced, no?' I asked her startled, my mouth dry with anxiety. My heart started pounding, my hands sweating. Finally, I could hear her breathing again.

'He has never been arrested', Lola said patiently, but firmly.

My mind was having trouble taking things in. 'What? Sorry, what did you just say?' I was thinking I must have misunderstood.

'No one arrested him and put him into the jail', she said slowly but in a high pitched voice to make sure I heard her this time.

I closed my eyes and took a deep breath to calm myself down. There was a feeling of muteness. Like my ears were plugged up as if I was underwater. I cannot remember our conversation past that moment. I sank down into my chair, blacked out, completely fixed on what I just heard. My eyes dropped to the floor.

We then exchanged a few more words and I promised I would call her again. I hung up the telephone, leaned back and looked around. I felt empty and stared at the wall for the next couple of minutes. I did not know where to put my mind. I mulled over what she had told me. I thought about Lola's life and the end result of her justice journey some thirty years after the crime had been committed. I remember repeating to myself, 'Justice? Is this justice?' I was enraged. I took up pen and paper and made notes, bullet points, a trajectory of her life over the past three decades. It was the one-page skeleton draft of Lola's life that would soon turn into this book. It took me less than a year to write it. I had never written a manuscript that fast before. Anger kept pressing on me to write more, to research, to read, to investigate where Lola's rapist could possibly be but more importantly why no one had arrested him. I understood that my feelings of 'being upset' were my vehicle that kept me alert and pushed me to investigate this situation and write about it. The more I investigated, the more unsettled I became, but I was also more determined than ever to document Lola's story and share it with the world.

The political conditions in BiH have failed survivors such as Lola. They have not enabled or supported their recovery but rather taken their toll on their physical and mental health. The lingering effects of the sexual violence committed against Lola in 1992 continue to affect not only her but her children and grandchildren. This is the story of Lola's protracted interaction with the legal and other state institutions which hold the power to officially legitimise her suffering and compensate her for it. It is also the story of her attempts over many years to gain for herself and her children, state-recognition as the civilian victims of the war. My study does not claim that Lola's experiences are representative of other women victims' experiences, but her story does shed new perspectives on the meaning of the often intangible term of 'dealing with the past'. It brings to light the dark knowledge[11] about the hidden obstacles women and their children may face when deciding to strive to achieve some degree of legal satisfaction for the rape crimes committed against them during the BiH war. It also showcases the level of endurance and tenacity it takes to seek justice but not necessarily receive it through the legal system. The war in BiH is over but the wounds from war remain raw. The aim of this book is to ensure that women survivors are not forgotten and their wounds are acknowledged and taken care of. The book also serves as a reminder that some women continue to live in fear of the threat of danger from their wartime perpetrators, even those prosecuted and sentenced decades after the crimes were committed.

Structure of the Book

Chapter 2 lays out the historical and theoretical context for this study. It provides an overview of the wartime rape trials and transitional justice mechanisms in BiH. The chapter reviews the literature on sexual violence in war in BiH and situates my study among the wealth of knowledge that has been produced by feminist scholars and practitioners working on this issue. Chapter 3 frames the book. In this chapter, I narrate Lola's story of victimhood and position myself within the study. Here, I also outline the methodology used in order to process and analyse the data I collected. In Chapter 4, I analyse how Lola fought for years to become recognised as a victim of crimes against humanity in the eyes of the law, enduring complex and victim unfriendly bureaucratic processes. In Chapter 5, I argue that while criminal trials for war crimes before national courts have received some scholarly attention, there has been scant attention devoted to the actual outcomes of such trials for beneficiaries. This chapter seeks to expand on the transitional justice scholarship by opening a more nuanced conversation about the impact that the lack of criminal trials' finality has on its victims. In the final chapter, Chapter 6, I argue that narratives such as Lola's provide a much more illuminating account of the real-life impact that transitional justice mechanisms have on survivors of wartime rape. It is important to listen to how women victims experience law and how the

---

[11] Simon Burnett and Annemaree Lloyd, 'Hidden and Forbidden: Conceptualising dark knowledge' (2020) 76(6) *Journal of Documentation* 1341.

law's paradoxes and anomalies affect them. The crux of this chapter is to emphasise that women such as Lola live in 'not-war not-peace time', after the guns have fallen silent. The enduring legacies of war are tangible and raw, the experience of war atrocities keeps pressing into their everyday lives. Navigating post-war lives through the minefield of painful memories is often a difficult and exhausting exercise but victims such as Lola use different techniques to keep themselves aloft and live their lives the best they can.

CHAPTER 2

War and Rape

MUSLIM WOMEN, CROAT WOMEN, SERB WOMEN

One of the key features of the armed conflict in Bosnia and Herzegovina (BiH) that attracted significant attention from international and feminist scholars was the pervasive use of rape and other forms of sexual violence. According to United Nations (UN) reports, scholars and practitioners in the field, there were around 20,000 women who were raped during the BiH war between 1992 and 1995.[1] Many rapes occurred in camps and other places of detention. Most women victims of wartime sexual violence were Bosnian Muslim women, but Serb and Croatian women were also victimised by different military and paramilitary groups. However, Serb women victims never attracted scholarly attention and their experiences with war and its aftermath remain neglected.[2] The reasons for such neglect can be found in the early reporting that identified victims and

---

[1] In 1992, the United Nations (UN) established an Expert Commission to investigate human rights violations occurring in the former Yugoslavia, and particularly in BiH. Finding evidence of 'a very high number of rapes and sexual assaults', the Commission concluded that 'the earlier projection of 20,000 rapes made by other sources is not unreasonable'. See *UN Security Council, Letter dated 24 May 1994 from the Secretary-General to the President of the Security Council*, UN SCOR, UN Doc S/1994/674 (27 May 1994) [87] <https://www.icty.org/x/file/About/OTP/un_commission_of_experts_report1994_en.pdf> ('*Letter from the Secretary-General to the President of the Security Council*').

[2] See Olivera Simic, *Silenced Victims of Wartime Sexual Violence* (Routledge, 2018).

villains. In 1994 while the war was still raging, the UN Commission of Experts reported that Serbs were in a different category from other warring parties because they had used rape and sexual violence in the war but as 'the product of a policy'.[3]

Although it was noted that rape and torture could not be exclusively pinned against Serb forces, the systematic nature of abuse was identified by the UN in Serb-run detention camps. The first accounts of women raped in war were published in 1992 and these were of Bosnian Muslim women.[4] They were singled out as a group of women who had undergone 'massive, systematic, and organised' rape during the war in BiH.[5] These reports had a ripple effect and significantly shaped identity-making processes in BiH. They institutionalised ethnic divisions and cemented the importance of ethnic categories in the war and post-war narrative.[6] However, these narratives did not tell the full story of wartime rape in BiH or the 'messy realities' of the local context in which women survivors live.

As Kay Schaffer and Sidonie Smith recognise in the contestation over human rights, only certain stories emerge and are able to lay claim to human rights and justice.[7] In a world of imbalanced power relationships, 'only certain speakers of crimes and injustice are able to have their narratives championed by the human rights community'.[8] These narratives in turn promote calls for greater development of a narrative victimology which focuses on the experiences of being intentionally wronged by

---

[3] *Letter from the Secretary-General to the President of the Security Council* (n 1) [313].

[4] Elissa Helms, *Innocence and Victimhood: Gender, Nation, and Women's Activism in Postwar Bosnia-Herzegovina* (University of Wisconsin Press, 2013) 27.

[5] Security Council, SC Res 798, UN SCOR, 3150th mtg, UN Doc S/Res/798 (18 December 1992) [2].

[6] See Lea David, 'Policing Memory in Bosnia: Ontological Security and International Administration of Memorialization Policies' (2019) 32(2) *International Journal of Politics, Culture and Society* 211.

[7] Kay Schaffer and Sidonie Smith, *Human Rights and Narrated Lives: The Ethics of Recognition* (Palgrave Macmillan, 2004) 3.

[8] Galya Ruffer, 'Testimony of Sexual Violence in the Democratic Republic of Congo and the Injustice of Rape: Moral Outrage, Epistemic Injustice, and the Failures of Bearing Witness' (2013) 15(2) *Oregon Review of International Law* 225, 240.

others.⁹ My scholarly interest has been in the narratives of 'the other'; those that are not necessarily championed and widely embraced. I draw on such testimonial discourses to explore possibilities of everyday justice, repair and social transformation[10] for those who remained silent for far too long.

International human rights and advocacy organisations such as Human Rights Watch and Amnesty International also reported the crimes committed in camps targeting Bosnian Muslim and Croat women 'who had been singled out for humiliation on account of their nationality and sometimes as a form of retribution'.[11] As Janine Natalya Clark argues, scholarship and discourse on the use of rape in the war in BiH 'have overwhelmingly focused on Serb perpetrators and Bosniak (female) victims. Serb and Croat experiences of rape ... have been heavily marginalised'.[12] The foreign media coverage of distraught Bosnian Muslim women invoked empathy and implicitly linked the war suffering to (Muslim) women.[13] As Dubravka Zarkov notes, not all women in the former Yugoslavia were equally 'rapable' either before the eyes of the world or their apparent communities.[14] These early and subsequent reports and later volumes of research have cemented a view that Bosnian Muslim women were the 'authentic' and almost sole victims of wartime rapes in BiH. The international community, including many feminist scholars, have persistently disregarded the fact that Serb women were also repeatedly and forcibly detained and gang raped during the wars in Croatia and BiH.[15] These stories did not make the headlines and such losses

---

[9] Antony Pemberton, Pauline GM Aarten and Eva Mulder, 'Stories as Property: Narrative Ownership as a Key Concept in Victims' Experiences with Criminal Justice' (2019) 19(4) *Criminology and Criminal Justice* 204.

[10] On the relationship between justice and the everyday, see Pilar Riaño Alcalá and Erin Baines, 'Editorial Note' (2012) 6 *International Journal of Transitional Justice* 385.

[11] 'Bosnia-Herzegovina: Rape and Sexual Abuse by Armed Forces', *Amnesty International* (Web Document, 21 January 1993) <https://www.amnesty.org/en/documents/eur63/001/1993/en/>.

[12] Janine Natayla Clark, 'Working with Survivors of War Rape and Sexual Violence: Fieldwork Reflections from Bosnia-Hercegovina' (2017) 17(4) *Qualitative Research* 424.

[13] Helms (n 4) 99.

[14] Dubravka Zarkov, 'Sexual Violence Against Men in Contemporary Warfare' in Indira Rosental et al. (eds) *Gender in International Criminal Law* (Oxford University Press, 2022) 110.

[15] Ibid.

stayed 'ungrievable'.[16] As a result, one-sided narratives that promoted only Bosnian Muslim women were the victims in this war, dismissed other narratives that could have potentially evolved. Judith Butler calls such trends as the 'derealization of loss' which creates public sphere in which certain forms of public grieving are 'prohibited'. She argues that, '[t]he public will be created on the condition that certain images do not appear in the media, certain names of the dead are not utterable, certain losses are not avowed as losses, and violence is derealized and diffused'.[17] This choice to privilege one narrative over the other is 'never innocent' but always 'intensely political'. Annick Wibben goes even further and claims that such insistence on one point of view, on a singular narrative is 'itself a form of violence'.[18]

BiH is still going through the transition to a democratic state. Its state institutions are fragile and very often paralysed by political parties due to established veto mechanisms and existing power-sharing models. The country remains ethnically segregated and 'one of the most divided post-conflict societies in the twenty-first century, with ethnic divisions enshrined in its constitution'.[19] According to the Dayton Constitution, BiH is not a state of its citizens but of Bosniaks, Croats, Serbs and 'Others'.[20] Bosnian citizens are accordingly divided into categories of victimhood and perpetration. Women victims of wartime rape suffered from such division too. Serb women victims' narratives have been dismissed and publicly silenced, making any attempt towards reconciliation challenging, if not impossible. The dominant narratives prevented

---

[16] See Judith Butler, 'Rethinking Vulnerability and Resistance', in Judith Butler, Zeynep Gambetti and Letitia Sabsay (eds), *Vulnerability and Resistance* (Duke University Press, 2016) 24.

[17] Judith Butler, *Precarious Life: The Powers of Mourning and Violence* (Verso, 2004) 37–38.

[18] Annick Wibben, Feminist Security Studies: A Narrative Approach (Taylor & Francis, 2010) 2.

[19] Uroš Čvoro, *Post-Conflict Monuments in Bosnia and Herzegovina: Unfinished Histories* (Routledge, 2020) 1; See also Florian Bieber, 'Nationalist Mobilization and Stories of Serb Suffering', (2002) 6(1) *Rethinking History* 95; Annika Björkdahl and Susanne Buckley-Zistel, *Spacialising Peace and Conflict: Mapping the Production of Places, Sites and Scales of Violence* (Palgrave Macmillan, 2016).

[20] *Constitution of the Federation of Bosnia and Herzegovina* (Annex 4 of the General Framework Agreement for Peace in Bosnia and Herzegovina) *Dayton Peace Agreement* (signed 14 December 1995), Preamble.

other narratives—narratives of 'the other' women—from being articulated in the public spaces. The proponents of the dominant war narratives were worried that if these other histories were articulated, the dominant narrative would somehow lose out.

In the years since war ended, I have become increasingly committed to gaining a better understanding of what Lola and other women like her went through. Little has been written about the Bosnian Serb women who were imprisoned with their children in detention and rape camps. In-depth individual stories of Bosnian women survivors of wartime sexual violence are rare, in particular their stories of fighting for justice in the aftermath of war. The stories of women other than Bosnian Muslim women are even more scarce and still need to be told.

My previous work on Bosnian Serb women survivors of wartime rape did not cover the experiences of women victims as witnesses but analysed the notion of the 'authentic victim': who can and who cannot be seen and heard as a victim.[21] It built on the arguments made elsewhere that women who belong to the 'perpetrator nation' have not been recognised and acknowledged as victims of rape since they were the mothers, daughters and sisters of perpetrators.[22] They have been the invisible and disposable communities 'designed [to be] expandable and driven out of sight'.[23] As a result of this, Bosnian Serb women victims belong to 'communities of [the] excluded' people.[24] The notion of victim does not simply signify someone who has been victimised but also speaks to a set of assumptions about the act of harm itself and the victimiser, becoming a 'pathway to assistance, sympathy and the shedding of responsibility for violence'.[25] As Tshepo Madlingozi argues, defining victims as '"good" and "bad"

---

[21] Ratna Kapur, 'The Tragedy of Victimization Rhetoric: Resurrecting the "Native" Subject in International/Post-Colonial Feminist Legal Politics' (2002) 15 *Harvard Human Rights Journal* 1; Simic, *Silenced Victims* (n 2).

[22] Alexandra Stiglemayer (ed), *Mass Rape: The War Against Women in Bosnia-Herzegovina*, tr Marion Faber (University of Nebraska Press, 1994).

[23] Rob Nixon, *Slow Violence and the Environmentalism of the Poor* (Harvard University Press, 2011).

[24] See Christopher Scanlon and John Adlam, *Psycho-social Explorations of Trauma, Exclusion and Violence: Un-housed Minds and Inhospitable Environments* (Routledge, 2022).

[25] Erica Bouris, Complex Political Victims (Kumarian Press, 2007) 31; Kevin Hearty, '"Victims of" Human Rights Abuses in Transitional Justice: Hierarchies, Perpetrators and the Struggle for Peace' (2018) 22(7) *The International Journal of Human Rights* 888.

or "innocent" or "guilty", "worthy" or "unworthy" may be less about victims' needs and circumstances and more about making a statement on the "justifiability" of the harms inflicted and the causes and consequences of the conflict within which their victimisation occurred'.[26] My recent work has as Zarkov noted, made an 'attempt of righting ... [the] invisibility' of Serb women victims of wartime sexual violence.[27]

Although criminal law sees individuals as being responsible for crimes, the reality is, as Roman David claims, that perpetrators and victims of crimes are both a part of a wider community of people. Members of such a community may identify with the victim or the perpetrator due to reasons of 'race, class, gender, political organization or nation'.[28] This means that beyond the experiences of the people involved in a criminal trial, the wider community will be impacted by a guilty or innocent verdict because 'justice for a victim and a transgressor inevitably means justice for the social groups to which they belong'.[29] It can therefore be expected that 'in-group members would welcome judgments that award them a collective victim status and resist judgments that condemn members of their in-group as perpetrators'.[30] Such rationale further purports that 'being associated with wrongdoing goes against the efforts of the in-group to maintain or achieve a positive social identity'.[31] In the case of the former Yugoslavia, as the UN has observed, 'all sides viewed themselves as victims, not as perpetrators' which has cultivated a desire for revenge and provided justification for pursuing own ethnic group interests and

---

[26] Tshepo Madlingozi, 'Good Victim, Bad Victim: Apartheid's Beneficiaries, Victims and the Struggle for Social Justice' in Wessel le Roux and Karin van Marle (eds), *Law, Memory and the Legacy of Apartheid: Ten Years after AZAPO v President of South Africa* (Pretoria University Law Press, 2007) 107.

[27] Zarkov (n 14).

[28] Roman David, 'International Criminal Tribunals and the Perception of Justice: The Effect of the ICTY in Croatia' (2014) 8(3) *The International Journal of Transitional Justice* 476, 479.

[29] Ibid.

[30] Ibid 481.

[31] Ibid 481–2.

actions.³² In such a social environment of divided ethnic realities, international crimes committed by one's own forces are considered legitimate or to an extent, at least justified.³³

The politicisation of victimhood in BiH resulted in competing interpretations of the causes of war and was contested through notions of 'guilt' and 'innocence' and endless discussions over the 'hierarchy of victimhood'.³⁴ Within this hierarchical conceptualisation of victimhood, only Bosnian Muslim women and men are seen as 'true' victims of the war. Bosnian Serb women's experiences of violence and suffering never attracted 'outpourings of sorrow, outrage, or anguish'.³⁵ Their narratives had been faceless and barely noticed as they were considered as 'somehow deserving' of their fate due to 'their belonging' to the Serb 'culprits'. The boundaries between Serb men perpetrators and Serb women victims has been blurred with culpability spread and extended to the Serb ethnic group as a whole. Against this backdrop, Bosnian Muslim women have dominated the public arena of victimhood in which their narratives have been constructed and reproduced. On the other hand, Bosnian Serb women have been relegated to private spaces, their voices muffled and silenced. Such reductive framing of victimhood narrows the space for compassion and a more nuanced understanding of the complexities of war and victimhood.³⁶

If Serb victims are mentioned at all in the literature, it just barely acknowledges the fact that Serb women were also victims, yet overall there has been little or no interest in their experiences.³⁷ Serb women were

---

³² Ibid 485.

³³ Marko Milanovic, 'Understanding the ICTY's Impact in the Former Yugoslavia', *EJIL: Talk! Blog of the European Journal of International Law* 5. 11 April 2016, https://www.ejiltalk.org/understanding-the-ictys-impact-in-the-former-yugoslavia/.

³⁴ See Simic (n 2); Helms (n 4).

³⁵ Simic (n 2).

³⁶ Cheryl Lawther, '"Let Me tell You": Transitional Justice, Victimhood and Dealing with a Contested Past' (2021) 30(6) *Social & Legal Studies* 890.

³⁷ Dario Vidojković, 'Ne dozvolimo da se ugasi, Udruženje žena žrtava rata Republike Srpske"!' *Basta Balkana* (online, 3 September 2017) <https://www.bastabalkana.com/2017/02/ne-dozvolimo-da-se-ugasi-udruzenje-zena-zrtava-rata-republike-srpske/>.

denied the status of victim[38] and only perceived as inherently and collectively 'guilty' for the crimes committed by Serb males. They bore 'guilt by association'; identified as members of the 'perpetrator nation' and as such, deemed to carry the collective responsibility for the Serb wartime atrocities, regardless of whether they were aware of and/or supported those crimes.[39]

By virtue of their belonging or association to a particular community, Serb women were deemed 'politically' guilty and collectively responsible[40] and as such, stripped of victimhood. They were seen as not entitled to victimhood because they had been portrayed as subscribing to Serb nationalist politics. Serb women, including women victims of sexual abuse, are seen as an accomplice to the male aggressor—as their 'symbolic representations'[41] and as an extension to the Serb male perpetrators. For these reasons, the transitional justice industry has not yet descended upon their lives.[42] Here, ethnicity and gender collide and cannot be dismantled. As Tanya Serisier argues, 'being heard relies on dominant narratives of race and class rather than an acceptance of women's right to be free of sexual violence and to be heard when they speak of it'.[43] Similarly, Tamara Tompkins underlines that 'rape, like genocide, will not be deterred unless and until the stories are heard'.[44] Such stories should not be sought from one ethnic group or another, but from all women who share the same victimhood experience.

---

[38] See Odia Kane, 'The Denial of Victimhood: Exploring the Attitudes Surrounding Collegiate Black Women and Rape' (Conference Paper, *National Conference of Black Political Scientists Annual Meeting*, 13 November 2018).

[39] See Karl Jaspers, *The Question of German Guilt*, tr EB Ashton (Fordham University Press, 1965).

[40] See Hannah Arendt, 'Collective Responsibility' in SJJW Bernauer (ed), *Amor Mundi: Explorations in the Faith and Thought of Hannah Arendt* (Martinus Nijhoff Publishers, 1987) 43; Hannah Arendt, 'Organized Guilt and Universal Responsibility' in Hannah Arendt (ed), *Essays in Understanding: 1930–1945* (Harcourt Brace, 1994) 121.

[41] Doris E Buss, 'Rethinking "Rape as a Weapon of War"' (2009) 17(2) *Feminist Legal Studies* 145, 148.

[42] Roxani Krystallii, 'Narrating Victimhood: Dilemmas and (In)Dignities' (2021) 23(1) *International Feminist Journal of Politics* 125.

[43] Tanya Serisier, *Speaking Out: Feminism, Rape and Narrative Politics* (Palgrave Macmillan, 2018) 90.

[44] Tamara L Tompkins, 'Prosecuting Rape as a War Crime: Speaking the Unspeakable' (1995) 70(4) *Notre Dame Law Review* 845.

Scholarly and feminist interest in Lola's and other Serb women victims' stories was simply never there. Their narratives disturb the official narrative of war in BiH in which Serb-lived experiences of victimhood were collectively silenced because 'perpetrators' can never be deemed as victims and as such are not worthy of being listened to. While cases of wartime rape in BiH continue to feature in local and international narratives of victimisation, it is the stories of Bosnian Muslim women that dominate these narratives. Yet, the experiences of Serb women also need to be heard. Different experiences of victimisation are important because they provide possibilities for transethnic solidarity and for connection across different groups and different histories.[45]

THE TRIALS

BiH women victims of wartime rape paved the way in international criminal law and jurisprudence by testifying before the first ad hoc international courts set up after World War Two, the Nuremberg and Tokyo tribunals. The creation of the International Criminal Tribunal for the former Yugoslavia (ICTY) as an ad hoc court to try war crimes in the region made history in international humanitarian law. Wartime sexual violence in BiH gave momentum to the rise of a global campaign against sexual violence in armed conflicts within international justice and advocacy.[46] After the Nuremberg and Tokyo trials, the ICTY was the first ad hoc tribunal to try war crimes and prosecute sexual violence and rape in war. As a result, feminists around the world 'began to pay an enormous amount of attention to wartime rape'.[47]

The ICTY was created to prosecute violations of international humanitarian law committed in the territory of the former Yugoslavia during the 1990s. It was the first time since the Nuremberg and Tokyo Trials that the international community held individuals accountable for violations

---

[45] Michael Rothberg, *Multidirectional Memory: Remembering the Holocaust in the Age of Decolonization* (Stanford University Press, 2009).

[46] Cynthia Cockburn, 'The Gendered Dynamics of Armed Conflict and Political Violence' in Caroline Moser and Fiona C Clark (eds), *Victims, Perpetrators or Actors: Gender, Armed Conflict and Political Violence* (Zed Books, 2001) 13.

[47] Karen Engle, *The Grip of Sexual Violence in Conflict* (Stanford University Press, 2020) 1.

of human rights instead of nation states.[48] Its mandate was to 'contribute to the restoration and maintenance of international peace and security' by providing justice and promoting peace and reconciliation.[49] Many of the ICTY's indictees 'were those at the highest levels of political and military responsibility'.[50] It prosecuted a 'broad sweep of crimes, targeting all groups, and addressing the most notorious examples of ethnic cleansing and even genocide'.[51] However, the ICTY has had a dubious success in achieving its transitional justice goals. The advocates of the ICTY argued that the Court's proceedings would 'establish a historical record [and] help facilitate processes of reconciliation ... [however] narratives of denial and victimhood remain deeply entrenched'.[52]

Shelley Inglis, UN Rule of Law Officer, admitted that one of the major flaws of the ICTY was that it failed to engage with 'the local national perspective[s] ... [of the] successor states as well as local ethnic communities'.[53] The ICTY trials gave unprecedented attention to sexual violence in war and for the first time, victims came forward to testify in such cases. Their appearance before the Court marked a new era in the history of international humanitarian law.[54] In 2005, just ten years after the Dayton Peace Agreement ended the war in BiH, the War Crimes Chamber in Sarajevo was established to prosecute war crimes and elevate the work of the ICTY. The ICTY and local courts, as tools of retributive justice, have

---

[48] Kathryn Sikkink and Hun Joon Kim, 'The Justice Cascade: The Origins and Effectiveness of Prosecutions of Human Rights Violations' (2013) 9 *Annual Review of Law and Social Science* 269, 271.

[49] Rachel Kerr, Centre for International Policy Studies, *Lost in Translation: The ICTY and the Legacy of War Crimes in the Western Balkans* (Policy Brief no 19, July 2012).

[50] Rachel Kerr, 'International Criminal Justice' in Olivera Simic (ed), *An Introduction to Transitional Justice* (Taylor & Francis Group, 2016) 47, 59.

[51] Ibid.

[52] Kerr, *Lost in Translation* (n 49) 12–3.

[53] Kirsten Campbell, 'Reassembling International Justice: The Making of "the Social" in International Criminal Law and Transitional Justice' (2014) 8(1) *International Journal of Transitional Justice* 53, 56–7.

[54] Nicola Henry, 'Witness to Rape: The Limits and Potential of International War Crimes Trials for Victims of Wartime Sexual Violence' (2009) 3(1) *International Journal of Transitional Justice* 114, 115.

played a significant role in the investigation, prosecution and adjudication of war crimes.[55] Some of the ICTY's stated objectives were:

> To bring to justice persons allegedly responsible for serious violations of international humanitarian law; to render justice to the victims; to deter further crimes; [and] to contribute to the restoration of peace by holding accountable persons responsible for serious violations of international humanitarian law.[56]

The ICTY indicted 161 individuals with crimes and convicted 92 of them.[57] Out of these, 78 individuals or 48% of the 161 accused, faced charges of sexual violence and 32 were convicted on these charges.[58] By individualising guilt, the perpetrators were identified as criminals, which debunks the aura of invincibility they previously held.[59] War criminal prosecutions lend their hand in upholding key features of international law, as well as maintaining the rule of law. By holding those who committed war crimes accountable, no matter who they are, the Court signalled to the local communities that such violations will not go unpunished. In turn, this sentiment was meant to assist in upholding citizens' trust in legal institutions. Prosecutions also assist victims in achieving some kind of closure by seeing those who wronged them brought to justice. The ICTY did not suffer from the risk of its defendants evading justice, however the reality before the local national courts in BiH has been strikingly different. Around 130 defendants prosecuted for war crimes and crimes against humanity before national courts have not only

---

[55] Organization for Security and Co-operation in Europe, *Delivering Justice in Bosnia and Herzegovina: An Overview of War Crimes Processing from 2005 to 2010* (Report, 19 May 2011).

[56] See the UN's general information on the ICTY: 'About the ICTY', *United Nations International Criminal Tribunal for the former Yugoslavia* (Web Page) <https://www.icty.org/en/about>.

[57] Zoran Arbutina, 'The Legacy of the ICTY Tribunal in the Hague', *Deutsche Welle* (online, 29 November 2017) [9] <https://beta.dw.com/en/icty-hague-tribunal-ends-prosecutions-of-yugoslav-war-crimes-but-legacy-lingers/a-41587892>.

[58] 'Crimes of Sexual Violence: In Numbers', *United Nations International Criminal Tribunal for the former Yugoslavia* (Web Page, September 2016) <https://www.icty.org/en/features/crimes-sexual-violence/in-numbers>.

[59] Elizabeth B Ludwin King, 'Does Justice always Require Prosecution: The International Criminal Court and Transitional Justice Measures' (2013) 45(1) *The George Washington International Law Review* 85, 91.

escaped imprisonment but simply disappeared 'into thin air' after being prosecuted and sentenced.[60]

Ilija Jurić, Lola's rapist, is one of those defendants who never served his sentence.

Lola was among the first women to testify before the Court of BiH about the rapes of Serb women in the Posavina region. She had contributed to successfully proving her rapist's guilt and the court sentenced him to six years imprisonment for committing the war crime of rape. Her rapist was not a stranger to her. He was someone she knew intimately: her former neighbour, an acquaintance. In 'new wars',[61] civil wars blur the front lines with homes and neighbourhoods. These are the wars in which civilians bear the brunt of the violence. They become rational targets in such wars, instead of being unintended 'collateral damage'. This is because 'new wars' are driven by often extreme forms of identity politics.[62] As Kimberly Theidon argues, 'the enemy is a son-in-law, a godfather, an old school mate, or the community that lies just across the valley'.[63] BiH was a textbook example of such a war.

The trials for the rapes of Bosnian Serb women in the Posavina region that started in 2014 saw Marijan Brnjić prosecuted and sentenced for his crimes, which brought some closure to his women victims. Brnjić was sentenced and is currently serving his twelve-year jail sentence in a local prison.[64] By the end of 2021 a total of 644 cases involving 978 defendants had been completed before the state Court. The number of

---

[60] Emir Velić, 'Mnogi optuženici za ratne zločine u BiH su još uvijek na slobodi', *Istinomjer* (online, 17 November 2021) <https://istinomjer.ba/mnogi-optuzenici-za-ratne-zlocine-u-bih-su-jos-uvijek-na-slobodi/>; 'Uzivaju u slobodi i ne kriju se: Objavljen spisak i lokacije svih osoba koje traži Sud BiH zbog ratnih zločina', *Slobodna Bosna* (online, 21 September 2021) <https://www.slobodna-bosna.ba/vijest/216337/uzi vaju_u_slobodi_i_ne_kriju_se_objavljen_spisak_i_lokacije_svih_osoba_koje_trazi_sud_bih_zbog_ratnih_zlochina.html>.

[61] See Mary Kaldor, 'In Defence of New Wars' (2013) 2(1) *Stability: International Journal of Security and Development* 4; Mary Kaldor, *New and Old Wars: Organised Violence in a Global Era* (Polity Press, 1st ed, 1999).

[62] Ibid.

[63] Kimberly Theidon, *Intimate Enemies: Violence and Reconciliation in Peru* (University of Pennsylvania Press, 2013) xiii.

[64] *Prosecutor v Marijan Brnjić* et al., Appeals Division of the Court of Bosnia and Herzegovina, S1 1 K 016706 16 Krž, 22 April 2016.

ongoing cases at the end of 2021 was 245.[65] In the proceedings before the BiH local courts in the period between 2004 and 2016, 123 perpetrators were convicted of wartime sexual violence. In many cases, sexual violence was one of several charges.[66] These trials for the 1990s wartime rapes are still ongoing before the local courts and information about these cases and the perpetrators are largely accessible in local media.[67] While millions of dollars have been spent by the international and local criminal trials to prosecute a few perpetrators,[68] there is a lack of scrutiny into the execution of the local courts' judgments.

TRANSITIONAL JUSTICE PROCESSES IN BOSNIA AND HERZEGOVINA

Transitional justice is a field of international law which involves not just prosecuting human right violations but also other methods which help countries transition from a time of war to a time of peace, and from an era of authoritarianism to an era of democracy.[69] National and international trials and criminal justice are just one example in a plethora of transitional justice mechanisms that are available to survivors of mass atrocities. Others, such as restitution, reparations, institutional reforms, truth commissions, satisfaction and guarantees of non-occurrence, also play a significant role in dealing with past crimes to varying degrees in post-conflict countries. Transitional justice is defined by the International Center for Transitional Justice as 'the set of judicial and non-judicial

---

[65] Mission to Bosnia and Herzegovina, Organisation for Security and Co-operation in Europe, *War Crimes Processing in Bosnia and Herzegovina (2004–2021)* (Report, 30 June 2022).

[66] Mission to Bosnia and Herzegovina, Organization for Security and Co-operation in Europe, *Towards Justice for Survivors of Conflict-Related Sexual Violence in Bosnia and Herzegovina: Progress before Courts in BiH 2004–2016* (Report, 20 June 2017) 9.

[67] Marija Tausan, 'Bosnia Convicts Serb Ex-Soldier of Wartime Rape', *Balkan Insight* (online, 18 November 2022) <https://balkaninsight.com/2022/11/18/bosnia-convicts-serb-ex-soldier-of-wartime-rape-2/>; Amila Zunic, 'Bosnian Wartime Jail Guard Pleads Not Guilty to Rape', *Balkan Insight* (online, 24 August 2022) <https://balkaninsight.com/2022/08/24/bosnian-wartime-jail-guard-pleads-not-guilty-to-rape/>.

[68] The ICTY was spending around 200 million dollars a year to prosecute dozens of people. See Rupert Skilbeck, 'Funding Justice: The Price of War Crimes Trials' (2008) 15(3) *Human Rights Brief* 6, 1.

[69] Kerr, 'International Criminal Justice' (n 50) 47, 48.

measures that have been implemented by different countries in order to redress the legacies of massive human rights abuses includ[ing] criminal prosecutions, truth commissions, reparations programs, and various kinds of institutional reforms'.[70] This means international criminal justice has a narrower focus than transitional justice, which is 'to put an end to impunity for the perpetrators of these crimes and thus to contribute to the prevention of such crimes… [and] provide a forum for retributive justice on behalf of the victims'.[71] As a mechanism of transitional justice, criminal trials can assist the transitional process by 'individualising guilt and thereby preventing collective accusations that imply an entire people was responsible for the conflict'. Prosecuting political and military leaders can 'debunk the aura of invincibility and impunity they may have previously held… and announce[s] to the nation and the world that this new government upholds human rights and the rule of law'. These proceedings may, in turn, deter others from committing human rights violations by showing them that such crimes will be punished.[72]

Although it has been long acknowledged that criminal justice is not necessarily the key transitional justice mechanism anymore,[73] it still dominates in some emerging democracies. Trials and prosecutions as transitional justice principal mechanisms are driven by the interests of the state rather than being 'victim-centred'.[74] In BiH, criminal justice has been the main state-led tool used to deal with past atrocities committed during the 1992–1995 civil war. Prosecutions have been privileged over reparation, a mechanism that primarily serves the needs of victims. There were several failed attempts to establish a truth commission in the country,[75] while other mechanisms such as reparations have been approached not as

---

[70] Niké Wentholt and Europa Südost, 'Mirroring Transitional Justice: Construction and Impact of European Union ICTY-Conditionality' (2017) 65(1) *Regensburg* 77, 78.

[71] Kerr, 'International Criminal Justice' (n 50) 54.

[72] Ludwin King, (n 59) 85, 91.

[73] Ruti G Teitel, 'Transitional Justice Genealogy' (2003) 16 *Harvard Human Rights Journal* 69.

[74] Simon Robins, 'Failing Victims: The Limits of Transitional Justice in Addressing the Needs of Victims of Violations' (2017) 11(1) *Human Rights and International Legal Discourse* 41.

[75] Jasna Dragović-Soso, 'History of a Failure: Attempts to Create a National Truth and Reconciliation Commission in Bosnia and Herzegovina, 1997–2006' (2016) 10(2) *International Journal of Transitional Justice* 292.

a national strategy, but piecemeal projects of each of the two BiH entities. The Dayton Peace Agreement that ended the war in BiH was signed in Dayton, Ohio by the presidents of BiH, Croatia and Serbia on 21 November 1995. The Agreement divided the state of BiH into two entities: the Federation of Bosnia and Herzegovina and the Republika Srpska. Both entities are politically autonomous to an extent, and each has its own constitution. The Federation of BiH is predominantly populated by Bosniaks (Muslims) and Croats (Catholics), while the Republika Srpska is largely populated by Serbs (Orthodox). They both jointly administer the Brčko District.

Nearly three decades after the war has ended, BiH still lacks a national legal framework that ensures effective access to full reparation for all civil victims of war crimes.[76] Symbolic reparations, such as street vigils, exhibitions, street performances, films and arts[77] have been implemented in an ad hoc manner depending on the willingness of donors to support symbolic justice projects. These initiatives have largely been rolled out by local human rights NGOs, activists and artists.[78] Furthermore, the BiH government has never issued a public apology to any victims of war crimes including victims of wartime sexual violence[79] or acknowledged

---

[76] Special Rapporteur on the Promotion of Truth, Justice, Reparation and Guarantees of Non-Recurrence, 'Preliminary Observations from the Official Visit to Bosnia and Herzegovina' *OHCHR.org* (Media Release, United Nations Office of the High Commissioner for Human Rights, 10 December 2021).

[77] See for example, the film *Grbavica: The Land of My Dreams* (Tanja Aćimović, 2006); the first appearance of the 'Women's Court—Feminist Approach to Justice' in Sarajevo, 7–10 May 2015 <http://www.zenskisud.org/en/>; the photographic exhibition 'My Body, A War Zone: Breaking the Silence Surrounding Sexual Violence in Conflict', *Peace Insight* (Blog Post, 1 September 2015) <https://www.peaceinsight.org/en/articles/my-body-a-war-zone-breaking-the-silence-surrounding-sexual-violence-in-conflict/?location=western-balkans&theme=women-peace-security>; the documentary theatre performance 'Crossing the Lines', see Olivera Simic 'Breathing Sense into Women's Lives Shattered by War: Dah Theatre Belgrade' (2010) 14 *Law Text Culture*, 117.

[78] See for example, Olivera Simic and Zala Volcic, 'In the Land of Wartime Rape: Bosnia, Cinema and Reparation' (2014) 2(2) *Griffith Journal of Law & Human Dignity* 377; Olivera Simic and Dijana Milošević, 'Enacting Justice: The Role of Dah Theatre Company in Transitional Justice Processes in Serbia and Beyond' in Peter D Rush and Olivera Simic (eds), *The Arts of Transitional Justice: Culture, Activism, and Memory after Atrocity* (Springer, 2014) 99.

[79] The government's apology is important to survivors. In 2019, the United Nations Committee Against Torture (CAT) instructed the government to do so but the government did not act on CAT's recommendation. See Committee Against Torture, *Decision*

their suffering in any other symbolic way. Despite receiving multi-billions of dollars in international aid for post-war recovery,[80] BiH remains a country wreaking with political instability, poverty and ethnic tensions which could easily spiral into another civil war.[81]

There is an agreement among transitional justice scholars and practitioners that, 'we still know too little' about what makes a transitional justice mechanism a success in the eyes of beneficiaries.[82] For too many victims of war in BiH 'retributive justice is justice'[83] and achieving justice is only meaningful and satisfactory in legal realms. This is not only because of the absence of other viable transitional justice mechanisms in the country, such as a truth commission or comprehensive reparation programmes but also because being a witness in criminal trials could trigger other transitional justice mechanisms in play such as reparations. Securing reparations is important to many victims in BiH and beyond, since getting material compensation for the harm means alleviating the tough socioeconomic conditions that many victims and their families live in.[84]

This perception is additionally informed by the post-Cold War emergence of 'a persistent seeking-justice discourse'[85] and global legalism which consists of the belief that law and legal institutions should play

---

adopted by the Committee under article 22 of the Convention, concerning Communication No. 854/2017, UN Doc CAT/C/67/D/854/2017 (22 August 2019).

[80] Daniel Daianu and Thanos Veremis (eds), *Balkan Reconstruction* (Routledge, 2001) 24.

[81] Julian Borger, 'Bosnia is in Danger of Breaking Up, Warns Top International Official', *The Guardian* (online, 2 November 2021) <https://www.theguardian.com/world/2021/nov/02/bosnia-is-in-danger-of-breaking-up-warns-eus-top-official-in-the-state>; Guy Delauney, 'Bosnian Leader Stokes Fears of Balkan Breakup', *BBC News* (online, 3 November 2021) <https://www.bbc.com/news/world-europe-59130945>.

[82] 'Editorial Note' (2014) 8(1) *International Journal of Transitional Justice* 1 ('Editorial Note').

[83] Judith N Shklar, *The Faces of Injustice* (Yale University Press, 1990) 94.

[84] Johanna Mannegren Selimovic, 'Perpetrators and Victims: Local Responses to the International Criminal Tribunal for the Former Yugoslavia' [2010] (57) *Focaal: Journal of Global and Historical Anthropology* 50; Isabelle Delpla, 'In the Midst of Injustice: The ICTY from the Perspective of Some Victim Associations' in Xavier Bougarel, Elissa Helms and Gerlachlus Duijzings (eds), *The New Bosnian Mosaic: Identities, Memories and Moral Claims in a Post-War Society* (Routledge, 2007) 211.

[85] Ruti G Teitel, 'Transitional Justice in a New Era' (2002) 26(4) *Fordham International Law Journal* 893, 896.

a central role in resolving various disputes and conflicts.[86] Since global legalism has suffered its setbacks[87] a holistic approach towards transitional justice has been promoted instead, holding that 'no mechanism is likely to be effective in isolation', encouraging a plurality of approaches which combine retributive and restorative conceptions of justice.[88] However, the legacy of thinking that criminal accountability and truth are necessary to right the wrongs of the past[89] has been prevalent in BiH. Among many survivors of wartime crimes, the logic remains firm that prosecuting human rights violations will result in convictions which will then diminish such violations.[90] International and national trials and criminal justice have been perceived by many victims as something to strive for—as the ultimate expressions of justice.[91] As one Bosnian survivor said, 'without justice and by that I mean *real justice* [retributive justice] … there can be no reconciliation'.[92] Such understandings of transitional justice are not unique to Bosnian victims of war crimes. For example, studying the experiences of Argentina after dictatorship, Terence Roehrig found that most of the citizens wanted to hold the perpetrators accountable for past crimes.[93] Globally, as Heather Douglas argues, every year millions

---

[86] See discussion on global legalism in Victor Igreja, 'Negotiating the Legacies of Intragroup Violence in Timor Leste' (2021) 15(2) *International Journal of Transitional Justice* 309, 315.

[87] Eric A Posner, *The Perils of Global Legalism* (University of Chicago Press, 2009).

[88] See International Center for Transitional Justice, *A Transitioning World* (Annual Report, 2008); Alexander L Boraine, 'Transitional Justice: A Holistic Interpretation' (2006) 60(1) *Journal Of International Affairs* 17; Pablo De Grieff, 'Theorizing Transitional Justice' in Melissa S Williams, Rosemary Nagy and Jon Elster (eds), *Transitional Justice: NOMOS LI* (New York University Press, 2012) 31; Rebekka Friedman and Andrew Jillions, 'The Pitfalls and Politics of Holistic Justice' (2015) 6(2) *Global Policy* 141.

[89] Alex Boraine, *A Country Unmasked* (Oxford University Press, 2000).

[90] Sikkink and Kim (n 48).

[91] Goran Basic, 'Conditions for Reconciliation: Narratives of Survivors from the War in Bosnia and Herzegovina', (2015) 17(2) *Journal of Criminal Justice and Security* 107.

[92] Ibid 116 (emphasis added).

[93] Terence Roehrig, 'Executive Leadership and the Continuing Quest for Justice in Argentina' (2009) 31(1) *Human Rights Quarterly* 721, 722.

of women 'turn to law as an integral part of their strategy to live lives free and safe from violence'.[94]

Likewise as Jasna Dragović-Soso notes, Bosnian victims have had a 'preference for judicial processes over truth and reconciliation projects'.[95] The majority of victims have seen the necessity of testifying in trials solely for the purpose of achieving accountability for perpetrators 'first and foremost'.[96] The last two decades have seen an unprecedented rise in mechanisms and institutions of transitional justice, yet how these affect the lives of victims who use them still needs scrutiny. Many perpetrators of war crimes in BiH still walk free: many are seen as 'war heroes' rather than war criminals.[97] In such a context one of the symbolic measures in transitional justice, the process of 'blaming and shaming', is not necessarily applicable in BiH. On the contrary, it is dangerous and can trigger verbal and physical abuse towards people who try to do so. For example, several NGOs from Serbia who openly campaigned against BiH Serb war criminals being glorified as heroes were verbally and physically abused.[98] Such a socio-political context during 'the-time-of not-war-not-peace'[99] gives victims little hope that their suffering will ever be fully acknowledged and their dignity reinstated. 'Celebrating' war criminals tells victims that the violence they survived is condoned and thus glorified.

---

[94] Heather Douglas, *Women, Intimate Partner Violence, and the Law* (Oxford University Press, 2021) 2.

[95] Dragović-Soso (n 75) 307.

[96] Ibid.

[97] Barbora Hola and Olivera Simic, 'ICTY Celebrities: War Criminals Coming Home' (2018) 28(4) *International Criminal Justice Review* 285.

[98] See Martha Moreno Guerrero, 'Women in Black, Thirty Years of Defying Serbian Nationalism', *Atalayar* (Web Page, 1 November 2021) <https://atalayar.com/en/content/women-black-thirty-years-defying-serbian-nationalism>; Tanjug, 'Attack on Activists at the Headquarters of Women in Black in Belgrade, Serbia', *War Resisters' International* (Web Page, 12 October 2010) <https://wri-irg.org/es/story/2010/attack-activists-headquarters-women-black-belgrade-serbia?language=en>; OMCT, 'Urgent Interventions: Physical assault against 9 members of the Youth Initiative for Human Rights (YIHR)', *OMCT SOS-Torture Network* (Web Page, 27 January 2017) <https://www.omct.org/en/resources/urgent-interventions/physical-assault-against-9-members-of-the-youth-initiative-for-human-rights-yihr>.

[99] Carolyn Nordstrom, *Shadows of War: Violence, Power, and International Profiteering in the Twenty-First Century* (University of California Press, 2004) 165.

War criminals who have perpetrated sexual violence, have largely been invisible from the judicial narratives which foreground the victim and where she becomes subject to interrogation. While Lola was interrogated and had to speak for herself, her wartime rapist paradoxically, did not even have to say a word: his attorney was paid to speak for him. Instead of calling Lola's rapist a 'war criminal' he should be called a 'war rapist' since Lola is a victim of wartime rape. Sexual violence in war is not just a 'women's issue' and should not erase the question of men's violence and male rapists. Framing war criminals who committed sexual violence crimes as rapists is necessary to shift the focus from the female victim to the male rapist which tends to get erased in 'wartime sexual violence against women' narratives.

This study moves beyond unprecedented contributions of national, hybrid and international courts and institutions that have been created over the past few decades, and instead brings focus on 'what we don't know and what these institutions can't do'.[100] It challenges the norm of accountability, unpacks the vulnerability of the transitional justice doctrine and focuses on the obstacles to upholding the rule of law in emerging democracies. While it has been acknowledged that 'the implementation of every significant transitional justice initiative has fallen short in meeting the expectations of victims and their advocates',[101] learning from mistakes can contribute to righting the wrongs in the future.

My study also brings to the fore the concept of a 'violence continuum' or 'continuum of sexual violence' which suggests that women's experience of sexual harm cannot be contained within legal parameters and does not remain fixed in one moment of one act.[102] As Christine Chinkin argues, 'The consequences of rape continue beyond the actual attack or attacks, often lasting for the rest of women's lives. As well as the degradation, pain, and terror caused at the time, the fear engendered remains long after'.[103] Bosnian women survivors remain trapped in the continuum of violence through their country's political, economic and social processes

---

[100] Jill Stauffer, *Ethical Loneliness: The Injustice of Not Being Heard* (Columbia University Press, 2015) 6.

[101] 'Editorial Note' (n 82).

[102] Liz Kelly, 'The Continuum of Sexual Violence' in Jalna Hanmer and Mary Maynard (eds), *Women, Violence and Social Control* (Macmillan, 1987) 46.

[103] Christine Chinkin, 'Rape and Sexual Abuse of Women in International Law' (1994) 5(3) *European Journal of International Law* 326, 329.

that are enmeshed in their everyday life. Most survivors live either below or on the poverty line. Impoverishment and patriarchal repression have become common denominators of their lives in their conflict-ridden homeland. Their lives continue to be shattered by experiences of everyday insitutionalised subordination and marginalisation.

Valerie Preston and Madeleine Wong coined the term 'mobility of conflict zones' and argue that the female wartime experiences are evidence that conflict zones—although seemingly geographically fixed territories and clearly delineated from peace zones—have expansible boundaries, because violent practices are easily stretched far beyond the combat borders.[104] Cynthia Cockburn concludes that although the word *zone* connotes a fixed geographical territory with well-defined boundaries, the violence that women suffer is the result of social and political processes that operate across militarised and nonmilitarised places.[105] However, while the commencement of armed conflict draws public attention, armed conflict often has a much longer genesis in events that often passed unnoticed.[106] The legacy of war stretches beyond frontlines into peace times. The trauma from it knows no geographical or time zones.

Yet, the question as to what 'counts as violence and how it is acknowledged' remains contentious at a conceptual and empirical level.[107] The violence towards Lola has changed its forms since her sexual abuse occurred in the detention camp, but it has never disappeared. One brutal act of violence turned into a 'slow violence' which has dispersed across time and space and been inflicted by various state and non-state actors.[108] How Lola perpetually negotiates, makes sense of, inhabits or resists state-led 'slow violence'—masked as 'transitional justice processes'—will be revealed in later chapters here through her insights on the subject

---

[104] Valerie Preston and Madeleine Wong, 'Geographies of Violence: Women and Conflict in Ghana' in Wenona Giles and Jennifer Hyndman (eds), *Sites of Violence: Gender and Conflict Zones* (University of California Press, 2004) 152, 167.

[105] Cynthia Cockburn, 'The Continuum of Violence: A Gender Perspective on War and Peace' in Wenona Giles and Jennifer Hyndman (eds), *Sites of Violence: Gender and Conflict Zones* (University of California Press, 2004) 24.

[106] Ibid.

[107] Veena Das, 'Violence, Crisis, and the Everyday' (2013) 45(4) *International Journal of Middle East Studies* 798.

[108] Nixon (n 23).

matter. The feminist methodologies I use shift the focus from an epistemological stance and knowledge to lived and embodied experiences of women victims in the quest for possible connections between these different levels of violence. While Lola survived *behavioural* violence which James Gilligan defines as 'harmful actions of specific individuals',[109] she also experienced impersonal, produced and distributed violence within the power structures and institutions that govern societies; the form of violence that Johan Galtung coined as 'structural' or 'institutional violence'.[110] For Slavoj Žižek, it is the structural violence that provides 'the invisible' structural background context of injustice, out of which acts of behavioural/subjective violence emerge.[111] Examining *structures* of violence, as opposed to only examining individual physical manifestations of violence, calls into question 'which violence allegedly "ends" with peace accords, where that violence is located, and how it may continue to live on during the-time-of-war-not-peace'.[112]

There are a few empirical studies addressing the long-term multi-layered consequences of sexual violence in war which include physical, psychological, familial and socioeconomic effects.[113] Nicola Jones et al. draw particular attention to some of the wider effects of wartime rape and sexual violence, including the effect on family members who are forced to watch their loved ones suffer.[114] Rarely were these magnified in case studies that would generate empirical knowledge by analysing the lived experience narrated by a survivor. This book contributes to these studies and provides an analysis of the socio-legal effects by exploring how law and its failures may contribute to the long-term stress on the mental and physical well-being of victims. As Antony Pemberton, Eva Mulder and

---

[109] Gilligan defines behavioural violence as 'harmful actions of specific individuals'. James Gilligan, *Violence: Reflections on Our Deadliest Epidemic* (Jessica Kingsley, 1996).

[110] Johan Galtung, 'Violence, Peace and Peace Research' (1969) 6(3) *Journal of Peace Research* 167.

[111] Slavoj Žižek, *Violence* (Profile Books, 2008).

[112] Krystalli (n 42) 140.

[113] Janine Natalya Clark, *Rape, Sexual Violence and Transitional Justice Challenges: Lessons from Bosnia Herzegovina* (Routledge, 2017) 51.

[114] Nicola Jones et al., 'The Fallout of Rape as a Weapon of War: The Life-Long and Intergenerational Impacts of Sexual Violence in Conflict' (Research Report, Overseas Development Institute, 8 June 2014) 2–3.

Pauline Aarten argue, narrative criminology should move towards understanding criminal justice processes 'in the way they are encountered by victims as an element of their unfolding narrative'.[115] The scholars also argue that future victimological studies should allow for more attention to the way the experience of victimisation and its aftermath, and the interaction with the criminal justice system and social surroundings 'is embedded in the life story of people'.[116] The first-hand life stories offer 'counter-discourses' that are engaged in battle with the state 'over identity construction and representation'.[117] Such representations by the state are contested by survivors' narratives. My study is a contribution to this bourgeoning literature.

Lola's story tells us 'a different kind of war story'[118] that explores the violence that continues in justice bureaucracies. Such stories offer a different understanding of violence, 'its endings, and its afterlives'.[119] It is the story told first-hand which tells us how one woman has experienced the wrongdoing; how she understands her own experience and actions in relation to her identity and the wider collective to which she belongs.[120] As philosopher Susan Brison, in her first-person account of her own rape states:

> When the trauma is of human origin and is intentionally inflicted...it not only shatters one's fundamental assumptions about the world and one's safety in it, but it also severs the sustaining connection between the self and the rest of humanity.[121]

---

[115] Antony Pemberton, Eva Mulder and Pauline GM Aarten, 'Stories of Injustice: Towards a Narrative of Victimology' (2019) 16(4) *European Journal of Criminology* 391, 401.

[116] Ibid 406.

[117] Paul Gready, *Writing as Resistance: Life Stories of Imprisonment, Exile, and Homecoming From Apartheid South Africa* (Lexington Books, 2003) 190.

[118] Krystallii (n 42) 125.

[119] Ibid.

[120] See Pemberton, Mulder and Aarten (n 115) 392.

[121] Susan Brison, *Aftermath: Violence and the Remaking of a Self* (Princeton University Press, 2002) 40.

Susan Silbey has also emphasised the importance of 'getting across lived experience [of law] not some idealistic, legalistic, theoretical notion of what the law was supposed to be'.[122] Douglas is also adamant that we need to understand how legal systems are working on the ground if we want to make them work better for the people they are supposed to serve.[123] While strong emphasis in BiH has been on victims' trauma and victimhood which arguably contributes to 'a culture of passivity',[124] my study also underlines the resilience and strength in coping with and surviving abuse. The case study will show how some survivors, such as Lola, engage in practices that help them 'to navigate their way to the resources'[125] they need to reach their objectives. This is important to emphasise since in each story of oppression and suffering there runs a parallel history of opposition and defiance.[126] My study aims to highlight the complexities of lives often obscured by too much attention paid to the 'success' or 'failure' of mechanisms deployed in specific transitional justice communities. It uses alternative accounts of sexual violence in war 'to discourage advocates from assuming that stigma and shame are natural responses to rape'[127] and to question the matrixes that researchers and practitioners use to measure the meaning of 'successful' criminal trials and reparative programmes.

The study will demonstrate that victimhood and resilience are not necessarily mutually exclusive but may exist in different stages of survivors' lives, and are expressed and acted upon diversely. It will also dismantle the common assumptions that victims are robbed of agency and are perceived as communities that need to be rescued 'lacking the ability

---

[122] Simon Halliday and Patrick Schmidt, *Conducting Law and Society Research: Reflections of Methods and Practices* (Cambridge University Press, 2009) 215.

[123] Hazel Genn, 'Understanding Civil Justice' 1997 50(1) *Current Legal Problems* 155; Hazel Genn, *Paths to Justice: What People Do and Think About Going to Law* (Hart Publishing, 1999); Heather Douglas (n 94) 6.

[124] Janine Natalya Clark, 'Helping or Harming: NGOs and Victims/-survivors of Conflict-related Sexual Violence in Bosnia-Herzegovina' (2019) 18(2) *Journal of Human Rights* 246.

[125] Michael Ungar, 'Resilience, Trauma, Context, and Culture' (2013) 14(3) *Trauma, Violence and Abuse* 255, 256.

[126] Margareta Hydén, '"I Must have Been an Idiot to Let it Go On": Agency and Positioning in Battered Women's Narratives of Leaving' (2005) 15(2) *Feminism and Psychology* 169, 173.

[127] Engle (n 47) 17.

to make decisions about the future, or as people driven by destructive psychosis that renders them incapable or morally unworthy of positive contributions to peace-building'.[128] Both pain and growth, rather than irreconcilable differences are inextricably linked in the recovery from loss and trauma.[129] By using the case study of Lola, I raise a series of critical questions surrounding national trials and reparative programmes and their outcomes, and the meaning of lack of sentence execution in domestic courts in countries emerging from widespread violence.

---

[128] Patricia Lundy and Mark McGovern, 'Whose Justice: Rethinking Transitional Justice from the Bottom Up' (2008) 35(2) *Journal of Law and Society* 265; Tshepo Madlingozi, 'On Transitional Justice Entrepreneurs and the Production of Victims' (2010) 13(2) *Journal of Human Rights Practice* 212.

[129] Konstantinos Tsirigotis and Joanna Łuczak, 'Resilience in Women Who Experience Domestic Violence' (2018) 89(1) *Psychiatric Quarterly* 201.

CHAPTER 3

Lola's War

On the 8th of May 1992 Lola, a 29-year-old widowed mother, together with her sister and their children, were rounded up by a Bosnian Croatian special unit called *Vatreni Konji* [Fiery Steeds]. Together with other Serb women, children and men from her village Novi Grad, Lola and her family were forced out of their homes at gunpoint and pushed into vehicles that took them to the neighbouring town. Some villagers rode their horses with the few belongings they could grab before being rounded up and maltreated by soldiers. Lola and her three children were in a green Mazda car driven by her brother-in-law in a column formed together with other expelled people that stretched for miles. Her mother-in-law and father-in-law were also in a column. Once they arrived at their destination, Lola and her fellow villagers were searched for weapons. The men were then separated from the women and children and detained in the abandoned primary school while the women were rounded up with their children on a bare plot of land. Lola arrived at the camp with her nine-month-old baby daughter tightly clutched in her arms and four- and six-year-old daughter and son. Her children were among the youngest concentration camp detainees.

According to data collected by the war veterans' associations, Croatian soldiers on that day detained 1294 Serb civilians. Out of this there were 864 men, 326 women and 140 children from the Odžak County, the villages of Novi Grad, Gornja and Donja Dubica, Gornji Svilaj, Lipik, and

© The Author(s), under exclusive license to Springer Nature Singapore Pte Ltd. 2023
O. Simic, *Lola's War*,
https://doi.org/10.1007/978-981-99-1942-0_3

Trnjak. During their two months of detention, some 60 women were raped, 42 detainees were killed and the rest were tortured, starved and abused. For the crimes committed in these camps only a handful of people have been prosecuted before the local courts to date.[1]

The plot of land where women and children were brought to was fenced with barbed wire and became a makeshift concentration camp. An armed soldier tore Lola's daughter from her breasts and threw her onto the ground in search of weapons. Lola was screaming from the top of her lungs fearing the soldiers would kill the child. The soldiers ripped the baby's clothes off and asked Lola whether she had hidden weapons in them. After tossing and turning the baby and not finding anything, they let Lola pick up her distressed daughter from the ground. She was then sent with her children and other women to the surrounding abandoned houses where they were detained. Soldiers would come and go as they wished to the houses occupied by Lola and the other women. They would choose from among the women and take them to the nearby residences where they resided. There, these women were in turn gang raped.

For the next two months, women detainees were regularly raped—the perpetrators were their former neighbours, now turned members of the special military unit the Fiery Steeds, recruited from the 102nd brigade of the Croatian Defence Council (HVO). It was the founders of the HVO who had established the concentration camps to house Serbs from the Odžak County. The Fiery Steeds have been mentioned repeatedly in reports to the UN Commission of Experts as perpetrators of ethnic cleansing against Serb civilians. Their members raped and killed Serb civilians, looted and destroyed their property, including homes and religious establishments. Odžak County on the border of Croatia and Bosnia and Herzegovina (BiH) was the target of such attacks between April and

---

[1] Vid Blagojević, '60 Women Raped, Serbs Tortured in 132 Ways: 29 Years Have Passed Since the Persecution of the Serbian People in Posavina, 42 Camp Inmates Have Been Killed', *Новости* (online, 5 August 2021) https://www.novosti.rs/republika-srpska/vesti/995196/silovali-60-zena-mucili-srbe-132-nacina-progona-srpskog-naroda-posavini-proslo-29-godina-ubijena-42-logorasa-foto: It is extremely difficult to know exact numbers of judgments in such cases since there is no central data base in which judgements from all local courts are registered. Human rights activists who work on these issues have to count the cases manually by investigating archives and databases in each local court that prosecutes war crimes.

August 1992. It has also been well documented that members of this unit were frequently engaged in sexual assault and gang rape activities.[2]

In these camps, the children witnessed the abuse and torture of their mothers. They witnessed as their mothers were taken away from them in obvious distress, while being beaten, shoved and pushed into cars by soldiers. The children heard their screams and cries for help. When women were taken away to be raped, their housemates—the other women left behind—would take turns to care for each other's children. On the 4th of July 1992, after two months of abuse and torture, Lola and her three young children were released 'in exchange' for the Croatian civilian victims of war captured by the Serb army. This was the second time the military men belonging to different armies made judgements of life and death for Lola and her children. Their lives were 'exchanged' and thus preserved. Due to hunger and maltreatment Lola had lost twenty kilogrammes while in the camp. She was extremely malnourished, just skin and bones.

However, her suffering did not end with 'the liberation'. As Viktor Frankl writes, there are three phases of a prisoner's life. First, is arrival at a death camp. Second, is learning to adapt to the inconceivable and impossible. The third phase, release and liberation which does not necessarily mean an end to the imprisonment. It can continue in disillusionment, in bitterness, a struggle for happiness and meaning.[3] After he was 'exchanged' and 'liberated', her father-in-law who was in his sixties died a few weeks later from a cardiac arrest. The torture, the beatings and maltreatment he went through had broken his heart. This happened to many other victims of prolonged and repeated torture. Once released into freedom, they died from medical complications triggered by infections and wounds left untreated while in the camps.[4]

The suffering from sexual abuse was exacerbated by the fact that Lola and the other women actually knew who their rapists were; in fact they knew them well. Ilija Jurić, a young soldier and member of the Fiery Steeds unit, was a former neighbour and friend of Lola's deceased

---

[2] United Nations Security Council, *Final Report of the United Nations Commission of Experts Established Pursuant to Security Council Resolution 780 (1992)*, annex ('Annex III.A Special Forces') (28 December 1994).

[3] Viktor E Frankl, *Man's Search for Meaning* (Beacon Press, 1946).

[4] 'Victims of the Wars 1992–1995' *adpacem.org* (Web page, undated <https://adpacem.org/en/bosnia-and-herzegovina-our-support/victims-of-the-wars-1992-1995/>.

husband, Milan. Milan was 32 years old and had only been drafted into the war for a few days before he was killed as a soldier of the Serb army. Less than two weeks after Lola had buried him, and while still grieving, she was taken together with her children to the detention camp by Jurić and others.

Before the war, Lola, her husband and Jurić lived in the same *komšiluk* [neighbourhood] and would regularly pass by each other's houses. In BiH, *komšije* [neighbours] have almost the same significance as extended family.[5] Before the war *komšiluk* signified a close-knit community of nearby neighbours who all socialised together despite being members of different ethnic groups.[6] They borrowed tools and farm machinery from each another. They went to each other's weddings and funerals. In the villages, such as Lola's, neighbours helped each other during the hay season in the fields[7] and drank coffee in any spare time.[8] On her way to and from work on a nearby farm, Lola would regularly pass by Jurić's house and some of the other Fiery Steeds members houses. Sometimes she would wave her hand to greet some of their family members resting or working in the front yard. They all lived in the surrounding small villages packed one next to each other. As David Henig described it, '*komšiluk* is the space where people live with one another, rather than next to each other'.[9] In the court's decision on Jurić, the meaning of the term *komšiluk* was important—in terms of being able to assume and trust

---

[5] The idea of neighbourhood (komšiluk) as a social mechanism has been widely discussed in the anthropology of Bosnia. See more on pre-war social relations between people in Bosnia in: Elizabeth Neuffer, *The Key to My Neighbour's House: Seeking Justice in Bosnia and Rwanda* (Bloomsbury, 2003); Tone Bringa, *Being Muslim the Bosnian Way: Identity and Community in a Central Bosnian Village* (Princeton University Press, 1995); David Henig, '"Knocking on My Neighbour's Door": On Metamorphoses of Sociality in Rural Bosnia', (2012) 32(1) *Critique of Anthropology* 3.

[6] Xavier Bougarel, 'Twenty Years Later: Was Ethnic War Just a Myth?' (2013) 61(4) *Südosteuropa* 573, 574.

[7] Nevena Medic, 'Helpers Across the Ethnic Divide: The Role of Komšiluk in Rescuing During the Bosnian Conflict' (2021) 2(2) *Historia Moderna* 86, 95.

[8] On the importance of coffee culture in BiH, see Elissa Helms, 'The Gender of Coffee: Woman and Reconciliation Initiatives in Bosnia and Herzegovina' (2010) 57 *Focal— Journal of Global and Historical Anthropology* 17, 17–23; Olivera Simic, 'Drinking Coffee in Bosnia: Listening to Stories of Wartime Violence and Rape' (2017) 18(4) *Journal of International Women's Studies* 321.

[9] Henig (n 5) 10–15.

that someone would have known their neighbours well—in their statement that, '...the witness...knew the best accused Iliju Jurić (she was his first *komšinica*)...'.¹⁰

Lola's trust in people, in particular men, was broken after she had survived everything that had occurred at the hands of her once neighbours. She reported to her neuropsychiatrist that she feels very depressed, nervous and helpless. Her new post-war neighbours do not understand her. Lola reported that some of them even blame her for her misfortune. They told her, 'How come that they picked up you and not someone else?'¹¹ The literature shows that victims of sexual violence are particularly vulnerable to being judged and blamed for their attack, unlike many other interpersonal crimes such as muggings or robberies.¹² Many victims such as Lola, have to endure not just their own trauma but also the secondary victimisation due to negative reactions of those around them.¹³ When she finally reported what had happened, what she had endured, she was disbelieved. Another blow, another pain for Lola came from not being trusted by her own fellow ethnic group members. Even three decades after the war, women victims of wartime rape still do not want to come forward and testify due to 'societally imposed and internalised feelings of shame and blame' and a fear that the community will judge them.¹⁴

Before the war, Lola had completed her primary school education but had not had an opportunity for secondary studies.

---

[10] See *Prosecutor v Ilija Jurić, Appeals Division of the Court of Bosnia and Herzegovina*, S1 1 K 018179 16 Kžž, 21 March 2017 [21].

[11] Documents on file with author dated from 1998.

[12] Steffen Bieneck and Barbara Krahé, 'Blaming the Victim and Exonerating the Perpetrator in Cases of Rape and Robbery: Is There a Double Standard?' (2011) 26(9) *Journal of Interpersonal Violence* 26, 1785; Claire R. Gravelin, Monica Baldwin and Matthew Biernat, 'The Impact of Power and Powerlessness on Blaming the Victim of Sexual Assault' (2017) 22(1) *Group Processes & Intergroup Relations* 98–115.

[13] J E Williams, 'Secondary Victimization: Confronting Public Attitudes About Rape' (1984) 9(1) *Victimology* 66.

[14] 'In Bosnia and Herzegovina, Stigmatization Persists for Victims Of Wartime Sexual Violence', *Trial International* (online, 17 April 2020) <https://trialinternational.org/latest-post/in-bosnia-and-herzegovina-stigmatization-persists-for-victims-of-wartime-sexual-violence/>.

> To be honest with you I did not know that something like a 'high school' even existed at the time... We lived in a village. My father was a farmer and we all had to work the land. I have just worked all my life.... I hardly finished primary school. Each day as soon as I returned from school my mother would give me sheep and cows to take out to graze.... We had livestock and land to harvest... we ploughed the fields...we all worked hard, children and adults...I had no joy in my life ever. The whole of my life I have just worked hard and listened to others...I have never experienced anything nice in my life...I have never seen the sea, never travelled anywhere, never dressed up to wait for a New Year eve party...I just knew hard work and then war and mayhem and now this poverty...my whole life feels like nothing...I had no joy apart from my children...I thank God that they are good and healthy...they are all the happiness that I know.

When she was older, Lola worked at a local cattle farm together with her husband who was a supervisor at the farm. They had built a house nearby and had their three children together over a period of a few years. The house they had built for their family, with their own hands and on modest incomes, was robbed and demolished during the war. However, its construction frames remain, and stand among the wild grass, the flowers now grow from the earth beneath it. They serve as a testament of their past lives. Today, Lola lives some fifteen kilometres away from her pre-war home and sometimes passes by it when visiting her husband's grave nearby. To mourn him is to mourn more than a person: she mourns the family life gone forever with no will of her own. She also often passes by her perpetrator's pre-war home. She told me that his house is now abandoned with broken wooden blinds shut over its windows.

> It [the house] is still standing, but no one lives in it. I have never seen the blinds open on its windows. He lives abroad with his family.

Witnessing the Crime

Twenty years after the crimes were committed against Lola and other women in the Posavina region, Odžak County, the calls to investigate and establish the truth about the events of the past were enacted by the judiciary of the Republika Srpska. In 2012, the investigations into the crimes committed against Serb civilians from Posavina finally started. Lola, her sister and other women victims gave their statements to investigators. In January 2015 the state Court handed down an indictment against Jurić and others. After almost two years of legal proceedings, including several trips to Sarajevo made by Lola to testify against indictees, Jurić was finally prosecuted and sentenced in September 2016.[15] This 'victory' happened only after the successful overturn of a non-guilty verdict brought in November 2015, which released Jurić from all charges, including the wartime rape of Lola.[16] Lola waited a quarter of a century to see her perpetrator tried and convicted. In Lola's case, her truth-telling resulted in the judgement and sentencing, but her actions did not 'facilitate closure'.[17] On the contrary, they triggered the continuation of stress and suffering. As Eric Stover writes,

> Contemporary writings about the needs of survivors of mass atrocity are peppered with terms like 'healing,' 'closure,' 'forgiveness,' and 'reconciliation' and phrases such as 'coming to terms with the past' ... Indeed, a primary weakness of writings on justice in the aftermath of war and political violence is the paucity of empirical evidence to substantiate claims about how well criminal trials achieve the goals ascribed to them.[18]

During the criminal proceedings, Lola did not have a legal representative and rejected the witness protection that was offered to her. She clenched her hands into fists. '*No one was protecting me in 1992. No one needs to protect me now*'. With a defiance and pride she repeated this statement several times during our multiple conversations. Every time she told me this, her chin stiffened. There is no free legal aid for victims of wartime rape but paradoxically, the accused has a right to an attorney, whose full expenses are paid from the state budget.[19] Nonetheless, testifying before the court gave Lola an opportunity to break the silence and for her experience to be transformed from the private to public space. The shame and humiliation often experienced by women who have survived sexual abuse

---

[15] *Prosecutor v Ilija Jurić*, (n 10).

[16] *Prosecutor v Ilija Jurić, Court of Bosnia and Herzegovina*, S1 1 K 018179 16 Kžž, 9 November 2015.

[17] See Neil J Kritz (ed), *Transitional Justice: How Emerging Democracies Reckon with Former Regimes* (United States Institute of Peace Press, 1995).

[18] Eric Stover, *The Witnesses: War Crimes and the Promise of Justice in The Hague* (University of Pennsylvania Press, 2005) 11.

[19] Kristina Ljevak, 'Život u miru nakon silovanja u ratu' *Diskriminacija* (online, 24 October 2016) https://www.diskriminacija.ba/teme/život-u-miru-nakon-silovanja-u-ratu.

can in this way turn into virtue and dignity which gives power and control to individuals who testify.[20] The question is, how long has this feeling of 'power and control' lasted in Lola's case?

While Lola was satisfied that Jurić would finally end up in prison, she was disappointed to see the rest of her alleged wartime rapists walking free. She never anticipated that Jurić, in the end, would walk free too. Truth-telling may have given Lola a voice to share her experience and provide an account of her suffering, which had the potential to bring about public knowledge and an acknowledgement of what had happened. However, the aftermath of her trial spoiled any possible gains from reclaiming her sense of autonomy and dignity she had lost in the experience of being victimised. On the contrary, for Lola the act of public truth-telling did not mark the beginning of her individual healing[21] but a continuation, even the exacerbation of stress and trauma.

On 5 October 2015, Lola testified and repeated that she had been raped by Jurić and that among the soldiers who were also present when she was raped were the brothers P.G. and I. G., Marijan Brnjić and M. B.[22] She said that all of the alleged rapists had been wearing camouflage uniforms with the HVO emblems and that they had been carrying rifles. They did not use their real names among themselves but nicknames, and they wore balaclavas. Yet, apart from Jurić, all of them were acquitted. Similar to other cases of wartime sexual abuse in other jurisdictions, the judges were satisfied with the evidence that rape was inflicted, but the identity of the perpetrators could not be proved beyond reasonable doubt.[23]

---

[20] Jonathan Doak, 'The Therapeutic Dimension of Transitional Justice: Emotional Repair and Victim Satisfaction in International Trials and Truth Commissions' (2011) 11(2) *International Criminal Law Review* 263.

[21] Priscilla B Hayner, *Unspeakable Truths: Confronting State Terror and Atrocity* (Routledge, 2000).

[22] 'Witness Confirms Rape by Ilija Jurić', *The Srpska Times* (online, 10 June 2015) https://thesrpskatimes.com/witness-confirms-rape-by-ilija-Jurić/.

[23] The problem of identifying a perpetrator is an issue in other post conflict jurisdictions. See Jelke Boesten, *Sexual Violence During War and Peace: Gender, Power, and Post-Conflict Justice in Peru* (Palgrave Macmillan, 2014) 115.

Hence, many cases were dropped due to lack of evidence and the impossibility of establishing the identity of perpetrators before the criminal court.[24] Given that there are often neither eyewitnesses or supporting medical records in wartime rape cases, international tribunals have established that a conviction can be based on the victim's testimony alone.[25] However, certain BiH courts have responded to cases lacking corroborating evidence by subjecting victims to 'abnormally high standards of credibility and/or acquitting perpetrators'.[26] Lola felt she was not given space to tell her story and when she asked her perpetrator, '*Would you do it again?*' the judge intervened by shushing her quickly while instructing her that was inappropriate to ask. Lola found her whole experience of testifying intimidating and unsatisfactory. She wanted Jurić to give her some rational explanation for his actions which were so inhumane. Lola wanted to receive some assurance that Jurić would never do what he had done again. She wanted him to take responsibility for his actions, to say that he regrets them. This is precisely what most offenders are advised not to do as that would incriminate them and therefore make them accountable for what they had done.[27] Jurić never admitted to allegations made against him and denied that he had been in the detention camp at the time, let alone raped Lola.[28] For Lola however, she still needs his remorse

---

[24] Morten Bergsmo, Alf Butenschøn Skre and Elisabeth J Wood (eds), *Understanding and Proving International Sex Crimes* (Torkel Opsahl Academic EPublisher, 2012).

[25] *Rules of Procedure and Evidence for the International Criminal Tribunal for the Former Yugoslavia*, UN Doc IT/32/REV.50 (8 July 2015) r 96 ('ICTY Rules of Procedure and Evidence'). Rule 96 of the ICTY Rules of Procedure and Evidence provides: 'In cases of sexual assault: (i) no corroboration of the victim's testimony shall be required'. Kunarac also clarified Rule 96 of the ICTY Statute dealing with consent: see *Prosecutor v Kunarac, Kovac, and Vukovic (Judgment)* (International Tribunal for the Former Yugoslavia, Trial Chamber, Case No. IT-96-23/I-T (22 February 2001) [464] ('Kunarac').

[26] TRIAL International, *Rape Myths in Wartime Sexual Violence Trials: Transferring the Burden from Survivor to Perpetrator* (Report, 2017) 8.

[27] 'Remorse and Restorative Justice: Is It Needed?', *Restorative Justice International* (online, 28 November 2012) https://www.restorativejusticeinternational.com/remorse-restorative-justice-is-it-needed/.

[28] 'Jurić: Konacna presuda 26 Septembra', *Ratni Zločini Tranzicijska Pravda* (online, 9 September 2016) https://detektor.ba/2016/09/09/Jurić-konacna-presuda-26-septembra/.

and his conviction that he would never do the same again; that what he did he regrets.²⁹

Another indictee in her case, Marijan Brnjić was acquitted for raping Lola but was later prosecuted in another case for the rape of two women who were allegedly with Lola on the night when the gang raped occurred.³⁰ He was sentenced to cumulatively twelve years in prison. Brnjić received six years for each woman he raped.³¹ Lola testified in that case too. However, she still cannot understand how it was possible that the rapist was prosecuted for raping fellow women who were taken with her on the same night, to the same house to be gang raped, but then acquitted for raping her. Visibly disturbed, Lola wove her fingers together in front of her and told me:

> *Why did they not prosecute him for raping me too? I wanted to testify again and asked them to open the case again, but they said they cannot prosecute him twice.*

Jurić was solely convicted for raping and sexually abusing Lola in a house in Posavska Mahala on the night of the 4th of June 1995, when he was a member of the Croatian 102nd Brigade. The rest of the indictees that Lola and the other women survivors wanted imprisoned for sexually abusing them, were released due to a lack of evidence that the alleged perpetrators committed the crimes they were accused of.

Danger to Witness

After the legal proceedings began in 2015, Lola's life was in danger. As documented, witnesses in criminal prosecutions are prone to suffer

---

²⁹ See, Hershey H Friedman, 'The Power of Remorse and Apology' (2006) 7(1) *Journal of College and Character* 1.

³⁰ A Doe, 'Brnjicu potvrdjena kazna za silovanje Srpkinja', *Nezavisne.com* (Report, 8 June 2017) https://www.nezavisne.com/novosti/hronika/Brnjicu-potvrdjena-kazna-za-silovanje-Srpkinja/429785.

³¹ The average prison sentence for wartime rape before the Bosnian courts is four years of imprisonment: See TRIAL International, *Punishing Conflict-Related Sexual Violence: Guidelines for Combatting Inconsistencies in Sentencing* (Report, 2018) https://trial.ba/wp-content/uploads/2019/05/01_publication__en_page_by_page_WEB.pdf.

'retaliatory violence' regardless of whether they testify before international or domestic courts.[32] Victor Igreja notes that in some post-conflict contexts, alleged perpetrators 'roam the inner circles of victims or state institutions' and this may prevent survivors talking about the violations they suffered.[33] Having no witness protection, or legal representation, Lola was on her own. The only support came from the women's non-governmental organisation (NGO) *Snaga Žene* [The Power of Women] based in the Federation of BiH. The women working in this NGO offered psychosocial assistance to Lola and the other women witnesses in order to prepare them for the trials. Throughout the years of the trial they visited Lola several times and also donated a greenhouse to help her grow her own vegetables.[34]

A few months into the trial, Lola was ambushed by an unknown man who attempted to drag her into his car on her way to the city to do some shopping. On that day the street was deserted so no one witnessed the incident. It was usual for her to walk several kilometres to the shops. '*He must have followed me and attacked me when there was no one at the road at that moment*', Lola told me. The man knew the best time to attack Lola, leaving no witnesses. Lola resisted, she fought back with her fists and she screamed at him to let go of her. The man eventually gave up, but while still grasping Lola's left wrist from his driver's seat he pressed the accelerator pedal, leaving her frightened and bruised in the middle of the road. Lola stumbled and fell on the concrete. She called her friend to come and pick her up, and later on called the police. Shocked and in distress, she could not remember the car registration number. The culprit could not be identified and was never found.

If only I could remember his car registration number, they would find him. But it was not on my mind to look at the number. I was so distressed and terrified he may drag me into his car and take me away with him.

---

[32] Nancy Armoury Combs, *Guilty Pleas in International Criminal Law: Constructing a Restorative Justice Approach* (Stanford University Press, 2007) 42.

[33] Victor Igreja, 'Negotiating Relationships in Transition: War, Famine, and Embodied Accountability in Mozambique' (2019) 61(4) *Comparative Studies in Society and History* 774, 789.

[34] Interview with representative of NGO '*Snaga Žene*' (Olivera Simic, Phone Interview, 19 October 2022).

The feeling of guilt for not remembering the registration number remains with her and she has told me several times over the years how she regrets not being able to remember the number of offender's car. This incident, however, did not stop her from continuing with her case.

Due to similar experiences, many women are afraid to act as witnesses in criminal trials. The media has brought attention to the threats that some women and men witnesses have faced from indicted war criminals and their families.[35] It has been reported that witnesses have received phone threats and also threats in-person from their own doorsteps, from an indicted war criminal's family member who has threatened them in case they act as witnesses in the trial.[36] Such threats not only aim to intimidate particular witnesses but they send a broader message to all potential witnesses, not to give evidence at a trial. There have been documented cases where witness have died from heart attacks after receiving threats,[37] and even from the fear of receiving them, as happened to Lola's sister. Even if a witness enjoys the status of 'protected witness' and their identity is concealed, the indictees and their families or friends can still sometimes find out who they are and can then assault them, verbally and physically.

Although the disclosure of the identity of a 'protected witness' is a crime and the accused could be punished by imprisonment[38] the courts of BiH have so far only served a handful of judgements for such crimes. In one of the cases, the accused was a journalist who received only a six-month suspended sentence for this criminal offence.[39] In another case,

---

[35] 'Udruženje "Žena-žrtva rata" prijavilo tužiteljstvu i SIPA-i prijetnje žrtvama i svjedocima', *Klix* (online, 12 May 2008) https://www.klix.ba/vijesti/bih/udruzenje-zena-zrtva-rata-prijavilo-tuziteljstvu-i-sipa-i-prijetnje-zrtvama-i-svjedocima/080512087.

[36] Ibid; A Hadžić, 'Nove Prijetnje Svjedocima: Bošnjaci Vlasenice i Milića opet na meti optuženih ratnih zločinaca', *Izdvojeno.ba* (online, 4 February 2022) https://izdvojeno.ba/nove-prijetnje-svjedocima-bosnjaci-vlasenice-i-milica-opet-na-meti-optuzenih-ratnih-zlocinaca/.

[37] A. Hadžić, 'Pokušaj zastrašivanja svjedoka zločina u Zvorniku', *Politika* (online, 28 April 2022) https://politicki.ba/vijesti/pokusaj-zastrasivanja-svjedoka-zlocina-u-zvorniku/22916.

[38] The Criminal Code of BiH Article 240 prescribes that a person could be punished by imprisonment for a term between six months and five years: *The Criminal Code of Bosnia and Herzegovina* (*Bosnia and Herzegovina*) art 240.

[39] Džana Brkanić, 'Prijetnje svjedocima bez istraga', *Justice Report* (online, 6 November 2014) https://www.justice-report.com/bh/sadržaj-članci/prijetnje-svjedocima-bez-istraga.

a wife of an indicted war criminal disclosed the identity of a protected witness on her Facebook profile. The motivation in this case was retaliation for her husband's prosecution which saw him sentenced to 17 years in jail for the war crimes he committed in Višegrad. She received a two-year suspended sentence for this criminal offence.[40] Such lenient sentences for these serious offences of disclosing a witness's identity in the war crime trials, do not serve as any deterrent to other people who plan to intimidate witnesses. Thus, due to these threats and intimidations, victims either do not want to or are forced to withdraw from the criminal trials.[41]

Evading Justice

Once prosecuted, Jurić simply never showed up to serve his sentence and has never been summoned to do so. After the first-degree judgement was handed down in November 2015, which freed him from any accountability for the wartime rapes, he vanished into 'thin air'. However, in September 2016 he was found guilty after Lola appealed that first-degree verdict. In September 2021, five years after the final judgement was handed down that saw him sentenced to six years in prison, the Court of BiH publicly released a warrant. On the list of names on this warrant was Jurić and more than 130 other individuals who had previously escaped justice and never served their sentences for war crimes. The warrant was published in the local media and listed perpetrators with their full names and dates of birth. It also listed their potential locations. For Jurić, the Court stated that his location was 'unknown'[42] although, in the judgement itself, the judge stated that Jurić lives and works in one of the neighbouring countries. Even though the warrant had been published in several online local outlets, Lola did not know of its existence until I told

---

[40] *Prosecutor v Branka Šekaric*, S1 3 K 021481 17 K, Court of Bosnia and Herzegovina, 17 May 2017.

[41] See Mission to Bosnia and Herzegovina, Organisation for Security and Co-operation in Europe, 'Zaštita i podrška svjedoka u predmetima ratnih zločina u Bosni i Hercegovini: Prepreke i preporuke godinu dana nakon usvajanja Državne strategije za rad na predmetima ratnih zločina' (Report, January 2010) https://www.osce.org/files/f/documents/e/4/118894.pdf.

[42] 'Utočište u Srbiji: Objavljujemo spisak i lokacije svih osoba koje traži Sud BiH zbog ratnih zločina', *Patria* (online, 21 September 2021) https://nap.ba/news/84253.

her. Soon after the Court of BiH released the warrant, the International Criminal Police Organization (Interpol) released a Red Notice for Jurić,[43] advising any country that Jurić should be arrested, except Croatia where he is a citizen. Yet, eighteen months after the release of the Court BiH warrant and Interpol Red Notice, Jurić has still not been arrested. He is most probably in Croatia since he has its citizenship. However, even if the Croatian government arrests Jurić it is highly likely that the government would release him due to the unwillingness of the state to cooperate with BiH institutions in the extradition of the war criminals.

There is at least one case where the Croatian government released a prosecuted war criminal once he found himself on their territory. Marko Radić, a prosecuted war criminal, was transferred to serve his sentence in Croatia from BiH. BiH is a member of the European Convention on the Transfer of Sentenced Persons[44] which promulgates that each convicted person has a right to serve in full or in part of his/her sentence in the state of his/her citizenship. According to this Convention between BiH and other states, transfers are made each year. Also, there is a Memorandum about the mutual execution of the court decisions in criminal cases signed between Croatia and BiH. Radić was sentenced to twenty-one years in prison for war crimes and crimes against humanity and after serving seven years in BiH prison he was transferred to Croatia on approval of the then Ministry of Justice Josip Grubeš. Once transferred Radić was fully released after serving only two months in prison.[45] It remains unclear why Radić was transferred to Croatia in the first place because he is also a citizen of BiH, therefore he had already served his sentence in his country of origin.[46]

One of the major obstacles remaining in processing war crime cases is the unavailability and inaccessibility of the defendants to the relevant

---

[43] Anyone can use a search engine on the Interpol website and google for Jurić. See https://www.interpol.int/en/How-we-work/Notices/View-Red-Notices.

[44] *Convention on the Transfer of Sentenced Persons, Opened for Signature 21 March* 1983, ETS 112 (entered into force 1 July 1985).

[45] Faruk Vele, 'Ratni zlocinac Marko Maka Radic pusten na slobodu', *Tacno* (online, 25 February 2019), https://www.tacno.net/mostar/ratni-zlocinac-marko-maka-radic-pusten-na-slobodu/.

[46] 'Cilj transfera osuđenih osoba je izdržavanje kazne u zemlji porijekla, Marko Radić je državljanin BiH', *Inicijativa za monitoring Evropskih integracija* (online, undated), https://eu-monitoring.ba/cilj-transfera-osudenih-osoba-je-izdrzavanje-kazne-u-zemlji-porijekla-marko-radic-je-drzavljanin-bih/.

courts in BiH or their release from detention in Croatia. The problem of unavailability not only affects those like Jurić who have been prosecuted already, but also those who are parties in ongoing cases. It affects approximately thirty eight per cent of war crime cases across BiH at all jurisdictional levels.[47] The reasons for their inaccessibility are manyfold. Most of those who are unavailable are in the neighbouring countries, such as Serbia and Croatia. However, Croatia is not willing to cooperate with investigations and extradition of their citizens. In 2015 the Croatian Premier Zoran Milanović publicly stated that Croatia won't act on 'political indictments' from neighbouring countries. The government of Croatia explicitly rejected the statement of the BiH judiciary which accuses the Croatian army of its involvement in crimes during wars in BiH and beyond. The government stated that accepting such claims would be against Croatian 'national interests'. It gave instructions to the Ministry of Justice to take into account 'vital interest of Croatian state' when deciding upon requests for assistance in investigations or arrests from the BiH judiciary.[48] Since then most of the requests sent by the State Prosecutor Office to the Croatian Ministry of Justice were rejected on the pretext of being detrimental to the Croatian 'state interests'.[49] Croatian citizens are also protected from extradition by the Constitution of Republic of Croatia. In its Article 9, the Constitution promulgates that,

> A citizen of the Republic of Croatia may not be forcibly expelled from the Republic of Croatia nor deprived of citizenship, nor extradited to another state, except in the execution of a decision on extradition or

---

[47] Her Honour Judge Joanna Korner, *Improving War Crimes Processing at the State Level in Bosnia and Herzegovina* (Report, 16 September 2020); Mission to Bosnia and Herzegovina, Organisation for Security and Co-operation in Europe, War Crimes Processing in Bosnia and Herzegovina (2004–2021) (Report, 30 June 2022) https://osce.org/files/f/documents/d/1/494881_0.pdf; Haris Rovcanin, 'Absent War Crime Suspects Pose Problem for Bosnia's New Prosecutor', *BIRN* (online, 5 January 2023), https://balkaninsight.com/2023/01/05/absent-war-crime-suspects-pose-problem-for-bosnias-new-prosecutor/.

[48] 'Hrvatska se buni zbog "političkih optužnica"', *BN* (online, 3 June 2015) https://www.rtvbn.com/346453/Hrvatska-se-buni-zbog-političkih-optuznica%3E.

[49] Interview with a representative of the State Prosecutor's Office in Sarajevo (Oliveral Simic, Phone Interview, 7 October 2022).

surrender made in accordance with an international treaty or the *acquis communautaire* of the European Union.⁵⁰

Since BiH is not a member of the European Union and Croatia has no treaty with BiH on extradition, dual citizens, such as Jurić, are safe from being extradited. Many defendants deliberately relocated abroad and cannot be extradited by law which is a major obstacle to processing war crime cases. According to the Organisation for Security and Co-operation in Europe (OSCE), of the 245 cases in the post-indictment phase at the end of 2021, 100 defendants in a total of 94 cases were inaccessible to the relevant domestic courts.⁵¹ There are also cases where instead of being arrested, the indictee is allowed to leave the country. On the 28th of April 2022, the former commandant of the BiH Army, Sakib Mahmuljin was prosecuted to eight years of imprisonment under a doctrine called 'command responsibility'. In international criminal law command responsibility is a jurisprudential doctrine permitting the prosecution of military commanders for war crimes perpetrated by their subordinates. Mahmuljin was accused of knowing but not preventing the war crimes committed by the paramilitary forces 'El Mujahideen'⁵² which was under his command. The crimes of torture, inhumane treatment and unlawful killings were committed against Serb civilians and prisoners of war in Vozuća and Zavidovići.⁵³ Once prosecuted and sentenced, Mahmuljin left the country and went to Turkey to receive medical treatment. The Court of BiH had no

---

⁵⁰ *The Constitution of the Republic of Croatia*, (*Croatia*), (consolidated text, Official Gazette Nos 56/90, 135/97, 113/00, 28/01, 76/10 and 5/14).

⁵¹ Mission to Bosnia and Herzegovina, Organisation for Security and Co-operation in Europe, *War Crimes Processing in Bosnia and Herzegovina (2004–2021)* (Report, 30 June 2022) https://osce.org/files/f/documents/d/1/4948810.pdf.

⁵² The members of the El Mujahideen Unit, a detachment of Islamic fighters from Middle Eastern countries, killed at least 55 captured Bosnian Serb Army soldiers in the Vozuca and Zavidovici areas from July to September 1995 and decapitated some captured Serb soldiers: Jasmin Begic, 'Bosnian Army Ex-Commander Retried in "El Mujahideen" Fighters Case', *Balkan Insight* (online, 1 December 2021) https://balkaninsight.com/2021/12/01/bosnian-army-ex-commander-retried-in-el-mujahidee; 'Mujahideen Fighters 'Cut off Bosnian Serb Soldiers' Heads', *Balkan Insight* (online, 21 April 2016) https://balkaninsight.com/2016/04/21/bosnian-serb-soldier-recalls-mujahideen-cutting-off-heads-04-21-2016/.

⁵³ 'Sakib Mahmuljin osuden na osam godina zatvora', *Aljazeera* (online, 28 April 2022) https://balkans.aljazeera.net/news/balkan/2022/4/28/sakib-mahmuljin-osudjenna-osam-godina-zatvora.

prohibition measures imposed on him and stated that he was not sent to serve his sentence at the time he left for Turkey.[54]

The Court publicly stated in relation to this case that, 'The court notes that, during the criminal proceedings until the end of the proceedings, no prohibition measures were imposed on the convicted person'.[55] The Serb victims' associations were outraged that Mahmuljin could have left the country. They accused the Court of BiH of 'not imposing any measures prohibiting people from leaving Bosnia, but also [of] not issuing a referral act for serving the sentence after the second-instance verdict'. In this way the Court reportedly enabled Mahmuljin 'to escape under the pretext of [medical] treatment'.[56] This perhaps explains why almost thirty per cent of indictees or prosecuted war criminals are unavailable for prosecution and/or serving their sentences. Jurić also left the country since there were no measures in place to prohibit him from crossing the borders of national jurisdiction.

In BiH, thirty years after the war almost 600 cases involving over 4500 suspects remain unresolved.[57] With the passage of time, these cases are becoming harder to solve. Numerous suspects have never been arrested, nor have proceedings been brought against them. Some of these suspects have been living and working in BiH and some in other countries, while others may have died by now.[58] A study from 2019 uncovered that at least 20 suspected perpetrators had died while awaiting the trial or during

---

[54] Nejra Dzaferagic and Djordje Vujatovic, 'War Criminal's Escape Outrages Bosnian Serb Victims Associations', *Balkan Insight* (online, 11 August 2022) https://balkaninsight.com/2022/08/11/war-criminals-escape-outrages-bosnian-serb-victims-associations/.

[55] Ibid.

[56] Ibid.

[57] Organization for Security and Co-operation in Europe, '*OSCE Mission Presents Judge Korner's Report on War Crimes Processing at State Level in Bosnia and Herzegovina*' (Press Release, 16 September 2020) https://www.osce.org/mission-to-bosnia-and-herzegovina/463764.

[58] See Erna Mackic, 'Poor Cooperation Leaves Balkan War Crime Suspects at Large', *Balkan Insight* (online, 1 October 2018) https://balkaninsight.com/2018/10/01/poor-cooperation-leaves-balkan-war-crime-suspects-at-large-09-26-2018/; 'Bosnia Arrests Five More War Crimes Suspects As Sweep Continues', *RadioFreeEurope/RadioLiberty* (online, 7 December 2013) https://www.rferl.org/a/bosnia-war-crimes-suspects-arrests/31597717.html.

the trial.⁵⁹ On top of that, the age of the defendant becomes a mitigating circumstance, so many of the war crime suspects received lesser sentences because they were arrested in their older age and often suffered from some medical condition.⁶⁰

A Note on Methodology and Positionality

Cynthia Enloe reminds us that,

> One of the starting points of feminism is taking women's lives seriously. 'Seriously' implies listening carefully, digging dip, developing a long attention span, being ready to be surprised.⁶¹

I followed Enloe's advice and listened closely to what preoccupied Lola and how she spoke about her concerns. I listened to what she was saying, what she was testifying to, what truths she holds onto. I also respected what she kept to herself because some things need to remain unsaid. I chronicled Lola's transitional justice life trajectory in order to gauge from her lived experiences and the obstacles she faced on her way to achieve some form of justice for herself and her children. Acknowledging that victims' experiences are diverse and heterogenous, the use of a long-term case study of a woman survivor can offer an in-depth insight into the lived experience of 'working through' the post-conflict country's criminal justice system, a mechanism used by some survivors in BiH in the hope to gain justice. Lola gives us a vivid insight into what it is like to live through—and try to make sense of—violence and its aftermath. Her narrative offers a more complete picture of the workings of violence, negotiating with the past and confrontation with the violence that is still

---

⁵⁹ Emina Dizdarević, 'Another Bosnian Croat Defendant in Stolac Crimes Case Dies', *Balkan Insight* (online, 16 January 2020) https://www.balkaninsight.com/2020/01/16/another-bosnian-croat-defendant-in-stolac-crimes-case-dies/>; Milica Stojanovic, Haris Rovcanin and Anja Vladisavljevic, 'Cases Closed: Deaths of Ageing Balkan War Suspects Thwart Justice', *Balkan Insight* (online, 26 August 2021) https://balkaninsight.com/2021/08/26/cases-closed-deaths-of-ageing-balkan-war-suspects-thwart-justice/.

⁶⁰ *Prosecutor v Marko Samardžija*, Court of Bosnia and Herzegovina, X-KRŽ-05/07, 3 November 2006, 39.

⁶¹ Cynthia Enloe, *The Curious Feminist: Searching for Women in a New Age of Empire* (University of California Press, 2004) 4.

ongoing in different forms and multiple levels. This study validates her knowledge and her wish to make it accessible to women without it.[62]

A limited focus just on the trials fails to reflect on the real-world transitional justice experience of victims who are the main drivers of the legal procedures. Focusing solely on the administration of trials cannot address the long-term legacies and everyday difficulties that victims face in their struggles to bring themselves some form of satisfaction. Such a focus fails to uncover the full dimensions of wartime rape cases and the understanding of victims' lives in the aftermath of violence. Carolyn Nordstrom noted the ability of violence to 'escalate and to insinuate itself into the fabric of everyday life', and she rejects the idea that the battlefield is the only self-contained zone of violence.[63] According to Nordstrom, violence should be categorised 'along a continuum — from necessary to extreme and from civilised to inhumane'.[64] She argues further that,

> (…) the very place researchers choose for studying war is shaped by their notions of what constitutes, and does not constitute, political violence. The people who documented war from its sidelines, pen and paper in hand, went to the sites of military battles. They watched immediate and sometimes immense physical carnage. They were far less likely to trace all the circumstances that led each and every actor to converge on the battlefield; to follow these soldiers as they pursued their lives after the battle. They seldom passed the sites of physical fighting to document less honourable activities — the profiteering among commanders, the lies and deceits among soldiers, the torture behind closed doors. They documented the heroic and tragic. Nor did they find the lives of the soldiers' wives, sisters, and daughters as interesting as the lives of the soldiers themselves (…) There remains a tendency to see a soldier shooting at another soldier as constituting war's violence, while the shooting of a civilian, or the rape of a woman as a soldier returns to the barracks, is seen as peripheral — an accident, an anomaly. The civilian casualty and the rape are understood as different orders of violence situated along a continuum that demarcates both severity and im/morality.[65]

---

[62] See Liz Kelly, *Surviving Sexual Violence* (Polity Press, 1988).

[63] Carolyn Nordstrom, *Shadows of War: Violence, Power, and International Profiteering in the Twenty-First Century* (University of California Press, 2004) 68.

[64] Ibid 57.

[65] Ibid 58.

A longitudinal study into a woman wartime rape survivor is an important source for furthering our understanding of transitional justice processes in post-conflict countries. The study can show us how state-made transitional justice projects 'work in practice'[66] and what kind of effects and structural challenges they may present to survivors fighting for justice. Such studies are rare when it comes to sexual abuse survivors due to multiple issues and challenges they pose, such as the cost of such studies, lengthiness and extensive resources they require to be done well.[67] They are even rarer when it comes to 'unpopular' victims—victims who belong to 'perpetrator nations' or so-called 'wrong victims'[68] such as Serb victims in the context of the BiH war.

I met Lola for the first time in BiH in 2014 when I was doing research into the Serb women raped during the war between 1992 and 1995.[69] What is unique about Lola is that she was one of the few women to testify in the first of the handful of cases brought for the wartime rape of Serb women by the members of the Croatian army in the Posavina region, Odžak County. I gathered Lola's oral 'herstory' through multiple in-depth interviews with her on a number of occasions. I met with her in various places, such as at her home but also in public spaces such as cafes and restaurants. These conversations were undertaken between 2014 and 2022. Most of them can be described as semi-structured often starting with some broad questions that would lead Lola into telling her story.[70] I would ask her about her experience with the national legal system. For example, 'Can you tell me about your experiences as a witness?' I would then follow her narrative and try not to interrupt it unless I sought clarification on some points. I wanted to prioritise her perspectives and experiences of the legal journey on which she was set in order

---

[66] James Ferguson, *The Anti-Politics Machine: Development, Depoliticization, and Bureaucratic Power in Lesotho* (University of Minnesota Press, 2nd ed, 1994) xiv.

[67] Rebecca Campbell et al., 'Longitudinal Research with Sexual Assault Survivors: A Methodological Review' (2011) 26(3) *Journal of Interpersonal Violence* 433.

[68] Miriam Gebhardt, *Crimes Unspoken: The Rape of German Women at the End of the Second World War* (Polity, 2016).

[69] Olivera Simic, *Silenced Victims of Wartime Sexual Violence* (Routledge, 2018).

[70] William C Adams, 'Conducting Semi-Structured Interviews' in Kathryn E Newcomer, Harry P Hatry and Joseph S Wholey (eds), *Handbook of Practical Program Evaluation* (Jossey-Bass, 4th ed, 2015) 492.

to understand how she made sense of the country's legal and administrative system, their actors and her relationship with them.[71] This method allows researchers to explore participants' thoughts, to collect open-ended data, beliefs and feelings about a particular topic and to delve deeply into personal and sometimes sensitive issues.[72] Over the past years, I developed a trusting and positive relationship with Lola. Building rapport[73] and gaining each other's trust allowed her to freely express her ideas about law, justice, reparation, politics and memory. A majority of the interviews were recorded but not all. Sometimes, it was not feasible or appropriate to use a digital voice recorder. If I was meeting Lola in a public space, I did not use a voice recorder but made extensive notes immediately after our meetings.

Since 2005, I have been undertaking socio-legal ethnography research in BiH, studying the long-term effects of wartime violence and in particular sexual violence that has been used as a tactic of war. Over the years, I have conducted extensive fieldwork in places where the violence took place. I have been returning to these places multiple times to conduct interviews with survivors and gain an understanding of their first-hand experiences in coping with trauma and rebuilding their lives in a new post-war state. I believe in the power of 'close observation' and in giving space for women's accounts in order to gauge the personal and political implications of post-war women's lives.[74] I am interested in survivors' lived experiences, feelings and the meanings they attach to events that tore their lives apart. I apply feminist standpoint theory in my work, the starting premise is that authority is rooted in individual's personal knowledge and perspectives. Sandra Harding calls this 'strong objectivity'. It is

---

[71] Catherine Kohler Riessman, *Narrative Methods for the Human Sciences* (Sage Publications, 2008); Claire Anderson and Susan Kirkpatrick 'Narrative Interviewing' (2016) 38 *International Journal of Clinical Pharmacy* 631.

[72] Melissa DeJonckheere and Lisa M Vaughn, 'Semistructured Interviewing in Primary Care Research: A Balance of Relationship and Rigour' (2019) 7(2) *Family Medicine and Community Health* 1.

[73] George E Marcus, 'From Rapport Under Erasure to Theatres of Complicit Reflexivity' (2001) 7(4) *Qualitative Inquiry* 519.

[74] See Cynthia Enloe, *The Big Push: Exposing and Challenging the Persistence of Patriarchy* (Myriad Editions, 2017) 99.

the notion that the perspectives of marginalised and/or oppressed individuals can help to create more objective accounts of the world.[75] Standpoint theory gives voice to marginalised groups, such as women survivors of wartime sexual violence to challenge the status quo.[76] They are placed in a unique position to point to patterns of behaviour that those immersed in the dominant group culture are unable to recognise.[77] To understand the women's facts and perspectives and to document their lived reality is a part of a feminist legal method.[78]

Janine Natalya Clark argues that 'survivors [in Bosnia] have become wary of researchers, and particularly of *stranci* [foreigners]',[79] so the fact that I am a female, who was born and grew up in the former Yugoslavia and BiH, and who experienced the warfare myself played a meaningful role in building a rapport with Lola. Together with my immediate family members, I have that particular experience of the historical trauma which is enmeshed in my everyday life; a specific positionality that affects my experience of researching aspects of war in my country of origin. My unique and personal experience is 'always the starting point for a phenomenological analysis' and I use it in drawing, analysing and theorising themes that I explore in my work.[80]

Lola and I share a number of intersectionalities: We shared the state we had both known and lost. We both speak the same language and we are of the same ethnic origin. I read out loud parts of the draft of this book to Lola, so that we could check and review passages for representation and factual accuracy. As I read, I was simultaneously translating passages into the Serbian language since Lola does not speak or

---

[75] Sandra Harding, *Whose Science? Whose Knowledge?* (Cornell University Press, 1991); Sandra Harding, 'Rethinking Standpoint Epistemology: What is "Strong Objectivity?"' in Ann E Cudd and Robin O Andreasen (eds), *Feminist Theory: A Philosophical Anthology* (Blackwell Publishing, 2005) 218.

[76] Patrice M Buzzanell, 'A Feminist Standpoint Analysis of Maternity and Maternity Leave for Women with Disabilities' 26(2) *Women and Language* 53.

[77] Brenda J Allen, 'Feminist Standpoint Theory: A Black Woman's (Re)view of Organizational Socialization' (1996) 47(4) *Communication Studies* 257.

[78] Sara Ahmed, *Living a Feminist Life* (Duke University Press, 2017) 26.

[79] Janine Natalya Clark, 'Working with Survivors of War Rape and Sexual Violence: Fieldwork Reflections from Bosnia-Hercegovina' (2017) 17(4) *Qualitative Research* 424.

[80] See Johanna Mannergren Selimovic, 'The Stuff from the Siege: Transitional Justice and the Power of Everyday Objects in Museums' (2022) 16(2) *International Journal of Transitional Justice* 220.

read English. I have knowledge of shared cultural codes, norms and histories which allows me easier access to research subjects and establishing relationships with them. I believe my gender in conjunction with a shared ethnic background has played a key role in developing an easy and trustful relationship with Lola. In fact, our shared ethnicity is, I suggest, even more important than gender in building the trust. In the postwar BiH, the perceptions of victimhood are based primarily on ethnicity. Ethnicity more than gender denies or approves someone's victimhood and can close or open the door to forging new social relationships. Being perceived as 'the ethnic other' may present challenges to researchers who are cultural insiders.[81] Similarly to Serb men, the Serb women victims, as mentioned before, were not attributed victimhood but denied it. Such denial created close alliances and solidarity between Serb women and Serb men rather than Serb and Muslim women victims or rape and other war crimes. As a result, Serb women's experiences of victimhood remain overlooked, under-documented and ignored. They have been neglected by academics, activists and practitioners and considered more 'Serb' and 'less' women narratives.[82]

Lola is convinced that the reason why she was left with no support in her struggle for justice is because of her ethnicity and not her gender. She has a strong pride in her ethnic origin and identity and is certain that,

> This [lack of judicial enforcement] happens only to Bosnian Serbs. They [Muslims and Croats] fared better after the war. Their women and veterans have been recognised, have better pensions than us [Serbs]. I don't hate anyone. Everyone who committed crime must be accountable, but it looks like only Serbs committed crimes. Who committed a crime against me then? Who?

---

[81] See Hariz Halilovich, 'Behind the Emic Lines: Ethics and Politics of Insiders' Ethnography' in Lejla Voloder and Liudmila Kirpitchenko, *Insider Research on Migration and Mobility: International Perspectives on Researcher Positioning* (Ashgate, 2014) 87.

[82] See Stewart M Coles and Josh Pasek, 'Intersectional Invisibility Revisited: How Group Prototypes Lead to the Erasure and Exclusion of Black Women' 2020 6(4) *Translational Issues in Psychological Science* 314.

Her face turned warm as she was speaking. Lola shares a common view held by Serbs that they are seen as an object of hatred by non-Serbs in BiH and beyond.[83] Not only Serb perpetrators, but the whole ethnic group was 'defined as aggressors in the early 2000s'.[84] Being seen as the main culprits in the war, Serb victims, both males or females, have also been shunned and ignored by researchers. As Helms argues, there is no denying that Bosnian Muslim women were the most numerous among survivors of sexual violence, but through different modes of dominant representations they have become 'the only victims'.[85] The focus on victimhood meant that Bosnian women were exemplified by Muslim women, leaving women of Serb, Croat, Roma and other ethnic backgrounds invisible as victims.[86] In the case of Serb women, as I mentioned before, they were also seen as culpable for the violence perpetrated by the male members of the ethnic group they belong to: their fathers, brothers, sons, husbands.[87] Since researchers did not flock to interview Serb women victims of wartime rape in BiH, Lola and the other Serb women that I interviewed in my earlier projects did not suffer from the so-called 'research fatigue' that some scholars noticed with their interlocutors.[88] Lola repressed an untold truth that she struggled to articulate after the violence took root in her mind and body. Her anger and shock turned inward and congealed in her flesh, unable to escape. Only many years afterwards did she slowly begin to find a language to express her pain.

---

[83] Miron Rezun, *Europe's Nightmare: The Struggle for Kosovo* (Praeger, 2001) 16; Richard West, *Tito and the Rise and Fall of Yugoslavia* (Faber and Faber, 2012).

[84] Paul Rock, 'On Becoming a Victim' in Carolyn Hoyle and Richard Young (eds), *New Visions of Crime Victims* (Hart, 2002) 1, 17.

[85] Elissa Helms, *Innocence and Victimhood: Gender, Nation, and Women's Activism in Postwar Bosnia-Herzegovina* (University of Wisconsin Press, 2013) 27.

[86] Ibid 44.

[87] Alexandra Stiglemayer (ed), *Mass Rape: The War Against Women in Bosnia-Herzegovina*, tr Marion Faber (University of Nebraska Press, 1994).

[88] Tom Clark, '"We're Over-Researched Here!": Exploring Accounts of Research Fatigue within Qualitative Research Engagements' (2008) 42(5) *Sociology* 953, 955; Jelke Boesten and Marsha Henry, 'Between Fatigue and Silence: The Challenges of Conducting Research on Sexual Violence in Conflict' (2018) 25(4) *Social Politics: International Studies in Gender, State & Society*, 568. See also Janine Natalya Clark, 'Storytelling, Resilience and Transitional Justice: Reversing Narrative Social Bulimia' (2022) 3(2) *Theoretical Criminology* 131.

Over the past three decades, researchers have remained keen to ask survivors questions and while some grow weary of telling their stories, 'others tell their stories again and again and again'.[89] Chris Coulter terms these accounts as 'NGO narratives',[90] since the way in which war victims speak of their victimhood has become 'formulaic and standardized'[91] driven by the need to present themselves as 'victims' to humanitarian organisations. There are problems with both: those who are only included in and those excluded from such conversations. Experts in wartime sexual violence have recently warned about the danger of selecting a 'chosen few' survivors that 'become speakers on behalf of all survivors' and in turn risk 'silencing those who are not among the 'chosen few'.[92] Those who experienced highly traumatic events, such as sexual violence and recount their stories multiple times, often did not see any benefits it doing so.[93] Some were disappointed.

> I am sick of telling my story. It makes them [those working in the field of transitional justice] feel good to show that they are helping us. They don't really want to change things and what good does telling our stories over and over do?[94]

---

[89] Anette Bringedal Houge, 'Violent Re-Presentations: Reflections on the Ethics of Re-Presentation in Violence Research' (2022) *Qualitative Research*, 13.

[90] Chris Coulter, *Being a Bush Wife: Women's Lives Through War and Peace in Northern Sierra Leone* (PhD Thesis, Uppsala University, 2006) 22, 48.

[91] Rosalind Shaw, 'Linking Justice with Reintegration Engagement? Ex Combatants and Sierra Leone Experiments' in Rosalind Shaw, Lars Waldorf and Pierre Hazan (eds), *Localizing Transitional Justice: Interventions and priorities after mass violence* (Stanford University Press, 2010) 111, 124.

[92] Maling Bode et al., 'Response to the Draft of the "Global Code of Conduct for Investigating and Documenting Conflict-Related Sexual Violence"', *Response to Draft Mura Code* (Web Page, January 2021) [6] https://responsetodraftmuradcode.wordpress.com.

[93] Rosalind Shaw, 'Memory Frictions: Localizing the Truth and Reconciliation Commission in Sierra Leone' (2007) 1(2) *International Journal of Transitional Justice* 183, 203.

[94] Tshepo Madlingozi, 'Good Victim, Bad Victim: Apartheid's Beneficiaries, Victims and the Struggle for Social Justice' in Wessel le Roux and Karin van Marle (eds), *Law, Memory and the Legacy of Apartheid: Ten Years After AZAPO v President of South Africa* (Pretoria University Law Press, 2007) 107, 213.

Some researchers argue that even if their research has little impact on the lives of those included in it, it may be significant for 'the category of persons they are taken to represent'.[95] On the other hand, there are those who have never met researchers before, who have never been sought out to tell their stories. Lola was one of such victims. It is important to develop a deeper understanding of what led to Serb women victims' invisibility; their erasure and exclusion from the Bosnian women wartime rape narrative. Their narratives have been indistinguishable from Serb male nationalistic narratives of victimhood and perpetrator-hood that have been unpopular and ignored. Ethnic identities were transformed into newly created political identities that became inseparable from the victim/perpetrator dichotomy made during and cemented after the war.[96]

In my many conversations with Lola I never intended on asking her about her wartime rape experience as such and we never talked about the rapes in any detail. Many women survivors of wartime rape expect researchers to ask such questions and feel 'fatigue and frustration' for reducing them to 'the violence they had suffered'.[97] Survivors intuitively feel that researchers have an interest in them as long as they are willing to describe 'this particular violent rupture in their lives'.[98] Engaging in such reflections is beyond the scope of this study but they raise serious ethical, analytical and moral questions for researchers in the field who are investigating the BiH war; a war that is notoriously remembered for mass sexual violence.[99]

I did not want to focus on the intimate and invasive violence Lola suffered for several reasons. First, I did not want to re-traumatise Lola by asking her to tell me the graphic, cringing details of the occasions when she was brutally raped. I wanted to humanise rather than dehumanise

---

[95] Mary Maynard, 'Methods, Practice and Epistemology: The Debate about Feminism and Research' in Mary Maynard and June Purvis, *Researching Women's Lives from a Feminist Perspective* (Routledge, 1994) 17.

[96] Claudine Kuradusenge explores newly created identities in Rwanda after genocide and how these prevent reconciliation process between Hutus and Tutsis. See Claudine Kuradusenge, 'Denied Victimhood and Contested Narratives: The case of Hutu Diaspora' (2016) 10(2) *Genocide Studies and Prevention: An International Journal* 59.

[97] Ibid 3.

[98] Ibid.

[99] Anette Bringedal Houge and Inger Skjelsbæk, 'Securitising Sexual Violence: Transitions from War to Peace' in Kate Fitz-Gibbon et al. (eds), *Intimate Partner Violence, Risk and Security: Securing Women's Lives in a Global World* (Routledge, 2018).

her by providing readers with a detailed description of the violence that reduced her to an object of sexual torture. I agree with researchers who are wary about sensationalism and academic voyeurism[100] when writing about sexual violence in war and did not see any purpose in asking Lola about the crime as such and the details of it. There is so much more to Lola's life. She is a mother, sister, grandmother, neighbour, bread-maker, housewife, farmer and woman fighting for justice. Lola occupies these multiple identities and reducing her just to the victim of rape does not do her justice.

Second, I was interested in her understanding and lived experience of transitional justice processes in BiH. There was no need to re-traumatise Lola to obtain data about her experience by asking her for detailed descriptions of the most traumatising events in her life. I could not ethically and analytically justify asking such questions by reducing her rich life experience to that particular event. Maybe Lola expected me to ask those questions and not to steer into other directions. Maybe she was perplexed that I did not 'go there' but our conversations were open-ended, and she could talk about it if she wanted to. She just never did, and I respected that. I wanted to honour her story and be careful about not bringing things up that she had not told me about. I was very aware that there might be things that she did not touch upon because they were too distressing.[101]

In that respect, Lola's narrative had many silences. Absent was any mention of the act of rape that happened on 'that night'. We talked about events leading to 'that night' and her being taken by the soldiers to the house where she was raped. We talked about her life before and after the act of violence and about some aspects of her life in detention, but neither of us zoomed in on the act of sexual violence as such. I thought there was much to learn by listening to what a woman victim can tell us about her first-hand experience with legal, administrative and restorative processes in the country she lives in, and also by observing her body language imprinted with traumatic memories. The account of violence and pain

---

[100] Janet Liebman Jacobs, 'Women, Genocide, and Memory: The Ethics of Feminist Ethnography in Holocaust Research' (2004) 18(2) *Gender and Society* 223.

[101] Heather Morris talks similarly about her experience in her interviews of Holocaust survivor. See Heather Morris, *Stories of Hope: Finding Inspiration in Everyday Lives* (Manilla Press, 2020) 165.

that she holds onto is inscribed on her body.[102] As some survivors in BiH stated, too much focus on sensational offence has distracted researchers from looking at socio-legal and political challenges survivors have to deal with every day in post-conflict BiH.[103] Focusing on the crime undermines other aspects of survivors lives and experiences. As Veena Das argues, there are the stories that 'remain in the shadows' when we focus too narrowly on particular harms or time periods of violence.[104] There are stories within the stories: stories that are not told, that we can feel in the air, that we can only anticipate, stories surrounded by the wall of silence. These stories are important too.[105] As Jelke Boesten argues, 'silence that is imposed either by lack of hearing or stigma furthers the problem of wartime sexual violence since it affirms tolerance for and impunity of such violence'.[106] Breaking the silence of Serb women survivors is important not only for the breakdown of shame and blame they suffer from but for the normative framework that imposes it[107]; the framework that has constructed Serb women as somehow deserving their victimhood.

To rectify this problem in this study, I first and foremost focus on Lola as a woman and examine the ripple effects of the violence she survived. I asked Lola to tell me about her experiences as a witness in a criminal trial, of her fight to obtain the status of a civilian victim of war, about her health and her life in BiH before and after the war. We also talked about her hopes, challenges and obstacles to receive any form of justice in the past thirty years. Having said all this, we both knew that the act of violence still forms the centre of her justice experience; one cannot disentangle these two. Nonetheless, while the act has been present in our talks—in the deafening silence between our words—we did not articulate it and rarely called it by its name. I believe that sharing silence with

---

[102] See Sara B Cobb, *Speaking of Violence: The Politics and Poetics of Narrative in Conflict Resolution* (Oxford University Press, 2013) 22.

[103] Houge (n 89) 12.

[104] Veena Das, 'Language and Body: Transactions in the Construction of Pain' (1996) 125(1) *Daedalus* 67.

[105] See Psiholuminis Prijedor, 'Vladan Beara - Sekundarna traumatizacija i rad sa sekundarno traumatizovanim osobama – predavanje' (YouTube, 21 April 2020) https://www.youtube.com/watch?v=R9a-IshWrH4.

[106] Jelke Boesten, *Sexual Violence During War and Peace: Gender, Power and Post-Conflict Justice in Peru* (Palgrave Macmillan, 2014) 87.

[107] Ibid.

interviewees is as important as sharing conversations. We did our best to become comfortable with the discomfort that would rise up and crash down like a tidal wave.

The heaviness of the past act of violence although not verbally articulated in any detail was present in our conversations. We breathed it in like air, we could almost touch it but we decided to ignore it. I wanted to document and understand what everyday life looks like for a woman survivor in post-conflict BiH. I wanted to learn how Lola understands and practices transitional justice mechanisms; what sort of social and economic challenges she faces and what kind of bureaucratic manoeuvrability she has had to exercise to achieve some form of justice for her and her children. As Isser states,

> actual practice and everyday experience, far more than any written laws, determine the nature and quality of justice accessible to the population ... [E]mpirical practice rather than written codes must serve as our starting point in any rule-of-law assessment – we need to examine the justice landscape as the population sees and acts in it.[108]

My positionality in this project, however, comes with its caveats. While being a cultural insider provides advantages to the research, it may also affect professional 'objectivity and validity of knowledge' produced.[109] My dual roles and personal experiences of war in BiH are embedded in my personal positionality and reflexivity and my emotional and social investment into the research topic. Rather than distancing me from 'the phenomenological realities of social suffering of those I write about'[110]

---

[108] Deborah H Isser, 'Conclusion: Understanding and Engaging Customary Justice Systems' in Deborah H Isser (ed), *Customary Justice and the Rule of Law in War-Torn Societies* (United States Institute of Peace Press, 2011) 325, 327.

[109] Linda Tuhiwai Smith, *Decolonizing Methodologies: Research and Indigenous Peoples* (University of Otago Press, 1999); Andrew Gary Darwin Holmes, 'Researcher Positionality: A Consideration of its Influence and Place in Qualitative Research' (2020) 8(4) *Shanlax International Journal of Education* 1.

[110] See Hariz Halilovich, 'Missing People and Missing Stories in the Aftermath of Genocide: Reclaiming Local Memories at the Place of Suffering' in Mina Rauschenbach, Julia Viebach and Stephan Parmentier (eds), *Localising Memory in Transitional Justice: The Dynamics and Informal Practices of Memorialisation after Mass Violence and Dictatorship* (Routledge, 2022) 209; Hariz Halilovich, 'Etika, ljudska prava i istraživanje: Etnografija u posljeratnoj Bosni i Hercegovin Ethics' (2008) 45(2) *Narodna Umjetnost: Hrvatski Časopis za Etnologiju i Folkloristiku* [*Croatian Journal of Ethnology and Folklore*] 165.

this allows for a broader narrative to emerge. To avoid bias that may come from my position, while my main method was qualitative research, I also collected and analysed many secondary sources to corroborate and gain a deeper understanding of Lola's 'experiential experience'; of what she has seen, heard and felt. By situating her story in the border context of sexual violence in war and nuances of dealing with it, her lived expertise can inform policy making and teach transitional justice lessons. In my research, I drew on local media reports, official court documents, legislative records, country reports, publications and reports of human rights organisations and scholarly studies.

My research methodology includes a focus on the actual experiences of those seeking justice and understands research as an ongoing process over time that both informs policy and measures impact.[111] While this book is based on one woman's story, and as such is not representative of other women's experiences, the book overcomes this limitation by offering in-depth analysis of judicial and non-judicial mechanisms that were practised with an aim to achieve some form of justice. Afterall, feminist theorising starts from women's experiences of everyday life and telling of women's stories is vital to 'feminists' resistance to abstraction'.[112] As Annick Wibben argues, telling individual women's stories serves as a correction to 'the generalizing and universalising tendencies that work to institute bias and obscure responsibility'.[113] 'Bottom-top' narratives can encourage a broader understanding of how victims and affected communities cope and try to manage their trauma. Personal and collective storytelling can become one way in which women assert their participation in the public sphere and claim new identities.[114]

There have been many books written using excerpts from women's narratives, but as Kelly McWilliam argues, in large groups of stories, individual stories 'can lose their distinctiveness and become, collectively, banal'.[115] Similarly, Nancy Thumim writes, if you 'look at too many of

---

[111] See Isser (n 108) 344–345.

[112] Annick Wibben, *Feminist Security Studies: A Narrative Approach* (Routledge, 2011), 2.

[113] Ibid.

[114] Kay Schaffer and Sidonie Smith, *Human Rights and Narrated Lives: The Ethics of Recognition* (Palgrave Macmillan, 2004) 19.

[115] Kelly McWilliam, 'Digital Storytelling and the "Problem" of Sentimentality' (2017) 165(1) *Media International Australia* 77.

these self-representations at once [...] you could be overwhelmed; they may feel sentimental and even repetitive, but viewed individually, they can feel powerful'.[116] In that sense, the story of Lola may serve as a correction or addendum to the women's stories that have been told but also to the tales that have been shunned, judged and abandoned; of bruises nobody was willing to see and voices reluctant to be heard.

---

[116] Nancy Thumim, 'Exploring Self-Representations in Wales and London: Tension in the Text' in John Hartley and Kelly McWilliam (eds), *Story Circle: Digital Storytelling Around the World* (Wiley, 2009) 205, 216.

CHAPTER 4

Becoming a Victim in the Eyes of the Law

THE LAW AND ITS VICTIMS

Lola still talks vividly about what happened to her and her children during the war and her three-decade-long fight on various legal and administrative fronts. Her recount of events often has gaps, they are disjointed memories that do not follow chronological order. This is typical for women survivors of serious violations of human rights, including sexual violence.[1] Similar to narratives of physical violence, stories about how individuals have navigated the bureaucracies of law and justice are seldom linear, tidy or chronological.[2] Although Lola spoke freely, sometimes she would be brief and matter-of-fact with her various descriptions of events that affected her and her family during the war and its aftermath.

I had to draw her story together from these vignettes and memories that came and went, and from the research I undertook to fill the gaps. I would hear of things in snatched fragments, piecing them together slowly and over time. Severe forms of victimisation, such as rape, endanger

---

[1] TRIAL International, *Rape Myths in Wartime Sexual Violence Trials: Transferring the Burden from Survivor to Perpetrator* (Report, 2017) 8.

[2] Jenny Edkins, *Trauma and the Memory of Politics* (Cambridge University Press, 2003).

narrative identity; 'they cause a rupture in people's life stories'.³ As both Michele Crossley and Antony Pemberton et al. have argued, victims such as Lola, existentially struggle to make sense of the relationship between the person they were before, during and after their victimisation.⁴

Lola fought for years against complex bureaucratic processes to become recognised as a victim of crimes against humanity in the eyes of the law. She was determined to compete for legal recognition of her victimhood by navigating through the bureaucratic offices in which she sought redress.⁵ Such recognition is important to women because being 'legally defined'⁶ as victims entitles them the status of 'civilian victims of war' deserving compensation. The first basic requirement in the administrative and legal process of obtaining the status is providing proof of wartime victimhood. Many survivors have been refused this status since, according to the relevant ministerial bodies, they 'did not have enough evidence to support their [victimhood] statements'.⁷

Lola was exchanged as a prisoner of war together with her children, and she was then registered with the International Committee for the Red Cross (ICRC).⁸ This registration is proof of her suffering, yet in itself it was not considered enough. Next she needed to be able to convince the bureaucrats that she had suffered a bodily injury of over 60 per cent.⁹ Requirements such as this have resulted in many women failing to become

---

³ Antony Pemberton and Rianne Letschert, 'Victimology of Atrocity Crimes' in Barbora Holá, Hollie Nyseth Nzitatira and Maartje Weerdesteijn (eds), *The Oxford Handbook of Atrocity Crimes* (Oxford University Press, 2022) 461, 467.

⁴ Michele L Crossley, 'Narrative Psychology, Trauma and the Study of Self/Identity' (2000) 10(4) *Theory & Psychology* 527; Antony Pemberton, Eva Mulder and Pauline GM Aarten, 'Stories of Injustice: Towards a Narrative Victimology' (2019) 16(4) *European Journal of Criminology* 391.

⁵ Stephanie Fohring, 'Introduction to the Special Issue: Victim Identities and Hierarchies' (2018) 24(2) *International Journal of Victimology* 147.

⁶ Inger Skjelsbæk, *The Political Psychology of War Rape: Studies from Bosnia and Herzegovina* (Routledge, 2012).

⁷ Snezana Mitrovic, 'Zrtve ratnih mucenja u RS: Logorasi tesko ostvaruju svoja prava', *N1* (online, 6 November 2022) <https://ba.n1info.com/vijesti/zrtve-ratnih-mucenja-u-rs-imam-traume-i-teske-posljedice/>.

⁸ The decision of the Association of Former Camp Inmates, 'Odžak 92', No. 01-43/07, 12 December 2007 (original document in Serbian language on file with author).

⁹ *Zakon o Zaštiti Civilnih Žrtava Rata* [*Law on the Protection of Civilian Victims of War*] (Republic of Srpska) Official Gazette of the Republika Srpska, No. 24/10.

officially recognised as a victim in the eyes of the law. As a result, they have been denied modest welfare compounding their vulnerability and endangering their survival. Some persistent women like Lola, have fought for years to obtain this status. In Lola's case it took her eleven years to finally prove that her bodily damage reached the bureaucratic threshold and then to receive the status of 'civilian victim of war'.

She first submitted her claim in 2003. After four years in the procedure, in 2007 her claim was rejected. The Republika Srpska Ministry for the Veterans and Disabled Veterans (the Ministry) rejected her claim on the basis that the appointed medical commission which reviewed her medical certificates determined her disability to be only 50 per cent. Lola appealed the decision to the County Court and in February 2014 her appeal was accepted after reviewal of all medical documentation and finding that there was an error in the administrative procedure.[10] In the appeal decision, the Ministry accepted more up-to-date medical certificates which confirmed that she suffered from 60 per cent bodily injury. In the decision it was stated that Lola, after leaving the detention camp on the 4th of July 1992, was examined by a neuropsychiatrist and gynaecologist for the first time on the 7th of July 1992. It was confirmed by the general practitioner that Lola had lost a lot of bodily weight and suffered from anxiety. Extensive documentation about her medical condition was submitted and her anxiety, post-traumatic stress disorder (PTSD), nightmares and flashbacks from her time in the camp were all meticulously documented. Lola was also diagnosed with pains in her bones and back, headaches, apathy and listlessness.

In its decision, the Ministry explained the compensation calculator it used to determine lump sums a victim may be able to claim for her personal injury. The 60 per cent bodily damage was divided up along the following lines: 20 per cent was due to various chronic infections that Lola suffered since her maltreatment in the camp; the remaining 40 per cent was ascribed to an 'endogenous, multifaceted illness which started to manifest itself during her time in the camp as a civilian...and this proportion of disability she obtained as a result of conditions under which she lived in the camp'. All of these conditions had increased her 'general life disability'[11] as a result of the trauma she experienced in the camp. After

---

[10] The decision No. 16-03/4-1-4-534-39/13, 20 February 2014.

[11] Original decision on file with author.

leaving the camp, Lola only once tried to return to the workforce, guided and advised by her psychiatrist to find some work.

With her help, Lola was employed as a casual laundress in a local firm. Her psychiatrist thought that it would be good for Lola to get out of the home and interact with people. She even recommended Lola to the owner of the laundry business and Lola went a few times to work.

> *I had to stop working because my youngest daughter was only seven at the time. I had to leave her alone in the home to go to work. I had no one to look after her. I would prepare her food, and everything…but it did not work…it could not work…She was too little to be left alone for long hours…Every time I would return home from work I would found her sad and with patchy bald spots on her head from pulling her hair out. Some of these spots were sore and some were bleeding. I got frightened for my child and stopped working. That was all the work I had done after the war. It lasted a few days.*

Although Lola was still young and able bodied, the lack of support for child rearing restricted her ability to engage in any work outside of her home. The emotional distress was too much to bear and Lola never again returned to work. Lola's youngest daughter has suffered from a myriad of health issues related to internal organ infections all of her life. Three weeks after being released from detention on the 28th of July 1992, Lola's daughter then baby (less than one year old) was examined by a paediatric doctor and diagnosed with pains in her stomach and constipation. As a five-year-old, on 22 January 1996, Lola's daughter experienced night-time wetting and received another diagnosis of anxiety. Two years later, on the 12th of November 1998, she was again diagnosed with urinary infections from continued bedtime and now also daytime wetting. On the 14th of December 2007, she was found to have anxiety. In 2009 Lola's daughter submitted all of this medical documentation to support her request to obtain the status of 'civilian victim of war'. Her request, however, was rejected. She lodged a complaint and further submitted medical documentation about her regular trips to the doctor, paediatrician and nephrologist since 2000 onwards.[12] In 2009 the relevant body in their statement of reasons to act on her appeal and grant her status of civilian victim of war stated that,

---

[12] Decision on accepting complaint and granting status of civilian victim of war on file with author. Medical documentation also on file with author.

as a consequence of being detained in the camp as a nine months old baby and exposed to inhumane conditions, applicant suffered from a hunger because she was not being fed adequately...she suffers from psychological disorders which manifest themselves in irregular sleep, fear, uncontrollable crying with bodily psycho somatic illnesses manifesting themselves in an absence of regular stools for a few days in a row...all of this can be seen in the medical documentation and reports of paediatrician and nephrologists who confirmed chronic urinary and genital infections... these are all direct consequence of the time she spent in detention camp with her mother, brother and sister and conditions she was exposed to at a very delicate time of her development for her normal psychological and physical growth ... she continues to suffer from daytime and nighttime wetting, nightmares and urinary infections that became chronic.

Both Lola's daughters are now married, but she is more concerned for the younger one due to the chronic infections she has had to live with. She is worried that the conditions may have affected her reproductive organs too.

> *The older one has two children but the youngest has none. She is already five years married and cannot stay pregnant. I am so afraid. The soldiers dumped her into canal once next to the road we were marching on...I returned to pick her up and hid her under my shirt...I thought she would never be able to walk or talk...She got all these infections when we were imprisoned, as a little baby she's had urinary infections ever since...Being in and out of hospital. I am so worried about her. Maybe that is the reason she cannot have children now.*

The state body decided that her impairment was permanent and calculated that it was to the sum of 70 per cent.[13] Lola's youngest daughter thus received the highest impairment of them all.

Other women survivors who have not been able to achieve the legal status of victim are denied, what Adriana Petryna calls 'biological citizenship'. Petryna defines such citizenship as 'a massive demand for, but selective access to, a form of social welfare based on medical, scientific,

---

[13] Decision on file with author.

and legal criteria that both acknowledge biological injury and compensate for it'.[14] For those who 'do not make the cut', medical and political vulnerabilities are exacerbated.[15] Many women in BiH did not 'make the cut'. According to available data, the number of survivors who have received some form of reparations for sexual violence in war is approximately 1000.[16] This number is less than symbolic when taking into account the thirty years that have passed since the beginning of the war and the 20,000 women who were reportedly raped during the war.

In Republika Srpska where Lola resides, the former Law on the Protection of Civilian Victims of War (the former Law) provided a deadline of the 31st of December 2007 for submission of applications for the status of victim and its associated legal rights.[17] Article 35 of the former Law stipulated that requests for the status of civilian victim of war could be submitted within five years from the 7th of January 1994 or from the date when the person was injured, killed, died or disappeared. Persons who were sexually abused, tortured or detained were required to submit along with their request, medical documentation about their rehabilitation immediately after being sexually abused, injured or wounded.[18] Many women did not know about the deadline, did not possess the proper documentation and never submitted their claim. The former Law permitted the late submissions in certain circumstances but after the 31 December 2007 deadline expired, and for eleven years thereafter, there was no law that would enable victims to seek the status of civilian victim of war.

In March 2015 the first document that outlines the status of Serb women victims of wartime sexual violence was published by the Gender

---

[14] Adriana Petryna, *Life Exposed: Biological Citizens After Chernobyl* (Princeton University Press, 2003) 6.

[15] Ibid xxv.

[16] TRIAL International, *Bosnia and Herzegovina Study on Opportunities for Reparations for Survivors of Conflict-Related Sexual Violence: We raise our voices* (Report, March 2022) 7 <https://trialinternational.org/wp-content/uploads/2022/03/GSFReportBiH_ENG_Web.pdf>.

[17] International Commission on Missing Persons, *Vodič za civilne žrtve Rata: Kako ostvariti pravo na zaštitu kao civilna žrtva rata u Republici Srpskoj* (Report, 2007) <https://www.icmp.int/wp-content/uploads/2014/08/guidebook-wictim-of-war-rs-bos.pdf>.

[18] *Zakon o Zaštiti Civilnih Žrtava Rata* [*Law on the Protection of Civilian Victims of War*] (n 9) art 2.

Center Republika Srpska.[19] On the 21st of April 2015, the document was discussed and adopted before the Republika Srpska National Assembly.[20] This document is a summary of the first report ever written that documents and analyses the experiences of Serb women victims of wartime rape.[21] There are fourteen recommendations in the document and the first one suggests bringing a new law on civilian victims of war that would include and give rights to a special category of victims; victims of wartime rape and other forms of sexual violence. In 2016, the initiative for drafting a new law was submitted to the government of Republika Srpska and on the 5th of October 2018 the Law on the Protection of Victims of War Torture (the new Law) was enforced. The new Law for the first time recognises the victims of wartime sexual violence and guarantees monthly disability pensions to those who can prove their victimhood. Although the former Law was heavily criticised because of the absurdity of deadlines and other requirements that victims were supposed to meet, the new Law did not make it any easier for victims to achieve their rights.

It is still difficult for survivors to obtain the status because of the requirement that victims must have medical documentation about their bodily injuries that is no older than one year from the date they left the camp or other detention place. What this means is that victims of sexual abuse must possess medical documentation confirming that they were raped or tortured within one year from the period when the injury happened.[22] A similar but more acceptable condition exists for mental

---

[19] Centre for Gender Equality and Equality, 'Information on the Findings and Recommendations of the Study on the Position of Serbian Women Victims of the War Crime of Sexual Violence in Bosnia and Herzegovina' (Gender Centre of the Government of the Republic Serbia, March 2015) <https://www.vladars.net/sr-SP-Cyrl/Vlada/centri/gender centarrs/Documents/Informacija%20%20latinica_204855676.pdf>.

[20] SRNA, 'NSRS Razmtrano vise informacija', *PTPC* (online, 21 April 2015) <https://lat.rtrs.tv/vijesti/vijest.php?id=146170>.

[21] I was contracted by the Gender Center Republika Srpske to write the report above (n 19). The report was written but it has never been published for the reasons never revealed to me or my colleagues. The launch of the report scheduled at the Parliament House of Republika Srpske was cancelled at the last minute. I write more extensively about the incident in my book: Olivera Simic, *Silenced Victims of Wartime Sexual Violence* (Routledge, 2018) 2–3.

[22] *Zakon o Zaštiti Žrtava Ratne Torture Republike Srpske* [*Law on the Protection of Victims of War Torture*], (Republic of Serbia) Official Gazette of the Republika Srpska, No. 90/18, art 10(4).

illnesses: documentation of diagnosis was required within one year, but no later than ten years from the moment of injury.[23]

Keeping in mind that most instances of abuse happened between 1992 and 1993, it is irrational to expect that in war-torn BiH, each and every survivor could simply walk into the hospital or medical centre and obtain the necessary documents. Most hospitals were destroyed and survivors were preoccupied with trying to preserve their lives and the lives of their families during this time. Besides, those women who were fortunate enough to be registered with the ICRC and had access to health services immediately or soon after their release, such as Lola, did not necessarily want to talk in detail about what happened to them. Božica Živković-Rajilić is a victim of torture herself and the president of the first NGO in Republika Srpska called the 'Association of women victims of war' ('Association') which was established in 2012 to support women survivors of wartime torture. She recently stated,

> Some women gave their statements immediately after they were exchanged or after they came to the territory of Republika Srpska. However, in these statements they did not talk about all details…especially if this was the case of wartime rape. They did not think of going around and talking about what had happened to them just to get nothing in return…in particular women who had husbands, brothers, children…These were not the things to be talked about publicly and many women omitted to tell this segment of their story. I would like to appeal to those that they should tell it all now to the relevant bodies as they told us in our rehabilitation workshops.[24]

In her first several encounters with doctors, Lola did not disclose to them that she was raped. She only told her story to the women's NGO 'Duga' from Banjaluka which was the only active women and humanitarian NGO in 1992 when the war was raging. The women activists from 'Duga' assisted women victims who were in detention camps by providing them with psychological counselling and humanitarian aid.[25] Lola gave

---

[23] Ibid.

[24] 'Da li se primjenjuje Zakon o zastititi zrtava ratne torture', *ATV BL* (online, 30 April 2019) <https://www.atvbl.rs/vijesti/republika-srpska/da-li-se-primjenjuje-zakon-o-zastiti-zrtava-ratne-torture-30-4-2019>.

[25] 'Duga' was the first NGO established in Banjaluka and Republika Srpska in 1992. For several years it worked with women victims of war by providing humanitarian aid. In the 2000s, 'Duga' started to work as a psychosocial association that provides humanitarian aid

her first statement to 'Duga' in 1994 and she kept the copy of it and used it with other documentation to prove that she was a civilian victim of war and victim of wartime rape.

Živković-Rajilić stated that to get monthly compensation, the right to rehabilitation and free legal aid, one needed to prove the status:

> They [government] asked us to have police records that we were tortured and whatnot. That is additional burden and re-traumatisation. The biological clock did its work, so large number of victims could never claim their legal rights. This government does not care much about its victims.[26]

Živković-Rajilić also confirmed to me her frustration with the institutions' unrealistic expectation that all women victims were in the position to receive medical treatment or keep the paperwork necessary to prove their victimhood. She raised her voice while speaking to me,

> Who kept all those papers with them? A few women did but many more were dislocated, moved from one place to another…They lost their documents or these were destroyed during the war…This is why we fought that women who don't have such documents can go to the police station and give a statement. So, if a woman has no documents to prove her victimhood and some don't, she can go to the nearest police station in Republika Srpska and give her statement. With this statement she will go to testify to the court and act as a witness. This statement is also her proof of victimhood and she can get the status with it.

I asked Živković-Rajilić whether women may be reluctant to give statements because they do not necessarily want to testify in criminal proceedings. I told her that I noted that some of them may be emotionally distressed about it. Živković-Rajilić snapped and quickly dismissed my concern,

---

to all vulnerable population: 'Istorijat', *Humanitarno udruženje žena "Duga" Banjaluka* (Web Page) <https://dugasuvenir.com/istorijat/>.

[26] Marija Augustinović, 'Hiljade silovanih u ratu u BiH žive krijući traume' *Radio Slobodna Evropa* (online, 25 November 2021) <https://www.slobodnaevropa.org/amp/bih-zrtve-ratno-silovanje-stigma-diskriminacija/31578526.html>.

Emotions are not relevant here. What emotions? The law knows no emotions. If you give the statement, it will serve as a basis for criminal investigations. If you give a false statement you will be criminally investigated. Women who give statements must act as witness. We want perpetrators prosecuted. I and women in my Association all testified and are still testifying in cases before the courts. Around 150 people had been prosecuted for wartime crimes thanks to us. They all received only a few years of jail but still.[27]

Živković-Rajilić is a very well-known woman activist in Republika Srpska and BiH but controversial too. Due to her close ties with the Republika Srpska government and public talks which are always in line with the Serb nationalist politics, she does not network with other local women NGOs in Republika Srpska who are more critical of the government and its policies and do not necessarily follow the party lines. She is often invited by local media to discuss the challenges that women wartime victims face. The 'Association' that she governs is the first and only NGO in Republika Srpska that supports the women victims of wartime torture which, according to Živković-Rajilić has around 750 women members. The new Law empowered the 'Association' which received the status of public and state interest to help the government in determining the status for each victim that submits application. The 'Association' acts as a consultant body to the Republika Srpska's governmental institutions when making decisions about granting the status.[28] Živković-Rajilić and the 'Association' are in a unique position and have the power to shift things and lobby the government directly. However, her work is isolated from the rest of the local women's NGOs who do not see her as a partner to work with. Reluctance to engage in any joint project is mutual. They often have opposite views on issues affecting women victims. The most recent clash between the 'Association' and the rest of the local women NGOs was around the upcoming deadline for submission of requests for the status of civilian victim of torture. An application under the new Law

---

[27] Interview with Zivkovic-Rajilic (Olivera Simic, phone interview, 29 November 2022).

[28] *Zakon o Zaštiti Žrtava Ratne Torture Republike Srpske* [*Law on the Protection of Victims of War Torture*] (n 22) art 16(7).

must be submitted within five years from the date of its enforcement.[29] These deadlines were heavily criticised by local women's and human rights NGOs who argued that war crimes do not have a statute of limitations, therefore the deadlines should be abolished.[30] Their request was rejected by the government of Republika Srpska and the deadline for submission of application remains the 1st of October 2023. The lobbying, however, for abolishing the deadline by the NGOs and some survivors is still on going. According to some local NGOs, very few victims received the status by using the new Law since many women were not well informed about the procedure to submit requests or were not 'encouraged enough' to do so.[31]

The Center for Investigation of War, War Crimes and Missing Persons in Republika Srpska which was established in 2008 by the government of Republika Srpska received 542 individual requests for receiving a certificate declaring that one had survived torture during the war in BiH. According to Article 16 of the new Law the Center is responsible for issuing these certificates noting that someone was a victim of torture, and then this document can be used in order to prove one's victimhood.[32] 542 requests were received between October 2018 when the new Law was enforced until the 17th of November 2022. Out of 542 requests, 429 survivors received a certificate declaring that they had fulfilled the requirements for receiving the status of civilian victim of war. The rest were however rejected due to a lack of evidence.[33] With respect to gender,

---

[29] Udružene Žene Banjaluka [United Women Banjaluka], *Primjena Zakona o Zaštiti Žrtava Ratne Torture* (Internet Publication, 2020) <http://unitedwomenbl.org/wp-content/uploads/2020/06/1.pdf>.

[30] Vedran Maglajlija, 'Udruženja žrtava: Zakon o zaštiti žrtava ratne torture u RS-u diskriminatorski' *Aljazeera* (online, 29 June 2018) <https://balkans.aljazeera.net/teme/2018/6/29/udruzenja-zrtava-zakon-o-zastiti-zrtava-ratne-torture-u-rs-u-diskriminatorski>.

[31] Milorad Milojević, 'Žrtve ratne torture traže ukidanje roka za sticanje statusa u Republici Srpskoj', *Radio Slobodna Evropa* (online, 28 October 2022) <https://www.slobodnaevropa.org/a/bih-republika-srpska-zrtve-ratne-torture-ukidanje-roka-sticanje-statusa/32103819.html>.

[32] *Zakon o Zaštiti Žrtava Ratne Torture Republike Srpske* [*Law on the Protection of Victims of War Torture*] (n 22) art 16 (a).

[33] Snežana Mitrović, 'Zrtve ratnih mucenja u RS: logorasi tesko istvaruju svoja prava' *N1* (online, 6 November 2022) <https://ba.n1info.com/vijesti/zrtve-ratnih-mucenja-u-rs-imam-traume-i-teske-posljedice/>.

out of 546 requests, 323 were women and 223 men. Out of those 429 survivors who received the certificates, only 54 received certificates in the category of wartime sexual abuse[34] and of these 52 were women and two were men respectively. Within the first two years of its enforcement, around 200 women obtained the status using the new Law, but only 121 received the monthly pension as a form of material reparation.[35] Those who did not get the monthly payments received other privileges prescribed by law, such as free health checks, rehabilitation, medical examination and other services. Between October 2018 and October 2022, a total of 296 women received the status.[36]

Živković-Rajilić supported by the Republika Srpska institutions is fiercely against prolonging the deadline after October 2023. I asked her to explain the reason for her position on this issue.

> Who needs that law after the deadline passes? Thirty years has passed from the war. Lots of victims died. Thirty women out of 726 members of the Association died in the recent years, some from natural causes, some from COVID-19, two women committed suicide. Many of them had a status. Anyone who was victim had enough time to obtain the status. Who has an interest in such law after so many years, after thirty years since war? Only those ones who want to destroy Republika Srpska and its budget so the state goes bankrupt. Some 'so called victims' want to give fake statements and accuse as many Republika Srpska war veterans as possible for the rapes they did not commit. We cannot afford our people to be again accused of genocide and rapes all built on the fake testimonies that some women want to give. They want to portray us as war criminals, our men who defended us, our husbands, fathers. Imprisoned would end up men who are guilty for those crimes, but also those who are not and we cannot allow that. They portray the Republika Srpske as genocidal entity who must be abolished. We don't have time to go to the courts to prove they are wrong. Our men could end up sitting through the court procedures for five, six years until they prove they are innocent but we don't have any more that time. We are old and many of us are dying. So, we have to stop women giving

---

[34] Email correspondence with the Center on file with author (Olivera Simic, Email Correspondence, 17 November 2022).

[35] 'Zakon o Zaštiti Žrtava Ratne Torture: U RS po osnovu Zakona pravo ostvaruje 200 žena', *Paragraph* (Web Page, 2 June 2020) <https://www.paragraf.ba/dnevne-vijesti/02072020/02072020-vijest1.html>.

[36] Official document received from the Ministry of Veteran's Affairs on file with author.

false statements and accusing Serbs for crimes they never committed. We cannot allow that. We don't want to spend our last few years of life in the courtrooms fighting against their lies. We would win at the end with truth but we don't have extra years of our precarious lives to give in to those who want to destroy us.

Živković-Rajilić gave similar statements to some media outlets.[37] She firmly believes that some non-Serb women want to harm Republika Srpska institutions and bring the entity to a collapse. Interestingly, she is not isolated in those views. The Director of the Centre for Investigation of War, War Crimes and Missing Persons stated in the local media that 'the names of all witnesses who testified against prosecuted war criminals of Serb origin will be disclosed'.[38] He accused such witnesses of giving 'fake testimonies'.[39] After hearing such threats, potential witnesses are likely to be terrified, now too scared to come forward and give statements. So far, there have not been any indictments raised against the Director for the public threat of disclosing witnesses' identities.

While waiting to see justice over the last thirty years, many women victims have died or committed suicide.[40] Dr. Olga Draško, a well-known woman victim of wartime sexual violence and torture and a former prisoner of the notorious detention camp Dretelj, recently died from a poor health. Dr. Draško was Lola's friend and they often spoke to each other over the phone since they lived away from each other. They supported and comforted each other while fighting to receive some form of justice.

---

[37] Mladen Kremenovic, 'Srbe bi da upisu kao zrtve Srpske agresije', *Politika* (online, 17 November 2022) <https://www.politika.rs/scc/clanak/525517/republika-srpska-zrtve>; SRNA, 'Rajilic: Perfidna namjera da Srbe proglase zrtvama "Srpske agresije"', *PTPC* (online, 18 November 2022) <https://www.rtrs.tv/vijesti/vijest.php?id=493906>; ATV TV, 'Deset godina Udruženje žena žrtava rata: "Uradili smo mnogo"—Gost vijesti Bozica Zivkovic Rajilic' (Rutube, 7 December 2022) <https://rutube.ru/video/8bc1697c1adab38228a2b414e0f6e0a8/>.

[38] 'Sudije suda BiH od Tuzilastva trazile istragu zbog objave identiteta zasticenog svjedoka' *Faktor* (online, 30 Septemeber 2020) <https://faktor.ba/vijest/ko-je-podstrekivao-medije-sudije-suda-bih-trazile-istragu-zbog-objave-identiteta-zasticenog-svjedoka-/99272>.

[39] Ibid.

[40] N. Vidakovic, 'Žene žrtve rata: Preživjele zvjerska mučenja', *Nezavisne* (online, 10 February 2016) <https://www.nezavisne.com/zivot-stil/zivot/Prezivjele-zvjerska-mucenja/352972>.

> Olga was calling me, sending me text messages each time when I would go to the court. She was giving me support I needed.

Dr. Draško was a voice for the Serb women victims and spoke publicly about her ordeal, which is considered one of the most horrific sexual and physical torture ordeals that a woman victim could go through. She reportedly stated, 'I survived the most horrific torture which left permanent damage on my health and life'.[41] She spent a long stretch of time in and out of the hospital in an effort to heal her body and mind from the torture she endured. Dr. Draško lost her battle with the state to prosecute her perpetrator. He was acquitted of the charge of torture against her. She was only sixty-three when she died.[42]

Some women do not want 'to go back to the past'[43] but nonetheless undertake a painful bureaucratic journey struggling with the administrative and legal system to prove their victimhood. The new Law received a lot of criticism because it allows only the victims of torture who live in the territory of Republika Srpska and possess documents issued by the Republika Srpska institutions and agencies, the right to apply for the status.[44] Victims of torture who live outside of the Republika Srpska are not eligible to apply. Despite criticism of the new Law's discriminatory ethnic and residential criteria, there have been no amendments to it.

However, obtaining 'the status' does not mean an end to the 'biological citizenship' test. Another hurdle is the legal challenge. For a large segment of those who sought, or may be eligible to seek, reparations from the state, entitlement to compensation is contingent upon prosecution of individuals who were responsible for the crimes committed against

---

[41] 'RS: zastita zena-zrtava ratnog nasilja', *Vecernje Novosti* (online, 16 January 2013) <https://www.novosti.rs/vesti/planeta.300.html:415221-РС-Заштита-жена-жртава-ратног-насиља>.

[42] See 'Preminula Olga Draško: Borila se za istinu o stradanju Srba, Hrvati je mučili i silovali u logoru', *Telegraf* (online, 20 September 2019) <https://www.telegraf.rs/vesti/jugosfera/3104230-preminula-olga-drasko-borila-se-za-istinu-o-stradanju-srba-hrvati-je-mucili-i-silovali-u-logoru>; 'Mirsad Repak Found Guilty of Dretelj Crimes', *Balkan Insight* (online, 11 March 2020) <https://balkaninsight.com/2010/03/11/mirsad-repak-found-guilty-of-dretelj-crimes/>.

[43] 'Žiković Rajilić: Stalna borba za ostvarivanje prava žena žrtava rata', *Radio Televizija Gradiška* [Radio Television Gradiška] (online, 26 February 2020) <https://www.radiogradiska.com/zivkovic-rajilic-stalna-borba-za-ostvarivanje-prava-zena-zrtava-rata/>.

[44] Maglajlija (n 30).

them.⁴⁵ As Živković-Rajilić said, women are obliged to act as witnesses if they cannot otherwise prove their victimhood.

However, many survivors do not believe they will see their perpetrators prosecuted and for this reason they do not have the opportunity to seek compensation through the court proceedings.⁴⁶ While Lola's perpetrator was prosecuted and sentenced, she was not awarded damage compensation as her perpetrator cannot be located and his property cannot be assessed. At the same time as she fought to see her rapists brought to justice, Lola also tried to bring a civil suit against the authorities for compensation for the harm done to her and her children. She and many other victims were unsuccessful because the statute of limitations was invoked to dismiss such cases.⁴⁷ In 2009, Lola also tried, together with a number of other survivors, to get compensation from the Federation of BiH for the damage inflicted on her and her children. The basis of her claim was that the Croatian army which detained them was part of the BiH Army which had its headquarters in Odžak County. Her request was rejected on grounds of procedural error, but the main argument was that the statute of limitations precluded her from submitting the claim. Under the Law of Civil Obligations,⁴⁸ the limitation period is three years from the date that the injured party learns about the damage and the identity of the person who caused it. The objective deadline is five years from the date the damage was inflicted.⁴⁹ The Court stated that since Lola submitted her claim in 2009 and the damage was done in 1992, all the deadlines had passed for claiming non-pecuniary damages against entities.

---

⁴⁵ Kate Clark, The Nuhanovic Foundation, *War Reparations and Litigation: the case of Bosnia*, (Report, 2014) 11 <http://www.nuhanovicfoundation.org/user/file/war_reparation_and_litigation_-_bosnia-report_version_5_march_2015.pdf>.

⁴⁶ Emina Dizdarevic, 'Bosnian Wartime Sexual Violence Survivors "Feel Betrayed by System"', *Balkan Insight* (online, 4 November 2021) <https://balkaninsight.com/2021/11/04/bosnian-wartime-sexual-violence-survivors-feel-betrayed-by-system/>.

⁴⁷ Ibid; Sunneva Gilmore and Luke Moffett, 'Finding a Way to Live with the Past: 'Self-Repair', 'Informal Repair', and Reparations in Transitional Justice' (2021) 48(3) *Journal of Law and Society* 455.

⁴⁸ Law of Civil Obligations (Republic of Yugoslavia) *Official Gazette of Socialist Federal Republic of Yugoslavia*, No. 29/78, 39/85, 45/89 and 57/89, art 376 (on file with author).

⁴⁹ The Municipal Court of Sarajevo, No. 65 O P 108160 09 P, 18 June 2015 (on file with author).

The Court accepts another deadline as relevant too, this is the 23rd of December 1995, the date from which all obstacles to submitting a claim were removed (coinciding with the end of the war). However, even with this exception, the objective deadline for submitting a claim passed on the 23rd of December 2000. As a result, all deadlines had passed and Lola lost her case. In a recent decision of the United Nations Committee against Torture (the Committee), a complainant from BiH argued that the unrealistic timelines set out in the Law of Civil Obligations prevented victims of rape or any other form of torture or conflict-related crime from claiming their rights in the first several years post-war as there was instability and many still feared reprisals from public institutions.[50] Victims whose claims were rejected for the aforementioned reasons were then forced to pay between 2000 and 10,000 Bosnian Marks (BAM) for the courts expenses.[51]

The Committee reasoned that the statute of limitations makes it impossible for victims of torture and other forms of conflict-related violence to obtain damages. It further stated that due to the 'continuous nature of the effects of torture, statues of limitations should not be applicable as these deprive victims of the redress, compensation and rehabilitation due to them'.[52] The courts in BiH make it impossible to apply subsidiary liability, eventually leaving survivors without any enforceable right to redress and compensation.[53] Although the Committee recommended that the BiH government enable victims access to a fair and accessible compensation scheme, the government has not yet amended its laws to accommodate this recommendation.

On the contrary, judicial and legal representatives from both entities agreed that the court proceedings should be completely halted until a new joint law on the compensation of war damages is made and the courts adopts the same practice in the whole territory of BiH when dealing with

---

[50] Committee Against Torture, *Decision adopted by the Committee under article 22 of the Convention, concerning Communication No. 854/2017*, 67th sess, UN Doc CAT/C/67/D/854/2017 (22 August 2019) [2.9] ('*Decision concerning Communication No. 854/2017*').

[51] Approximately 1020 and 5110 euros respectively: *Decision concerning Communication No. 854/2017* [2.9] Most survivors, such as Lola, survive with very limited resources and these costs are between 5 to 20 times more than the monthly disability pension.

[52] *Decision concerning Communication No. 854/2017* [7.5].

[53] Ibid [2.17].

such cases.[54] Halting these proceedings was in the interests of both entities[55] but as yet, the law has not been drafted. Additionally in 2014, the Republika Srpska government amended, in an emergency procedure, the Law on Internal Debt and the Law on Executive Procedure. It did so with an aim to protect the entity from execution of final judicial judgments of applications by individuals illegally detained during the war for compensation of material and non-material war damages.

In 2014, the Court of BiH had received around 20,000 such requests against and altogether the claims amounted to approximately one billion euros.[56] The Republika Srpska entity Minister of Justice stated that by amending laws the judicial bodies 'wanted to protect the budget of Republika Srpska so that institutions and state officials in Republika Srpska could function. We suggested bringing those amendments as the only solution which can help us stop and prolong execution of these judgements'.[57] It was argued that this was necessary to 'keep stability of the Republika Srpska budget'.[58] This statement is a blunt admission that the Republika Srpska entity neither has enough funds in its budget to pay victims compensation nor does it see these payments as a priority.

It has been acknowledged that victims of sexual violence in the former Yugoslavia have experienced the greatest amount of difficulties in both obtaining some form of redress and in accessing assistance. Many women victims who have testified have been excluded from their families and communities, trapped in poverty and ongoing vulnerabilities, and together with their children have faced stigma and discrimination.[59] As

---

[54] 'Uskoro zakon na nivou BiH koji bi regulisao pojam ratne štete?', *Nezavisne* (online, 16 November 2013) <https://www.nezavisne.com/novosti/bih/Uskoro-zakon-na-nivou-BiH-koji-bi-regulisao-pojam-ratne-stete/218419>.

[55] Ibid.

[56] Erduan Katana, 'RS se zakonski štiti od isplata odštete logorašima', *Radio Slobodna Evropa* (online, 4 July 2014) <https://www.slobodnaevropa.org/amp/rs-se-zakonski-stiti-od-isplata-odstete-logorasima/25445828.html>.

[57] Ibid.

[58] 'Usvojen Zakon o unutrašnjem dugu Republike Srpske', *Ekapija* (online, 27 February 2014) <https://ba.ekapija.com/news/859801/usvojen-zakon-o-unutrasnjem-dugu-republike-srpske>.

[59] Peter Van der Auweraert, 'Reparations for Wartime Victims in the Former Yugoslavia: In Search of the Way Forward', *International Organization for Migration*

Antony Pemberton et al. argue, victims' rights will only benefit victims if their implementation in practice is secured.[60] The notion that 'anything is better than nothing' and thus allowing victims to participate but then 'disrespecting them or flagrantly failing to deliver their expectations' will, according to scholars, lead to secondary victimisation.[61] The bedrock principle of victims' procedural rights is to 'do no further harm',[62] but it appears this is being ignored.

FIGHTING (IN)JUSTICE

There are disparities in the treatment of women victims of wartime rape between two entities in BiH. Until recently Republika Srpska, where Lola lives, did not recognise survivors of sexual violence as a separate category under the umbrella of civilian victims of war, and the application deadline for those seeking reparations ended in 2007. With the new Law, women victims of wartime rape have been recognised as a separate category but as mentioned, there has been little change to the existence of the obstacles for achieving the status and rights attached to them. These barriers, including inconsistent requirements for medical documentation and proof of physical damage, have prompted the Committee Against Torture to order BiH to 'establish an effective reparation scheme at the *national* level'.[63] In its concluding observations on the combined second

---

(Internet Publication, June 2013) 13 <https://www.iom.int/sites/g/files/tmzbdl486/files/migrated_files/What-We-Do/docs/Reparations-for-Wartime-Victims-in-the-Former-Yugoslavia-In-Search-of-the-Way-Forward.pdf>.

[60] Antony Pemberton et al., 'Coherence in International Criminal Justice: A Victimological Perspective' (2015) 25(2) *International Criminal Law Review* 339, 357.

[61] Ibid 357; Judith Herman, 'The Mental Health of Crime Victims: Impact of Legal Intervention' (2003) 16(2) *Journal of Traumatic Stress* 159; Uli Orth, 'Secondary Victimization of Crime Victims by Criminal Proceedings' (2002) 15(4) *Social Justice Research* 313.

[62] Marc S Groenhuijsen, 'Victims' Rights in the Criminal Justice System: A Call for More Comprehensive Implementation Theory' in Jan JM van Dijk, Ron GH van Kaam, and Jo-Anne Wemmers (eds), *Caring for Crime Victims: Selected Proceedings of the Ninth International Symposium on Victimology* (Criminal Justice Press, 1999), 85–114.

[63] 'Compensation to War Crimes Victims in BIH a Matter of Willingness', *TRIAL International* (Internet Publication, 2 June 2021) <https://trialinternational.org/wp-content/uploads/2021/06/News_BiH_Compensation_20210506.pdf> (emphasis added).

to fifth periodic reports of BiH in 2011, the Committee recommended that the BiH authorities:

> Adopt the draft law on the rights of victims of torture and civilian victims of war and the strategy for transitional justice without delay in order to fully protect the rights of victims, including the provision of compensation and as full a rehabilitation as possible, with the aim of obtaining physical and psychological recovery and their social integration.[64]

While it has long been established that 'the legal basis to a right to remedy and reparations became firmly enshrined in the elaborate corpus of human rights instruments', it has also been recognised that implementing this right is 'in essence a matter of domestic law and policy'.[65] As Luis Moreno Ocampo said, 'the victims are at the mercy of their national state'.[66] Towards the end of 2010, the 'Programme for Improvement of the Status of Women Victims of Wartime Rape, Sexual Violence and Other Forms of Torture in BiH' was launched but is yet to be adopted by the state authorities.[67] This Programme was part of BiH's overall attempt to deal with the massive human rights violations that took place in the past.[68]

---

[64] Committee Against Torture, *Consideration of Reports Submitted by States Parties Under Article 19 of the Convention: Concluding Observations of the Committee Against Torture*, 45th sess, UN Doc CAT/C/BIH/CO/2-5 (20 January 2011). Similar recommendations were adopted by the UN Committee on the Elimination of Discrimination against Women (CEDAW) in 2013. See Committee on the Elimination of Discrimination against Women, *Concluding Observations on the Combined Fourth and Fifth Periodic Reports of Bosnia and Herzegovina*, 55th sess, UN Doc CEDAW/C/BIH/CO/4-5 (30 July 2013).

[65] Office of the United Nations High Commissioner for Human Rights, *Rule-of-Law Tools for Post-Conflict States: Reparations Programmes*, UN Doc HR/PUB/08/01 (2008) 15.

[66] Luis Moreno Ocampo, 'Stopping the Crimes While Repairing the Victims: Personal Reflections of a Global Prosecutor' in Jacqueline Bhabha, Margareta Matache and Caroline Elkins (eds), *Time for Reparations: A Global Perspective* (University of Pennsylvania Press, 2021) 291, 298.

[67] 'Bosnia and Herzegovina Must Uphold the Rights of a War Rape Survivor', *TRIAL International* (Web Page, 12 July 2017) <https://trialinternational.org/latest-post/bosnia-and-herzegovina-must-uphold-the-rights-of-a-war-rape-survivor/>.

[68] United Nations Population Fund, *Combating Sexual Violence in Conflict: Because Everyone Counts* (Report, 17 September 2012) <https://ba.unfpa.org/en/publications/combating-sexual-violence-conflict>.

In 2012 and 2013, the BiH Ministry of Human Rights and Refugees and the Ministry of Justice, with the assistance of the international community, launched an extensive state-wide Programme to improve the status of civilian victims of war (the Programme). The Programme comprised of the 'Draft National Strategy for Transitional Justice', a 'Programme for Survivors of Conflict-related Sexual Violence' and the 'Draft BiH Law on Protection of Victims of Torture'. According to Amnesty International, these documents were designed to provide a framework for non-judicial forms of justice, including a sustainable platform to provide redress for victims, to establish facts, to restore trust in institutions of governance and to protect collective memory.[69]

However, the Programme never gained sufficient political support for adoption at the state level and, as a result, was never formally adopted. There is clearly no interest and no commitment from the government to provide long-term assistance to survivors of wartime sexual violence. The legislative architecture is such that women need to navigate intersecting misogyny and ethnic discrimination that is embedded and inherited in the institutions. Clumsy or no institutional responses to victims needs show that women victims' interests do not feature highly in policy making and remain out of view.

The BiH government offers no support and has created no safe space for victims to secure accountability of perpetrators and heal from trauma. Lola's narrative prompts us to perhaps shift questions of accountability from a discourse of perpetrator's guilt back to the political terrain of state responsibility for its entrenched social inequality and negligence towards one of the most vulnerable groups of citizens. While the state has attempted to transfer accountability for Lola's suffering to her wartime rapist, its failure to arrest him means the state is responsible yet again for failing to protect Lola's life and safety. Yet, there is a little or no accountability of the state for such staggering system failures.

An effective reparations scheme at the national level remains to be adopted in BiH.[70] The stumbling block is the non-existence of a

---

[69] 'Bosnia and Herzegovina: Submission to the United Nations Committee Against Torture', *Amnesty International* (Internet Publication, 2017) <https://tbinternet.ohchr.org/Treaties/CAT/Shared%20Documents/BIH/INT_CAT_CSS_BIH_29189_E.pdf> ('Amnesty International Submission').

[70] Ibid 8; Alec Anderson and Chiara Zardoni, 'An investment in Bosnia and Herzegovina's future: Compensating survivors of wartime sexual violence', *Global Voices* (online,

state level approach to 'dealing with the past'[71] apart from the seemingly joint decision 'not to deal with the past' by intentionally and bluntly obstructing victims' access to compensation and rehabilitation. This is paradoxically the only agreement in the socio-political environment in which it is otherwise impossible to achieve a consensus on causes and consequences of war, who suffered the most, and who is to be blamed for it all.[72] All approaches to truth-seeking and truth-recovering remain grounded in competing ideological perspectives and three different ethno-national perspectives.[73]

In the absence of a formal state-wide reparations scheme, victims now have to rely on a complex system of social allowances and individual proceedings in criminal and civil courts if they wish to obtain some form of reparations, including compensation.[74] BiH is not alone in deceiving its victims. Survivors in Timor Leste (East Timor) for example, share a similar fate since the government has been very slow and reluctant to provide a comprehensive programme of reparations for victims of past atrocities.[75] In BiH where safety and economic security remains scarce and corruption and unemployment high, Lola relies on a token monthly social allowance to survive.

---

23 September 2021) <https://globalvoices.org/2021/09/23/an-investment-in-bosnias-future-compensating-survivors-of-wartime-sexual-violence/amp/>.

[71] Kevin Hearty, 'Truth Beyond the "Trigger Puller": Moral Accountability, Transitional (In)Justice and the Limitations of Legal Truth' (2021) 15(3) *International Journal of Transitional Justice* 658.

[72] Ibid.

[73] Louise Mallinder, 'Metaconflict and International Human Rights Law in Dealing with Northern Ireland's Past' (2019) 8(1) *Cambridge International Law Journal* 5.

[74] Amnesty International, *'We Need Support, Not Pity': Last Chance for Justice for Bosnia's Wartime Rape Survivors* (Report, 12 September 2017) <https://www.amnesty.org/en/documents/eur63/6679/2017/en/>.

[75] 'Remembering the Past: Recommendations to Effectively Establish The "National Reparations Programme" and "Public Memory Institute"', *Relief Web* (online, 27 February 2012) <https://reliefweb.int/report/timor-leste/remembering-past-recommendations-effectively-establish-"national-reparations">; International Center for Transitional Justice, *'Unfulfilled Expectations: Victims' Perceptions of Justice and Reparations in Timor-Leste'* Report, February 2010) <https://www.ictj.org/sites/default/files/ICTJ-TimorLeste-Unfulfilled-Expectations-2010-English.pdf>.

Well-Being and Justice

The emotional and psychological consequences of Lola's experiences were a recurring theme in our conversations. Now in her early sixties, Lola has a myriad of serious and ongoing health issues which she probably would not have had, were it not for the violence she experienced due to the lack of state protection of her life and well-being back in 1992. The lack of such protection, however continues today, thirty years after her ordeal in the detention camp. The past traumatic experiences continue 'to live in and through bodies'.[76] Lola has been diagnosed with a heart disease, anxiety, post-traumatic stress disorder (PTSD) and high blood pressure for which she must take daily medication. She uses tranquilisers and has been receiving irregular therapeutic treatment since 1994.

> *I sometimes go to counselling every two months, sometimes every four. My psychiatrist last time told me to come in four months. I have to take a taxi to go there. I don't have a car...My youngest daughter has but she works, she needs car. Sometimes she would drop me off, but I don't want to ask, to bother her...Everything has become so expensive. I need 20 KM [konvertibilna marka/convertible mark equivalent to 10 euros] to go from my village to the city to get a therapy session. Once it was 12 KM [equiv.6 euros]. Everything has become so expensive. The fuel too. So, I cannot afford to take taxi in both directions. I walk to the city five kilometres and then sometimes take a taxi back home. I cannot walk back anymore...I could before but now...my legs are weak. My bones hurt. I am tired of it all.*

Lola does not pay for her therapy herself but does need to pay for most of her medications. She has received some aid from the government for her ongoing mental and physical health illnesses.[77] BiH has a fragile

---

[76] Janine Natalya Clark, 'Social Ecologies of Health and Conflict-Related Sexual Violence: Translating "Healthworlds" into Transitional Justice' (2022) *Journal of Human Rights* 9.

[77] Many women victims of wartime rape never received any financial, psychological and medical support. See Augustinović (n 26). However, due to a number of NGOs in the Federation of BiH, women have a better chance of receiving some form of assistance. In Republika Srpska, the region where Lola lives, there are no state or non-state led associations that provide support to women like herself.

and inadequate health care system upon which so many survivors rely to sustain their survival and hopes for the future.[78]

Lola's lips pulled into tight sideways smiles. She clasped her hands together apprehensively, held her lids shut for a moment before opening her eyes wide. She holds me with them as she speaks:

> *No one ever paid for my medications. I spend every month's 100KM [50 euros] on medications since I must take them regularly. My monthly income as a civilian victim of war is 170KM [equiv. 85 euros] and as a family of fallen soldier I receive 256KM [equiv. 128 euros]. I can hardly survive on these funds.*

She nodded slowly, but the tension did not leave her face. When Lola's court case commenced she suffered a heart attack triggered by the stress of acting as a main witness in the trial. Lola nearly died. She now lives with only 37 per cent capacity of her heart function and has one coronary stent implanted. Her body narrates her story of victimisation; stored in her flesh and mind are old wounds mixed with the still fresh memories of seeing her perpetrator in the courtroom and now knowing that he is free but not knowing where is he hiding.

Lola lives in poverty in a house that she shares with her son, his wife and their three young children. Her two daughters live nearby. They all remain very close to each other for emotional support and physical survival.[79] Both of her daughters work causally in retail at the city's supermarket. They work in the refrigerated department of the store selling meat products.

> *I am worried about them working whole day in a cold space. They can get sick very easily. They do not want to move them somewhere else in the shop at least from time to time so they are not exposed to cold all the time… they are women. It's not good for them especially a younger one, she already has chronic infections.*

---

[78] Peter Locke, '*City of Survivors: Trauma, Grief, and Getting-by in Post-War Sarajevo*' (PhD Dissertation, Princeton University, 2009).

[79] See J David Kinzie, J Boehnlein and William H Sack, 'The Effects of Massive Trauma on Cambodian Parents and Children' in Yael Danieli (ed), *International Handbook of Multigenerational Legacies of Trauma* (Plenum Press, 1998) 211, 213.

Although Lola's younger daughter has a higher education degree, she has never gained employment in her profession. Both Lola and her daughter think she wasted her time and funds on education. Lola nervously tugged at her fringe. She rubbed her eyes and coughed before saying,

> *If she did not study, should would get employment earlier but she waisted years on her higher education...We all sacrificed so she can afford to pay accommodation, books, exams for four years. And what she got from it? She could never get job in her profession...She tried...But with no connections [in the government] it's impossible...Those years were waisted and she regrets she spent time and money on her studies. She could start working earlier and get her employment status running earlier...*

Lola's daughter is overqualified for the job in the supermarket but she has no choice than to accept it to earn a wage. Her husband is unemployed so she is the only breadwinner in her family. Lola's older daughter completed high school.

Lola has never remarried. Her house is shared by three generations living in three rooms and sharing one bathroom. Lola has one room for herself. Her living arrangements resemble the Slav socialist system called the *zadruga*, a traditional communal family structure with strong kinship ties practised mainly in the Balkan rural areas.[80] *Zadruga* signifies the family whose members shared equally in the labours and profits of a jointly owned estate, which was governed by an Elder.[81] An Elder was often the oldest male but in the case of Lola and many widowed households left after the war it is a woman Elder who governs the estate. Lola's family similar to the members of a *zadruga* support themselves with farming and stock-breeding and with owning livelihood jointly. This is the only way for Lola and her family to escape ultimate impoverishment.

---

[80] Keith Doubt, *Through the Window: Kinship and Elopement in Bosnia-Herzegovina* (Central European University Press, 2014) 99.

[81] See Rebecca West, *Black Lamb and Grey Falcon: A Journey Through Yugoslavia* (A&U Canongate, 2021) 489; Petko Hirstov, 'Imaginary Historical Pattern of Family and a Model for Construction of Political and Social Organizations—Extended Family (Zadruga) in Bulgaria' (2022) 6(3) *Genealogy* 59.

> We need to put the food on the table for all of us. No one is fully employed. My older daughter lives in the house next to ours, with only a fence running between us. Her husband is unemployed. My other son in law is unemployed too. They have two boys. There are lots of mouths to feed. We grow our own vegetables, have some chickens and two pigs. I make a bread and cook our meals. We cannot afford to buy food.

Lola's two brothers-in-law both live and work abroad, and do not provide any financial assistance or otherwise to Lola and their nephews.

> They could invite my unemployed son and two sons-in-law to work seasonally since none of them have regular jobs. They never send us any financial or other help although they have been living abroad for the past three decades.

Both of her daughters living on low-income casual jobs have to rely on each other's help to survive. Her youngest daughter was the first to receive the status of civilian victim of war in 2009. However she was first rejected and then after lodging a complaint she received the status.[82] Her older sister and brother were also rejected a few times but finally obtained the status and right to a monthly pension in 2014 and in 2020, respectively. Lola's older daughter is also diagnosed with PTSD and occasionally goes to counselling. She also has a history of different medical problems. As a teenage girl she was described by neuropsychiatrist as 'frightened, very cautious when meeting strangers, quiet, sad…careful, gives very short answers on questions, nervously fidgeting with her fingers, cannot listen to any talk about her father and does not mention him at all'.[83] It was stated in this report that Lola's children were present and were witness to their mother being beaten and tortured.

Each of Lola's children receive around 80 euros per month as compensation for the harm suffered during their time in detention. Lola blinked nervously,

> I am ashamed to tell someone when they ask me how much they get. It is a shame. I feel humiliated.

---

[82] Decision on file with author.
[83] Documents on file with author. The examination took place in 1998.

These funds are inadequate to cover the basic monthly costs of living. Lola feels angry and bitter because of the pitiful amount she receives from the government each month.

> *The state does not care about us at all. They give us nothing, but I have no choice but to take what they give me. I would rather not. But I have no choice. It's a shame they treat us like this.*

These payments are not reparations but a social welfare income. In the case of S.H. a woman victim of rape, allegedly perpetrated by a member of the Serb forces in 1995, the Committee on the Elimination of Discrimination against Women stated,

> the State party [Republika Srpska]…failed to provide her with timely recognition of her status as a victim and…the amount of the pension is not commensurate with the harm suffered by the author, comprising severe physical harm, including the impact on her sexual and reproductive health and rights, as well as psychological harm and material damage and prejudice.[84]

Other countries in the former Yugoslavia that experienced the war, such as Kosovo and Croatia, have secured higher monthly allowances for women victims of wartime rape. For example, in Kosovo, women who receive the status of survivor of wartime sexual violence are entitled to a monthly payment of 250 euros.[85] The Croatian government introduced a one off single payment of around 13,000 euros to all victims of sexual

---

[84] The Committee on the Elimination of Discrimination against Women, 'Views adopted by the Committee under article 7(3) of the Optional Protocol, concerning communication No. 116/2017 (26 August 2020) para 8.8.

[85] On 20 March 2014, Kosovo's Parliament approved amendments to the Law on the Status and the Rights of the Martyrs, Invalids, Veterans, Members of the Kosovo Liberation Army, Sexual Violence Victims of War, Civilian Victims and Their Families. These amendments provide for the legal recognition of civilian victims of sexual violence. See *Law on Amending and Supplementing the Law No. 04/L-054 on the Status and the Rights of the Martyrs, Invalids, Veterans, Members of Kosovo Liberation Army, Sexual Violence Victims of the War, Civilian Victims and Their Families* (Republic of Kosovo) Law No. 04/L-172. See also, Xhorxhina Bami, 'Rape Used as Weapon During Kosovo War, Says NGO', *Balkan Insight* (online, 26 October 2022) <https://balkaninsight.com/2022/10/26/rape-used-as-weapon-during-kosovo-war-says-ngo/>.

violence in war and also an additional monthly payment of 330 euros, plus free health insurance and health checks.[86]

Lola has sleeping difficulties and told me that she often '*hears someone banging on her bedroom door*' during the night which startles her from sleep. These health problems are not something unique to Lola but something other survivors report too. According to some studies, many survivors of wartime rape experience significant physical illnesses such as cardiovascular diseases, tumours and various types of cancers.[87] According to Siobhan O'Neill et al., there is a connection between some mental illnesses associated with PTSD and an increased risk of cancer.[88]

Lola also suffers from depression. At least once the illness almost pushed her over the edge. Lola told me that the morning after she was forcibly taken away by the soldiers and gang raped and tortured for the whole night, she dragged herself back to the house where she had left her children. She picked up her baby daughter and took her two other children by the hand. She was bleeding and had bruises all over her body. Her clothes were torn. She squeezed her son's hand tightly and her youngest daughter took her brother's other hand. She walked with them towards the river Sava with the intention of drowning them all. Lola's eyes were fixated on the river. Her throat was dry, her heart pounded. She had one foot in the river when her son suddenly turned to her and pulled her arm. He looked her in the eye, '*Mama, a de ćeš ti s nama?*' [Mum where are you taking us?]. The boy could sense the danger of the wild river that stretched before them. His question startled Lola, she turned around and looked her son in the eye. She then realised she could not bring herself to murder her children.

---

[86] On 29 May 2015 the Croatian parliament adopted the Law on the Rights of Victims of Sexual Violence during the Armed Aggression against the Republic of Croatia in the Homeland War (Republic of Croatia); See also, Sven Milekic, 'Croatia Plans Compensation for Wartime Sexual Violence Victims' *Balkan Insight* (online, 2 April 2015) <https://balkaninsight.com/2015/04/02/croatia-gives-reparations-for-wartime-sexual-violence-victims/>.

[87] Medica Zenica and Medica Mondiale, *'We Are Still Alive': Research on the Long-Term Consequences of War Rape and Coping Strategies of Survivors in Bosnia and Herzegovina* (Report, November 2014) 81.

[88] Siobhan O'Neill et al., 'Associations Between DSM-IV Mental Disorders and Subsequent Self-Reported Diagnosis of Cancer' (2014) 76(3) *Journal of Psychosomatic Research* 207.

Lola slowly turned around and stumbled back in the direction she came from. I observed her body as she took me into the past. She was shivering. Lola described this event so vividly that I could picture her and her young children walking down towards the river. She took a deep breath. Her eyes snapped open as if she had just woken up from a bad dream. This was not the first time Lola would be at risk of suicide. The members of the NGO 'Duga' noticed her extremely vulnerable psychological well-being during the several weeks they were offering her psychosocial assistance. In a recent book published by 'Duga' on the anniversary of their thirty years of humanitarian work, the authors used several women's victim stories as short case studies to portray their work from the wartime period. I recognised Lola's story described as one of the cases they dealt with. Although they used only her initials all of the personal and historical facts were clearly based on Lola's experience. Later, the women who worked in 'Duga' and who worked directly with her confirmed this.[89]

Heidi Hecht, a journalist from Germany and a humanitarian worker, volunteered to work with 'Duga' in 1992 and 1993. She was recognised as someone who investigated the crimes against Serbs.[90] Some of the first investigations and documentations of rape of Serb women including women from the Posavina region were documented by Hecht.[91] She met with a number of women victims of wartime rape including Lola. In the first half of 1993 Hecht sent a letter to the then mayor of Banjaluka, Minister of Health of Republika Srpska and Psychiatric clinic based in Banjaluka. The subject of the letter was: 'Rehabilitation of victims of war'. I bring here excerpts from her letter.

> After many talks with victims of war in Banjaluka and Novi Grad near Odžak, I strongly believe that they need a fast intervention or intensive care. With each passing day without psychotherapy there is an increasing risk that it will be impossible to integrate the victims into the society. We have to help these people so they can find a way into a normal life....I specifically ask for urgent help to L.D. (her full name was left out on purpose). I ask that you accept her and her three children in Banjaluka.

---

[89] Interview with the representatives of 'Duga' in Banjaluka (Olivera Simic, phone interview, 10 October 2022).

[90] Alexandra Stiglmayer, *Mass Rape: The War Against Women in Bosnia-Herzegovina*, tr Marion Faber (University of Nebraska Press, 1994) xv.

[91] Ibid 140–142.

She [Lola] is psychologically agitated (in a very difficult state of mind). She is raped in Novi Grad and her husband was killed in the war. According to my view, there is a risk of suicide in her case. We would all bear responsibility [for her suicide] if we would not help her through a pro-longed psychotherapy...[92]

Occasional suicidal thoughts and general apathy have followed Lola over the many years since her release from the camp. Her son, who was a six-year-old boy when detained together with Lola and his siblings is now the only bread winner in their household. The trauma he experienced at a young age from losing his father in the war, coupled with being taken to the detention camp and witnessing his mother being physically and verbally assaulted by his neighbours, left him with a life-long speech impediment. Four years after their release from the camp, in 1996, he was described by a neuropsychiatrist as 'a nervous child under neuropsychiatrist supervision' and as 'a very frightened child, bad student, stuttering, [who] has nightmares and insomnia'.

In 1998 he was further diagnosed with 'a very limited verbal expression, a dysarthric speech who cannot sit still in his chair'.[93] He was 12 years old at the time. He left the doctor's room with a diagnosis of PTSD. He was prescribed medications and referred to a speech pathologist. As we were going through her family medical documentation, Lola looked pale as she tried to put her pain into words,

> *Ever since our ordeal in the camp, he has been stammering. It is from fear that stayed with him. He never finished a high school because of it. He could not...He does not want to go to doctor or therapist. It is hard. He can be difficult to deal with...*

Her son, however, never received any mental health or another assistance from the state or anyone else. All his life, he has been either unemployed or casually employed without a steady job and salary. During the summertime he works in a workshop helping to deliver headstones to the neighbouring graveyards. During the winter the workshop is closed and his contract is terminated.

---

[92] Grozda Regodic, *U zagrljaju Duge* (Grafid, Banjaluka, 2021), 31–32. The initials included above have been changed to protect Lola's identity.

[93] Original documents on file with author.

> *In the winter he sits home with us. What else he can do? Sometimes neighbours call him to help them with slaughtering the pigs...he does that for them...this happens during the winter season when people prepare winter stores.. so, he earns something from time to time while waiting for spring and opening of the workshop again...*

He drinks and Lola is uncomfortable to admit that *'he has a problem with alcohol, he drinks a couple of beers every day'*. I asked her if he is physically violent. I looked into her troubled eyes. A furrow of tension gathered between them.

> *No, but he can say things and get angry. He can be a wonderful sometimes, but othertimes 'Oh, my God!' I wish I don't have to see and hear things in the house, but I have to calm him down. What else can I do? Where can I go? He should go to therapy, but he does not want. I have to calm him and everyone else in the house. They are more anxious than I am...and I in between them have to constantly calm down the tensions in the house... I wish sometimes that they are far from me so I don't have to hear and see everything... but what can I do... where I could go...*

Lola told me how she walked with him for five kilometres every morning to his primary school for years. In their small village there was no primary school and children would need to walk miles to get there. Later when he was in high school, she had to walk with him for several kilometres to the bus station where he would catch the bus. It could take him up to two hours to get to school. Each morning they had to wake up at 5am to start their journey. Once he was on the bus heading to school, Lola would return home on foot. By his second year of high school, her son had dropped out:

> *I walked with him every morning. It was hard but I wanted him to study, to finish the school. I did not know that he did not attend the classes. One day I went to see his teacher and she told me that he spent more time outside of the school than in the classroom. He dropped soon after I found out this.*

Living in the same household with several generations is common, either from custom or due to poverty. Traditionally and mostly in rural areas, Bosnians have lived in agricultural communities with two or three nuclear families living together.[94] The BiH war impacted the family lives of many people who lost family members in the war. The war resulted in the death of many Bosnian men; thus resulting in an increase in the number of households headed by widows, such as Lola's.[95]

Lola's daughters go to counselling occasionally (as they cannot afford regular sessions and the medications), however her son persistently refuses to do so. He works casual and low-paid jobs to provide food for his young family. Lola is concerned about his future since he has no savings or pension to live on once he retires.

> *Although the pension is nothing in this country, it is still something. The owner of the workshop registers him with the state Employment Office just for these six months he works with him. Once winter comes in he terminates his contract and deregister him as he does not want to cover his expenses...in this way he avoids paying for his social and health insurance contributions when he does not work with him...And then he is officially again unemployed. But what he can do? Better to do something rather than nothing. He cannot complain, he can lose even this job if he complains... He has only monthly income of some 140KM [70 euros] as a civilian victim of war. And he started to receive this only from 2020 when he got the status. That's all.*

Lola's son but also her daughters and daughter-in-law are among the many people in BiH who find themselves in the precarious situation in which employment does not guarantee a way out of poverty. It is not just because a low wages and insecure private employment but also the low work intensity of individuals such as Lola's children. Her son has been working all his life casually with a minimum wage; often doing several

---

[94] See, Philip E Mosley, 'The Peasant Family: The Zadruga, or Communal Joint Family in the Balkans and Its Recent Evolution' in Robert F Byrnes (ed), *Communal Families in the Balkans: The Zadruga* (University of Notre Dame Press, 1976) 19; Tone Bringa, *Being Muslim the Bosnian Way: Identity and Community* (Princeton University Press, 1995) 41–42; William G Lockwood, 'Coverts and Consanguinity: The Social Organization of Moslem Slavs in Western Bosnia' (1972) 11(1) *Ethnology* 55, 58; William G Lockwood, *European Moslems: Economy and Ethnicity in Western Bosnia* (Academic Press, 1975) 58–59; Karl Kaser, 'The Balkan Joint Family Household: Seeking its Origins' in Karl Kaser (ed), *Household and Family in the Balkans: Two Decades of Historical Family Research at University of Graz* (Lit, 2012) 109.

[95] Nina Evason, 'Bosnian Culture', *SBS* (online, 2017) <https://culturalatlas.sbs.com.au/bosnian-culture/bosnian-culture-family>.

casual jobs to survive. He and other people with low levels of education are more at risk of low work intensity, low wages and poverty. Legal protections for people like Lola's son existing on temporary contracts which blur the line between formal and informal employment, and relying on the mercy of their employees, are poorly enforced.[96]

Lola's daughter-in-law also only has primary education and is unemployed. She casually works as a cook or in a laundry but she mostly stays at home with Lola taking care of the young children and doing the chores. During the war she was a refugee living abroad. After the war was over she returned to BiH. She met Lola's son upon her return and soon after learned that she was pregnant. She became a mother when she was barely seventeen years old.

> *I had to help them with a baby. She [daughter in law] was a child herself. She knew nothing about babies. I was bathing baby and helping her to feed a baby. Slept next to her to help out…What could I do? I don't know where my strength comes from anymore.*

She paused and looked down at the floor. I could see she drifted away with her thoughts, forgetting for a moment that she had company.

Lola's sister Nada, together with her children, were with Lola in the camp. Nada gave testimony of her own abuse during the investigation into the wartime rapes of women in the Posavina region. Similar to Lola's husband, Nada's husband was captured, tortured and killed by Croatian soldiers just prior to her being taken with her two sons along with other people to the camp. Nada died a few days after her wartime rapists were arrested. She had a heart attack, brought on by the surprise and shock of hearing the news about the arrests. She had been living in fear since the investigations had begun. She imagined her rapists would seek revenge against her and her sons. When she gave a statement to the local media, Nada did so through tears, 'We are forgotten and unprotected'. She also declared she was ready to go to the Hague, to testify and tell her story before the International Criminal Tribunal for the former Yugoslavia.

Nada was in the camp with her two young sons and experienced enormous fear for their lives. The Croatian soldiers threatened they would kill them by using a roasting spit as a torture instrument in order to make

---

[96] See, Nikolina Obradovic, Mirna Jusic and Nermin Oruc, *In-Work Poverty in Bosnia and Herzegovina* (European Social Policy Network Report, 2019).

their death as painful as possible. Nada reported that she watched as they sharpened the head of the wooden spits and threatened they would kill her sons by slowly forcing the spit into their bodies and roasting them alive.[97] Nada knew that these threats were real since this and similar methods of torture had been performed by Ustashe, a Croatian fascist organisation on the Serb population during World War Two.[98] Nada's husband died horrifically at the hands of the Croatian soldiers after being exposed to several hours of torture.

Lola glanced at me and then down at her lap. She swallowed hard while her face contorted in anguish. Tears pooled in her eyes. She began hesitantly but then her voice became fuller as she spoke about her sister:

> *She was afraid when investigators were collecting evidence, preparing the case, and interrogating her. That all affected her. She started to have hallucinations that Jurić and others followed her. She was afraid to go out, to work in the field. She started to have delusions that they could come any day to attack her and seek revenge for testifying against them. Poor soul. Her heart could not bear anymore. On the day of the arrest of the perpetrators, she had a heart attack and died…Only one of her sons obtained the status of civilian victim of war. The other son still to this day did not. He tried. He submitted paperwork a few times but there was always, according to the government, some papers missing… He did not apparently had all documents they needed… he is very sick mentally and they want to put him in a mental hospital… But we are all against it… He will die there…*

She sobbed for a moment, the last few words catching in her throat. Lola blinked and picked at her nails. Her hands were imprinted with deep fine lines and calluses from hard work. Her face flushed red. An inner pain was written all over Lola's face. The panic. The dread. The fear of what was to come. Her nephews only have her, and the one that suffers from severe mental illness visits her often. He lives nearby. She feels helpless as there is nothing she can do for him. He lives alone and his health is deteriorating rapidly. He does not go to the doctors regularly and is terrified

---

[97] D M, 'Zastita zena-zrtava ratnog nasilja' *Novosti* (online, 16 January 2013) <https://www.novosti.rs/vesti/planeta.300.html:415221-PC-Заштита-жена-жртава-ратног-насиља>.

[98] 'The Jasenovac Extermination Camp', *Holocaust Education and Archive Research Team* (Web Page, undated) <http://www.holocaustresearchproject.org/othercamps/jasenovac.html>.

of being put into a psychiatric hospital. Lola's children and her sister's son are all children from fallen Republika Srpska soldiers but they do not enjoy any privileges or benefits from the Republika Srpska government such as being prioritised for employment.

For Lola, the lines between good and evil, once clearly drawn, are now blurred. She stares at me. I felt my body stiffen a little. We sat silently for a few moments, each lost in her own thoughts. The trajectory of the various governments' inactions on women survivors' lives reminded me of Rob Nixon's work on 'slow violence'. Although Nixon writes about 'slow violence' in the context of environmental catastrophes and its impact on people's health over years if not decades, his definition 'provoke(s) us to expand our imaginations of what constitutes harm'.[99]

An analogy to man-made violence can be drawn from the deterioration of women's health over the years as a direct result of government inaction. As Nixon explains, 'By slow violence I mean a violence that occurs gradually and out of sight, a violence of delayed destruction that is dispersed across time and space, an attritional violence that is typically not viewed as violence at all'.[100] Lola and other women survivors are victims of such dispersed mental and bodily destruction that is hard to qualify as violence and assign accountability for. Jurić, a prosecuted but never punished rapist, hijacked justice and made a mockery of the legal system. This is not to say that Lola could not find her own way to live; to 'self-repair'.[101] On the contrary, Lola reintegrated socially and moved on with her life defying the assumption that only transitional justice mechanisms can help victims regain their lives.[102]

---

[99] Thom Davies, 'Slow Violence and Toxic Geographies: "Out of Sight" to Whom?' (2022) 40(2) *Environment and Planning: Politics and Space* 409.

[100] Rob Nixon, *Slow Violence and the Environmentalism of the Poor* (Harvard University Press, 2011) 2.

[101] Gilmore and Moffett (n 47).

[102] Laurel E Fletcher and Harvey M Weinstein, 'Transitional Justice and the "Plight" of Victimhood' in Cheryl Lawther, Luke Moffett and Dov Jacobs (eds), *Research Handbook on Transitional Justice* (Edward Elgar Publishing, 2017) 244.

CHAPTER 5

Crime with No Punishment

Transitional justice processes in the form of trials determine what is and what isn't included in official accounts and consequently collective memory.[1] As argued, the court 'must understand its place and voice in the larger social and political processes of delegitimising discriminatory policies, setting the historical record straight, and exposing profound social and institutional failings'.[2] By individualising guilt, the court identifies the perpetrators as criminals and debunks the aura of invincibility they previously held.[3] Post-conflict prosecutions also assist victims to achieve some closure, by seeing those who wronged them brought to justice. By holding those who committed mass atrocities accountable, the government sends a message to the community that such violations will not go unpunished. This sentiment will in turn assist in upholding citizens' trust

---

[1] Shoshana Felman, 'Forms of Judicial Blindness: Traumatic Narratives and Legal Repetitions' in Austin Sarat and Thomas R Kearns (eds), *History, Memory and the Law* (University of Michigan Press, 2002) 25.

[2] 'Changing the Narrative: The Role of Communications in Transitional Justice', *Institute for Integrated Transitions* (online publication, 2019) <https://ifit-transitions.org/wp-content/uploads/2021/03/Changing-the-Narrative-The-Role-of-Communications-in-Transitional-Justice.pdf>.

[3] Elizabeth B Ludwin King, 'Does Justice Always Require Prosecution: The International Criminal Court and Transitional Justice Measures' (2013) 45(1) *The George Washington International Law Review* 85, 91.

in legal institutions. Yet, as important as judgements may be, they provide a limited language for understanding the lives of its main protagonists. Lola's case tells us that only upon their closer inspection there is a more complex story to outcomes of the trials for wartime rapes in Bosnia and Herzegovina (BiH).

Mark Drumbl notes that criminal prosecutions in the aftermath of collective violence represent a focal point where retributivist, deterrent and expressivist interests converge and overlap: those prosecuted are on trial because they deserve to be punished for their past misdeeds, because punishing them will deter others from engaging in these harmful acts and because punishing them expresses the immorality of their actions.[4] The interplay between these different interests means that a criminal trial not only makes a moral judgement of past wrongdoing, but it also creates a public record of that wrongdoing for future reference which should in turn deter others from committing these same harms.[5] As Anette Bringedal Houge argues from an expressivist perspective the importance of prosecution is not to punish perpetrators per se but to define their actions as morally wrong for the sake of the future.[6]

United Nations Deputy Secretary-General Amina Mohamed stated at a 2017 United Nations Security Council (UNSC) Women Peace and Security debate that,

> We have a solemn responsibility to convert a centuries-old culture of impunity into a culture of accountability and deterrence... All our words, laws and resolutions will mean nothing if violations go unpunished in practice.[7]

---

[4] Mark A Drumbl, *Atrocity, Punishment, and International Law* (Cambridge University Press, 2007) 149.

[5] Kathryn Sikkink, *The Justice Cascade: How Human Rights Prosecutions Are Changing World Politics* (W W Norton & Company, 2011); Carlos Santiago Nino, *Radical Evil on Trial* (Yale University Press, 1998); Nicola Henry, *War and Rape: Law, Memory and Justice* (Routledge, 2011) 21.

[6] Anette Bringedal Houge, 'Narrative Expressivism: A Criminological Approach to the Expressive Function of International Criminal Justice' (2019) 19(3) *Criminology & Criminal Justice* 297.

[7] Security Council, Women and Peace and Security, 7938th mtg, UN Doc S/PV.7938 (15 May 2017) 4.

The landmark UNSC Resolution 1325 promulgated on the 31st of October 2000[8] addresses the impact of war on women and stresses the importance of their equal participation and full involvement in all efforts for the maintenance and promotion of peace and security. Resolution 1325 calls on all parties to conflict, to take special measures to protect women and girls from gender-based violence, particularly rape and other forms of sexual abuse in situations of armed conflict.[9]

Following Resolution 1325, the UNSC has adopted nine additional resolutions on Women Peace and Security,[10] five of which directly address conflict-related sexual violence. The most recent, UNSC Resolution 2467, was promulgated in October 2019. It explicitly calls the States to end impunity and prosecute those responsible for crimes against humanity *'noting with concern* that only limited number of perpetrators of sexual violence have been brought to justice'[emphasis original].[11]

Holding individuals criminally responsible for their actions or affiliations through criminal trials could demonstrate that the new regime is different from the previous regime, operating on principles of the rule of law and trustworthiness.[12] It has been argued that criminal accountability brings 'positive changes to the state'[13] and has the potential to help diminish human rights violations.[14] The law strives for finality and

---

[8] Security Council, SC Res 1325, UN Doc S/RES/1325 (31 October 2000).

[9] Ibid para 10.

[10] These resolutions are often referred to as belonging to two sets of categories. The first group of resolutions promotes women's active and effective participation in peacemaking and peacebuilding. The second group, beginning with the adoption of SCR 1820 in 2008, aims to prevent and address conflict-related sexual violence. See, 'Security Council Resolutions on Women, Peace and Security: Normative Frameworks', *Peacemaker.UN.org* (Web page, undated) <https://peacemaker.un.org/wps/normative-frameworks/un-security-council-resolutions>.

[11] Security Council, SC Res 2467, 8514th mtg, UN Doc S/RES/2467 (23 April 2019).

[12] Cynthia M Horne, 'Trust and Transitional Justice' in Lavinia Stan and Nedelsky (eds), *Encyclopaedia of Transitional Justice* (Cambridge University Press, 2nd ed, forthcoming).

[13] Siphiwe Ignatius Dube, 'Transitional Justice Beyond the Normative: Towards a Literary Theory of Political Transitions' (2011) 5 *The International Journal of Transitional Justice* 177, 181.

[14] Kathryn Sikkink and Hun Joon Kim, 'The Justice Cascade: The Origins and Effectiveness of Prosecutions of Human Rights Violations' (2013) 9 *Annual Review of Law and Social Science* 269.

judgement.[15] However, what if judgement does not mean finality? What happens if the punishment never eventuates?

What should women survivors, such as Lola, make of it? If the law's objective of achieving finality is embodied in conviction and conviction fails to materialise, then what is its purpose? What if the courts fail to follow through by upholding the norm of criminal accountability after conviction? The trial assigned blame and responsibility to Lola's rapist, but it never punished him. By not demonstrating the legal prohibition of sexual and gender-based violence and its 'moral repugnance',[16] the law becomes morally corrupt. It tricks us into believing that accounts are settled; that Lola was recompensed for the harm she suffered.

Imposing sentences on legally convicted perpetrators means imposing hardship on them to satisfy the victims' desire for retribution. For many victims in BiH, retributive justice is fundamental[17] and they want to see perpetrators suffer for the pain they inflicted. However, in emerging democracies criminal justice systems are 'often in shambles' and domestic courts may be ill-equipped to undertake prosecutions for war crimes.[18]

The feelings of rage and grief that victims of sexual violence may have, are also intergenerational and affect not only the person it was perpetrated against but their families, communities and other people who were forced to witness such crimes taking place.[19] Moral anger and a determination to do something in return, to make a perpetrator pay for the wrongful deed with his own suffering, are common responses to the harm suffered.[20] Lola and her children have been living with these feelings for the past thirty years. They still have not seen their perpetrators get what they believe they deserved for the harm they inflicted. As a result, their grief and anger have not been ameliorated. Furthermore, the failure to

---

[15] Lawrence Douglas, *The Memory of Judgment: Making Law and History in the Trials of the Holocaust* (Yale University Press, 2001) 4.

[16] Catherine O'Rourke, *Gender Politics in Transitional Justice* (Routledge, 2013) 241.

[17] Diane Orentlicher, *Some Kind of Justice: Bosnian Expectations of the ICTY* (Oxford University Press, 2018).

[18] Nancy Amoury Combs, *Guilty Pleas in International Criminal Law: Constructing a Restorative Justice Approach* (Stanford University Press, 2007) 42.

[19] Stephanie Shillinglaw, *Sexual Violence in Conflict: Delivering Justice for Survivors and Holding Perpetrators to Account* (Report, September 2019) 2 <https://www.wiltonpark.org.uk/wp-content/uploads/WP1651-Report-1-1.pdf>.

[20] Trudy Govier, *Victims and Victimhood* (Broadview Press, 2015) 145.

prosecute perpetrators to the fullest ability of the law can also instil further distrust in the new government.[21]

As Nora Sveaass and Nils Lavik argue, reconciliation and social repair can only happen when there is a fair process of justice.[22] The desire for revenge is common in individuals in transitional societies who have suffered human rights abuses.[23] Such desire is a key reason for processes such as truth commissions and criminal trials to exist in these societies[24] as they aim to prevent continuing hatred and reduce the likelihood of conflict flaring up in future.[25] A trial with no penalty such as the one Lola experienced, can re-traumatise witnesses, provoke feelings of unfairness and undermine societal trust in state institutions.[26] As Lucila Edelman et al. argue, impunity has become 'a new traumatic factor' so detrimental that it renders closure impossible.[27] For survivors, such as Lola and her children and also for wider communities, impunity could contribute to a loss of respect for law and government.[28] Lola several times stated that she lost the trust and respect in the judiciary of BiH,

Justice? What justice?! The justice does not exist. There is no justice. If there was a justice I would not be where I am today. I don't know where is Jurić. It seems no one knows or cares.

---

[21] Maya Goldstein Bolocan, 'Rwandan Gacaca: An Experiment in Transitional Justice' [2004] (2) *Journal of Dispute Resolution* 355.

[22] Nora Sveaass and Nils Johan Lavik, 'Psychological Aspects of Human Rights Violations: The Importance of Justice and Reconciliation' (2000) 69(1) *Nordic Journal of International Law* 35.

[23] David Mendeloff, 'Trauma and Vengeance: Assessing the Psychological and Emotional Effects of Post-Conflict Justice' (2009) 31(3) *Human Rights Quarterly* 592.

[24] Kasaija Phillip Apuuli, 'The Prospect of Establishing a Truth-Telling and Reconciliation Commission in Uganda' (2013) 10 *US-China Law Review* 596.

[25] Olivera Simic, *An Introduction to Transitional Justice* (Taylor & Francis Group, 2nd ed, 2020).

[26] United Nations Development Programme, *Needs Assessment in the Field of Support to Witnesses/Victims in BiH* (Report, 25 July 2013) 53 ('*Needs Assessment Report*').

[27] Lucila Edelman, Diana Kordon and Dario Lagos, 'Transmission of Trauma: The Argentine Case' in Yael Danieli (ed), *International Handbook of Multigenerational Legacies of Trauma* (Springer, 1998) 447, 451.

[28] Yael Danieli, *Conclusion and Future Directions*' in *International Handbook of Multigenerational Legacies of Trauma* (Spring, 1998) 669, 686.

The longer impunity persists, the greater the spread of trauma over a long period of time across the plain of intergenerational transmission.[29]

Lola and her children have been living with impunity for the past three decades, however, in the years immediately after the judgement was rendered, their existing trauma may have exacerbated because the perpetrator's conviction never resulted in him actually serving the sentence. The rapist roams free. The only 'witness protection' Lola enjoys today is that she has been told to call the local police office if she receives 'strange text messages' on her cell phone and suspects these may be from *him*. Over the last several years she received a few suspicious texts and reported them to a local policewoman.

'What happens when you alert police about suspicious text?' I asked.

'Nothing. They take details and say they will investigate. I then never hear back from them', Lola told me in a matter-of-fact manner.

Loneliness and Testimonies

Victims' testimonies have increasingly been viewed as the 'life-blood' of war crime courts.[30] There is increasing recognition of the importance of victims' testimonies. A series of interviews had been conducted with victims of war crimes to understand their motivation for testifying. Some of the common motivations were found to be 'to tell the truth', 'to speak on behalf of the dead' and 'to make the trial an example to prevent future war crimes'.[31] As well as the empowering and cathartic nature of providing witness testimony, it also lends its hand to strengthening the prosecution's case as witnesses' testimonies have become, in some cases, integral to establishing the occurrence of a crime.[32]

After Lola and other women were released from the detention camp, the 'Duga' activists took them to have medical examinations at a local hospital. However, none of Lola's doctors at the time documented that

---

[29] Edelman, Kordon and Lagos (n 27) 460.

[30] Patricia M Wald, 'Dealing with Witnesses in War Crimes Trials: Lessons from the Yugoslav Tribunal' (2002) 5 *Yale Human Rights and Development Law Journal* 217, 219.

[31] Ibid 233.

[32] Ibid 219.

she had been sexually assaulted while in the camp. At the time, she did not want to tell them. Many other women also did not want to report the crimes of rape to the medical staff. Thus, although Lola first gave her testimony in 1994 to the women's association 'Duga', it would be another twenty years before her perpetrators were arrested.[33]

While justice has been excruciatingly slow, Lola never lost her hope that one day she will see it. In the Sarajevo courtroom in 2015, Lola came eye-to-eye with her rapist for the first time in all those years. She was alone on one side of the courtroom and Jurić, his attorney, the secretary, and the judge on the other. This was a difficult and intimidating encounter.

Lola tightened her shoulders while raising her chin up as she spoke.

I was alone in front of all of them. I was looking him [Jurić] *in the eye. I cannot describe that feeling. You can imagine how I felt. I felt sick and terrified. No one was there to support me.*

I saw a new feeling pass over her face: the past lingering, keeping her on guard, threatening to disrupt her life all over again. Her eyes were no longer focused on me, her vision was someplace else. Something had shifted. I waited. A silence stretched between us. She shook her head and then suddenly froze.

He was there ... I saw him. I begged him to leave me alone.

Lola told the judges that she was convinced that he was among the several others who had raped her on the night. She had known him well from the neighbourhood and was in no doubt that she had recognised him, then and now.

Lola:	*I worked in the farm. I worked in shifts. I would sometimes pass by his house even four times a day. Every day I was passing by his house. Sometimes he was coming to our house to ask my deceased husband for some tools, something for his tractor....*
Prosecutor:	Good. Had Ilija Jurić had a family, do you remember?

---

[33] 'Bosnia Arrests Four Croat War Crimes Suspects', *Balkan Insight* (online, 22 April 2014) <https://balkaninsight.com/2014/04/22/bosnia-arrests-four-new-war-crimes-suspects/>.

Lola:	*I would see his mother in the front yard of their house. He had a father who worked in Austria. He had a sister, she had a long straight hair. He had a brother too.*
Prosecutor:	Good. How did Ilija physically looked back then?
Lola:	*He had a blond hair, a small face...He had a straight hair...hanging down over his forehead...*
Prosecutor:	Good. What was his build?
Lola:	*Medium build.*
Prosecutor:	Good. I would like to ask you now to look around the courtroom and tell me whether that man is present here today.
Lola:	*Here he is sitting in that suit. I know him well and he knows me well too...*[34]

Widowed, unemployed with a myriad of health issues and only primary school education, Lola found herself in the courtroom alone with no legal representative to support her. The support she received from the state run Department for Victim and Witness Protection was to debrief her for fifteen minutes before the trial. Lola's comments align with the Department's explanation of their role. As the Department itself reported, although they have a team of psychologists they do not provide psychological support, but 'only give their opinion about psychological state of mind of witness for the trial'. They noted that it is not their job 'to help witnesses to deal with their trauma or to talk about personal difficulties they deal with'. The team's job is to explain to the witness, the different phases of a trial and to be there when the witness is invited to testify. 'When the trial is over, our job is over', the director of the Department said.[35] Although testifying can open old wounds, witnesses have no further support after the judgement is promulgated. If witnesses need counselling the Department can help them by referring them to social workers or centres for mental health.[36]

---

[34] *Prosecutor v Ilija Jurić*, Appeals Division of the Court of Bosnia and Herzegovina, S1 1 K 018179 16 Kžž, 21 March 2017 (third degree verdict), 7 ('Prosecutor v Jurić (third degree verdict)').

[35] Devon Fine and Léa Périllat, 'Podrska svjedocima tokom sudjena za ratne zlocine' *Balkan Diskurs*, <https://balkandiskurs.com/2022/06/17/podrska-svjedocima-tokom-sudjenja-za-ratne-zlocine/>.

[36] Ibid.

Unlike in the Federation of BiH, until recently in the Republika Srpska, as mentioned before, there were no women's non-governmental organisations (NGOs) which could provide support to women victims of wartime rape. In the Federation of BiH however, there were dozens of support groups and organisations, the first of which were established during the war itself. This is perhaps understandable since the NGO landscape of the two entities was built on an unequal footing. Considered as a victim of the Serb 'ethnic cleansing campaign',[37] the Federation of BiH that houses the predominantly Bosniak and Croat population, received approximately ninety-eight per cent of all international aid.[38] Such assistance allowed for the establishment of hundreds of local human rights and women's NGOs in this entity.

The 'Association Women Victims of War', the first and only NGO that supports Serb women victims of wartime rape and torture was only established in December 2012, twenty years after the war started. The NGO has no funds to offer women legal assistance and could not offer any support to Lola during her legal proceedings. As the director of this NGO reported,

> We don't have the funds to run workshops which would offer psychological support and prepare women for testifying before courts. Yet women have been continuously invited by the judiciary to do so. Women without the support of a psychotherapist are at a risk of danger to their lives. Last year two women killed themselves because they could not bear the pain of reliving traumatic memories. Many women victims are dying naturally [due to their age and ill health] and they take the difficult truth with them.[39]

---

[37] Ivo H. Daalder, 'Decision to Intervene: How the War in Bosnia Ended', *Brookings.edu* (Article, 1 December 1998) <https://www.brookings.edu/articles/decision-to-intervene-how-the-war-in-bosnia-ended/>; Carl T Dahlman and Gerard Toal, *Bosnia Remade: Ethnic Cleansing and its Reversal* (Oxford University Press, 2011); Klejda Mulaj, *Politics of Ethnic Cleansing* (Lexington Books, 2008); Paul Mojzes, *Balkan Genocides: Holocaust and Ethnic Cleansing in the Twentieth Century* (Rowman & Littlefield, 2015).

[38] Paul A Marin, 'Bosnia is Beginning to Recover After Four Years of War, and is Offering the First Signs of Legitimate Business Opportunities', *Business of America: The Magazine of International Trade* (Washington DC, September 1997).

[39] Dario Vidojković, 'Ne dozvolimo da se ugasi "Udruženje žena žrtava rata Republike Srpske"!', *Basta Balkana* (online, 3 February 2017) <https://www.bastabalkana.com/2017/02/ne-dozvolimo-da-se-ugasi-udruzenje-zena-zrtava-rata-republike-srpske/> [tr author].

Lola relied on her fellow members of the 'Association of the Former Camp Inmates' (the Association) from Brod and Šamac to drive her to the court hearings in Sarajevo. The trip to Sarajevo is about 200 kilometres from where Lola resides. Milan, a member of the Association and Serb victim of torture himself, drove Lola in the early mornings to the court and returned the same day after Lola had given her testimony. The prosecutor's office lacks the funds to cover the basic witness travel expenditure such as food, accommodation, travel and other associated costs.[40] The Association which has very limited funds, scraped together some money to cover fuel and, as Lola told me, *'for something to eat'* while in Sarajevo.

After the hearings, Lola and Milan would have just enough funds to eat and return home the same day. Lola's feelings of anger and disappointment were thus extended beyond her perpetrators and their community to encompass her *own* community for leaving her alone with no support. With a pale face, Lola swallowed hard, her voice low almost breaking in grief.

> *No one helped me financially or emotionally to go through it all. I survived what I survived from the Ustashe and now I get this* [no support] *from my own people.* [She starts to cry]...*I gave everything for this country, my husband, myself, my children and got nothing...nothing at all...we don't have enough to survive, we live in a poverty, as beggars...*

Feeling betrayed from 'an enemy' is expected but what hurts Lola more is to be betrayed by her 'own'. This was for Lola even harder to swallow. She was emotionally and physically in pain, she felt, as she put it *'humiliated'*. Tired of seeing their mother's constant fight for justice, her two older children were not particularly supportive of her wish to continue with the battle to get at least one rapist sentenced. Lola's voice quivered and her eyes watered when she said:

> *My biggest support was my youngest daughter, the one who was a baby at the time. My other daughter and my son were not really supportive. They kept asking me 'Why do you need this, what are you doing all of this for?' I don't think they are ashamed of what happened to me. They are worried, and it is hard for them. I was on a TV few times and my son would get up and leave*

---

[40] *Needs Assessment Report* (n 26) 16.

the room each time I would start to speak about our ordeal. He cannot listen that.

It is no surprise that Lola's son had the most difficulty accepting his mother's public speaking about her victimhood. Feelings of helplessness and fear coupled with deep trauma can trigger negative feelings and may have left him confused and agitated.[41] When children witness torture, their responses are different from one age to another. Younger children may not have the vocabulary to articulate events they witnessed. As Michael Peel noted, 'age, gender, position in the family, cultural norms and many other variables'[42] can shape their reactions. Such children are also at greater risk of internalised effects such as anxiety and depression.[43] Young children such as Lola's son, who was six at the time when exposed to the traumatic events (the murder of his father and abuse of his mother), can lose some of their acquired developmental skills such as talking or walking.[44] Her son acquired a life-long speech impediment as a result of such exposure.

During the hearings, Lola had to describe in detail the events and her terror of being dragged away to be raped by the soldiers and separated from her young children. The children witnessed the maltreatment of Lola being forced into the car that took her to the place where she was to be raped and tortured.

> *They [soldiers] entered the house and yelled at me to get out of the house. I was crying and screaming. My three children, they were all young… They cursed our Chetnik mothers, telling me 'get out of the house, nothing will happen to the kids'. I had to…I got out, I left my kids behind, I had to get out…*

---

[41] Areti Tsavoussis et al., 'Child-Witnessed Domestic Violence and Its Adverse Effects on Brain Development: A Call for Societal Self-Examination and Awareness' (2014) 2 *Frontiers in Public Health* 175:1–5.

[42] Michael Peel (ed), *Rape as a Method of Torture* (Medical Foundation for the Care of Victims of Torture, 2004) 122.

[43] Melissa M Stiles, 'Witnessing Domestic Violence: The Effect on Children' (2002) 66(11) *American Family Physician* 2052.

[44] Aida Alayarian, 'Children, Torture and Psychological Consequences' (2009) 19(2) *Torture* 145.

> ...Then when he entered into the room in that house he ordered me to take my clothes off. I was begging, crying, he was kicking me with his fists on my face, my legs. He had thrown me on the floor...⁴⁵

For Lola and the other women who were taken along with her on that night, the court described them as 'traumatised witnesses because they felt enormous fear since in those moments of being forcibly taken away they had to leave their young kids behind'.⁴⁶ Lola tells me that her son seems to be emotionally frozen and numb at any mention of their wartime experience. According to Tsavoussis et al., witnessing abuse carries the same risk of harm to children's mental health and learning as being abused directly.⁴⁷ It is possible that the reason Lola's youngest daughter offered her the most support throughout the process is because she was a baby when detained. She may not have a conscious memory of the time in the camp while Lola's two other children, although young, could have vivid traumatic memories. According to Susan Suleiman, they were 'too young to have had an adult understanding of what was happening to them, but old enough to have *been there*' and have some kind of memories.⁴⁸

The reason they do not want to talk about the past and they do not want their mother to speak up either, is because they do not want to remember. They experienced a 'sudden transformation of their world from at least some degree of stability and security to utter chaos'.⁴⁹ While they may not be willing to talk about the past their bodies did 'keep the score'⁵⁰ since they are all dealing with a myriad of health-related issues, mental and physical. The topic of children who were not directly abused but suffered secondary victimisation by witnessing their parent(s) being

---

⁴⁵ *Prosecutor v Ilija Jurić (third degree verdict)* (n 34) 9.

⁴⁶ *Prosecutor v Marijan Brnjic (second degree verdict)*, Appeals Division of the Court of Bosnia and Herzegovina, S1 1 K 019816 17 Krž, 18 May 2017, 76.

⁴⁷ Peter Jaffe et al., 'Similarities in Behavioural and Social Maladjustment among Child Victims and Witnesses to Family Violence' (1986) 56(1) *American Journal of Orthopsychiatry* 142; Tsavoussis et al. (n 41).

⁴⁸ Susan R. Suleiman, 'The 1.5 Generation: Thinking about Child Survivors and the Holocaust' (2002) 59 (3) *American Imago* 277.

⁴⁹ Ibid.

⁵⁰ Bessel Van der Kolk, *The Body Keeps The Score: Mind, and Body in the Healing of Trauma* (Viking, 2014).

abused has not received much attention thus far. Their experiences remain under-researched and unrepresented in the literature on BiH war. This is perplexing since events are defined as trauma if 'the person experienced, witnessed, or was confronted with an event or events that involved actual or threatened death or serious injury, or a threat to the physical integrity of self or others'.[51] The reason why multigenerational trauma generally has been treated as a secondary phenomenon for so long may rely upon the view that it was not 'as obviously dramatic' as the experiences of first-hand traumatised people.[52]

Nonetheless, Lola's children's traumatic experiences also need to be validated as an essential step towards resolution and closure.[53] Nikolina Židek in her study on memory narratives among children who were emigrants in Argentina after World War Two discusses how children's narratives represent a synthesis of first- and second-generation experiences, and their own and their community's trauma.[54] Since children were too young to 'grasp the historical and political complexity of the experience',[55] their childhood memories become inseparable from their parents' and community's memories, especially when they try to make intellectual sense of their experience.[56] The children complement and merge them with memories of their parents and community and this is a reason for extending scholarly focus beyond individual survivors of conflict-related sexual violence and to give more attention to the wider 'ecosystems' that

---

[51] American Psychiatric Association, *Diagnostic and Statistical Manual of Mental Disorders: DSM-5-TR* (American Psychiatric Association Publishing, 5th ed, 2022).

[52] Yael Danieli, 'Preface' in Yael Denieli (ed), *International Handbook of Multigenerational Legacies of Trauma* (Springer, 1998) xvi.

[53] See Harry Stack Sullivan, *The Interpersonal Theory of Psychiatry* (W.W. Norton & Company, 1953); see also discussion of the young people from the former Yugoslavia about 'inherited trauma' 'Perspektiva sa mladima na SFF-u: 'Moramo zaustaviti prenosenje traume', *Radio Slobodna Evropa*, 25 September 2022, https://www.slobodnaevropa.org/a/perspektiva-mladi-sff/32051214.html.

[54] See Nikolina Židek, '"Nobody Asked Me How I Felt". Childhood Memories of Exile among the Croatian Post-WW2 Diaspora in Argentina' (2021) 8 (1) *Contemporary Southeastern Europe* 3–5; Michael Pickering and Emily Keightley, 'Communities of Memory and the Problem of Transmission' (2013) 16 (1) *European Journal of Cultural Studies* 115.

[55] Židek (n 54) 2.

[56] Ibid 1.

constitute people's environments.⁵⁷ To 'disconnect' victims' experiences from the complex web of their surroundings which revolves around their everyday lives, Janine Natalya Clark argues, 'is problematic'.⁵⁸

THE LAW AND ITS VULNERABLE VICTIMS

Narratives such as Lola's provide illuminating accounts that can influence the discourse on theorising transitional justice for survivors of wartime sexual violence. We can use such narratives to explore how ordinary victims with first-hand experience think about law and its meanings and how the law's 'paradoxes' affect them. Sally Engle Merry analyses the contours of what she describes as the 'paradox of legal entitlement' where working class people feel entitled to use the law to resolve their problems, yet they lose the power over their lives when they make use of this entitlement.⁵⁹ Lola used the law and in turn Lola's life became unsafe. She entrusted her safety to legal bodies but her life is now arguably more endangered.

Through the close examination of women's lived experiences with transitional justice mechanisms, we can recognise the complexities that lay beyond the reading of final judgements, which often provide a reductively simplistic official account of wartime rape. If prosecutions are a measure of 'successful justice', Lola's case would represent BiH's relative success in prosecuting conflict-related sexual violence.⁶⁰ Yet there is a post-trial life that is not inscribed in the judgement itself. Such lives of women victims are *invisible* and only a 'feminist curiosity'⁶¹ to look beyond the court's paperwork can bring them under the spotlight. The judgement itself renders Lola's transitional justice experience—with the trial and its

---

⁵⁷ Janine Natalya Clark, 'Beyond a "Survivor-Centred Approach" to Conflict-Related Sexual Violence?' (2021) 97(4) *International Affairs* 1067, 1068.

⁵⁸ Ibid 1073.

⁵⁹ Sally Engle Merry, *Getting Justice and Getting Even: Legal Consciousness Among Working-Class Americans* (University of Chicago Press, 1990).

⁶⁰ See Karen McVeigh, 'Hague Hails "Tremendous Start" to Sexual Violence Scheme Set Up with Jolie', *The Guardian* (online, 23 November 2018) <https://www.theguardian.com/global-development/2018/nov/23/william-hague-hails-tremendous-start-sexual-violence-scheme-angelina-jolie>.

⁶¹ Cynthia Enloe, *The Curious Feminist: Searching for Women in a New Age of Empire* (University of California Press, 2004).

aftermath—*unseen*. Its unfinished 'business' makes her feel undeserving of its finality, of gaining some sense of satisfaction that justice 'has been done'. She was fighting for justice for a quarter of a century and in its finality, she was cheated by the law.

Legal professions have a saying that while justice can be painfully slow, it is not unreachable. Yet, in Lola's case it was too slow and is still unreachable. The failure of justice confirmed her trauma as ongoing, inevitable and inescapable. The violations occurred thirty years ago but have never really ended in Lola's body and mind. The law did not offer salvation to Lola or retribution for the perpetrator—a remorseless war criminal escapee. Lola expected that the trial and sentence were an end of her legal journey, but its *finality* in fact has never been reached.

For Lola, the lack of the law's finality meant the death of her hopes of seeing justice in her lifetime. She transitioned from injustice to a glimmer of justice and then back to injustice. She went the full cycle through the transitional *in*justice process. Judith Shklar invites us to view injustice 'as an independent phenomenon in its own right'.[62] She argues that for too many victims the key concern is that an emphasis on justice is likely to exclude the personal details of what it felt like, their story, past and present, the imprints it left on their memory and body, and the particular and personal meaning that the event(s) had in their lives. This was true for Lola's experience; it was lost in the court case files.

Lola's story speaks of the *everydayness* of transitional justice for survivors of wartime rape in their struggle to receive some form of legal and symbolic recognition. As Veena Das has noted, 'everyday' is where much of the political work happens and the definition of violence should be expanded to include 'the everyday and the event, within its ambit'.[63] A constant and 'everyday' struggle against state institutions can be too much of an overwhelming burden for these women. As seen in Lola's and her children's case it can take years to achieve a minimum of justice. No wonder that some women have no strength or will to pursue it. For many of them, there is a present and ongoing impossibility of ever *seeing* justice delivered; of their perpetrators being punished. The moment of justice, represented by judgement being delivered, may offer a false sense

---

[62] Judith N Shklar, *The Faces of Injustice* (Yale University Press, 1990) 15.

[63] Veena Das, 'Violence, Crisis, and the Everyday' (2013) 45(4) *International Journal of Middle East Studies* 798, 800.

of respite from the reality of everyday poverty and other forms of structural violence which Lola and other women survivors experience on a daily basis.

To Lola the judgement offered a deceitful sense of justice and finality. She finds it difficult to understand why the state authorities never apprehended Jurić to make him serve his sentence. The prosecutor stated during the initial trial that Jurić has 'Croatian citizenship and that he works in Austria'.[64] He suggested that there were risks that Jurić could 'influence witnesses' and for this reason he was ordered to report to the police every week during the trial and not to leave his place of residence.[65] However, once the first-degree trial was over Jurić was released, and he immediately left the country. Despite Lola's testimony that it was Jurić who raped her, the Court in its first-degree judgement concluded that 'there is no doubt that [Lola] was brutally raped and physically tortured at the exact way that witness had described, but the court could not without reasonable doubt prove that accused Jurić raped her'.[66]

Prosecutor: You told us that Ilija Jurić entered and, keeping in mind it was evening, are you sure you could really see that it was Ilija Jurić himself?
Lola: *Yes, I could see.*
Prosecutor: How could you see?
Lola: *I could see, there was a moonlight bright like a day...The moonlight was bright, the window was from this side and I could see when they entered...and when they came in the front yard, when they came to pick us up, they had torches and we also recognised their voices...*
Prosecutor: Good.[67]

Lola told the judges,

---

[64] 'Zatražene mjere zabrane za Iliju Jurića', *Klix* (online, 10 December 2014) <https://www.klix.ba/vijesti/bih/zatrazene-mjere-zabrane-za-iliju-Jurića/141210121>.

[65] Džana Brkanić, 'Requested extension of banning measures against Jurić', *Detektor* (online, 23 February 2015) <https://detektor.ba/2015/02/23/zatrazeno-produzenje-mjera-zabrane-Juriću/>.

[66] *Prosecutor v Ilija Jurić*, Appeals Division of the Court of Bosnia and Herzegovina, No S1 1 K 018179 16 Kžž, 17 March 2016 (second degree verdict) 19.

[67] *Prosecutor v Ilija Jurić (third degree verdict)* (n 34) 8 [tr author].

5 CRIME WITH NO PUNISHMENT   117

I was covered in blood all over my body. They destroyed me. I felt defeated, humiliated, perverse.

Lola was not *just* raped; she was sodomised and tortured by eight men she knew well. Jurić committed war crimes when perpetrating his acts in serious breaches of international humanitarian law against civilians that dictate what human rights should be respected during the war.[68] He also committed crimes against humanity by targeting Lola as a woman belonging to a particular ethnic group.[69] Lola did everything that was expected of her: she testified and told the truth so the defendant could be 'successfully' prosecuted. She cooperated with investigators and risked her safety. She never imagined that her efforts would result in a prosecution with a sentence that her rapist would never have to serve.

No one has ever called or advised Lola to tell her why Jurić has not yet been arrested or even if he will ever be arrested in her lifetime. The inaction of the state has reverberated into an unanswerable echo of Lola's '*Why?*' question. Lola wants reasons, explanations, arguments. She wants her life to make sense, to understand the truth. Accepting that many of her questions will not be answered is a difficult prospect. Vladan Beara, a

---

[68] Such crimes are derived primarily from the *Geneva Convention (I) for the Amelioration of the Condition of the Wounded and Sick in Armed Forces in the Field of 12 August 1949* (entered into force 21 October 1950) ('*Geneva Convention (I)*'); *Protocol Additional to the Geneva Conventions of 12 August 1949, and relating to the Protection of Victims of International Armed Conflict*s (Protocol I), 8 June 1977 (entered into force 7 December 1978) ('*Additional Protocol I*'); *Protocol Additional to the Geneva Conventions of 12 August 1949, and relating to the Protection of Victims of Non-International Armed Conflicts (Protocol II)*, 8 June 1977 (entered into force 7 December 1978) ('*Additional Protocol II*'); *The Convention (II) with Respect to the Laws and Customs of War on Land and its annex: Regulations concerning the Laws and Customs of War on Land*, The Hague, adopted 29 July 1899 (entered into force 4 September 1900) ('*Hague Convention 1899*'); and *Convention (IV) respecting the Laws and Customs of War on Land and its annex: Regulations concerning the Laws and Customs of War on Land*, The Hague, adopted 18 October 1907 (entered into force 26 January 1910) ('*Hague Convention 1907*'). Their most recent codification can be found in article 8 of the *Rome Statute for the International Criminal Court*, opened for signature 17 July 1998, 2187 UNTS 90 (entered into force 1 July 2002) ('*Rome Statute*').

[69] The definition of 'crimes against humanity' is codified in article 7 of the *Rome Statute* (n 68): 'The notion encompasses crimes such as murder, extermination, rape, persecution and all other inhumane acts of a similar character (wilfully causing great suffering, or serious injury to body or to mental or physical health), committed "as part of a widespread or systematic attack directed against any civilian population, with knowledge of the attack"'.

psycho-therapist who has been working for the past twenty years with war veterans and civilians who survived the war in BiH explains why victims such as Lola need to make a meaning from their experiences.

> According to Ronni Janoff-Bulman, people who are traumatised have shattered basic assumptions. Their conceptual world is in a chaos. Before traumatization they believed that the world is a benign place where evil does not happen to good people if they did not deserve it. After traumatization, victims build new basic assumptions according to which the world is an evil place, that people are dangerous and malicious, that their self is less valuable. The victims also have a need to correct their own image of the world and of other people because life with such traumatic condition is very difficult. They feel a need to see the world as a place of order and logic, they need an explanation why something happened.[70]

No one has ever asked Lola how she felt after the trial—after all of it; after six years of her perpetrator avoiding justice, being on the run. She received only one phone call from a representative of an NGO who followed the trial. The phone call came immediately after the first-degree judgement was delivered and Jurić was released. According to Lola, she received the call after she stormed out of the courtroom upon hearing that she had lost her case and her rapists were freed from all the charges. Lola was shocked and in disbelief that this could happen. She was angry and said loudly in the courtroom, *'There is no justice, this is all a farce!'* Lola looked troubled as she recalled,

> *She* [an NGO representative] *called me to tell me that I should have not behaved disrespectfully towards the judges and the rest of the court by storming out and being visibly upset. Instead of providing me with support she criticised me for my reaction upon hearing that the criminal was not held accountable for his crime and subsequently released. Why would that be so rude? I was so angry!*

Lola was also criticised by Jurić's defence counsel who stated in their closing argument that 'the witness had a personal interest in Ilija Jurić

---

[70] Correspondence with Vladan Beara (Olivera Simic, email correspondence, 13 December 2022). Ronni Janoff-Bulman, *Shattered Assumptions: Towards a new psychology of trauma* (The Free Press, 1992); See also Michaela Schok, *Meaning as a Mission: Making sense of War and Peacekeeping* (Eburon Academic Publishing 2009).

being proclaimed guilty since that would allow her to submit a legal asset request'. They also added that she 'acted hostile towards the accused and expressed aggressiveness'.[71] Lola was turned from victim into a violent woman who made up the story of her wartime rape to receive material gain. However, the court corrected this blatant attack on Lola and stated the following:

> The court cannot disregard that the statement made by the defence counsel is absolutely unacceptable...they tried to build their defence on a theory that the victim was motivated by possibility of making a legal asset request. Their statement about aggressiveness and hostile demeanour of the witness towards accused actually proves the contrary. After surviving such humiliating acts by accused towards witness, and the nature of the act itself, her reactions are totally logical and expected.[72]

This step taken by the court to defend the witness was welcomed, however the words had already been spoken. Lola heard them and she was re-traumatised by them. She experienced secondary victimisation by encountering 'victim-blaming attitudes, behaviours and practices; in her interaction with professionals and institutions which resulted in additional trauma'.[73] We know that when a trial takes place it can give a particular atrocity sufficient exposure to embed itself in collective memory,[74] and can even enable victims to contribute to the historical record.[75] Cherif Bassiouni points out that law can only 'make' memory through witness testimony if there are surviving witnesses, if such witnesses can adequately recollect what happened, and if they actually testify despite fears over their

---

[71] *Prosecutor v Ilija Jurić (third degree verdict)* (n 34) 26.

[72] Ibid.

[73] See Echo A Rivera, Cris M Sullivan and April M Zeoli, 'Secondary Victimization of Abused Mothers by Family Court Mediators' (2012) 7(3) *Feminist Criminology* 234, 237, quoting Rebecca Campbell, 'What Really Happened: A Validation Study of Rape Survivors' help-seeking experiences with the legal and medical systems' (2005) 20(1) *Violence & Victims* 55, 56.

[74] Joachim J Savelsberg and Ryan D King, *American Memories: Atrocities and the Law* (Russell Sage Foundation, 2011) 169.

[75] Martha Minow, *Between Vengeance and Forgiveness: Facing History after Genocide and Mass Violence* (Beacon Press, 1998).

safety.[76] From Lola's case and also from other cases, we can conclude that just because victims tell their stories within the formal legal setting, this does not mean the transitional justice process is over or that justice has been done. It also means that giving Lola a voice within the justice system does not imply the ability or willingness of receivers to 'listen to and understand that voice, let alone empathize with it'.[77] On the contrary, one can argue that Lola may be worse off by telling her story. Testifying can have a 'cathartic effect', but it may also fail to do so, and 'may even inflict further harm [instead of] helping'.[78] While not looking at me but staring down at the floor, with her hands twisted in and out of each other anxiously, Lola told me,

> *He is free. I have two adult daughters now. I cannot think of something happening to them. I am mortified of thinking that he can do something to them basically anytime. I have grandchildren too who are now their age when we were taken and detained.*

This was the first time that Lola pointed out that her grandchildren serve as a daily reminder of her children when they were young and vulnerable to a terrible ordeal. She fears for their lives too.

Lola will stay locked in anxiety as long as Jurić enjoys impunity. Amnesty represents a general pardon from criminal and civil liability for politically motivated offences committed in the past.[79] While Jurić did not get *de jure* amnesty, he has been given de facto *amnesty* by being allowed to commit the crime of rape without being arrested. Lola and also a number of other women victims of wartime rape have negative experiences with the court's inability to arrest and jail rapists.[80] Mirsada

---

[76] M Cherif Bassiouni and Peter Manikas, *The Law of the International Criminal Tribunal for the Former Yugoslavia* (Transnational Publishers, 1996).

[77] Antony Pemberton, Eva Mulder and Pauline GM Aarten, 'Stories of Injustice: Towards a Narrative Victimology' (2019) 16(4) *European Journal of Criminology* 391, 407.

[78] Jill Stauffer, *Ethical Loneliness: The Injustice of Not Being Heard* (Columbia University Press, 2015) 56.

[79] John Clark, 'Northern Ireland: A Balanced Approach to Amnesty, Reconciliation and Reintegration' [2008] (January–February) *Military Review* 37.

[80] See Azra Husaric, 'Bosnian War Rape Survivors "Still Afraid to Speak Out"', *Balkan Insight* (online, 3 March 2021) <https://balkaninsight.com/2021/03/03/bosnian-war-rape-survivors-still-afraid-to-speak-out/?lang=sr>.

Tursunović is one of them. She testified against her wartime rapist, but after she had given her statement, the perpetrator left for Russia and never returned. She searched for years for him online, on social media platforms such as Facebook and recently found his profile which brought the trauma back. Mirsada reported, 'I started shivering, I logged out of my account quickly and later deleted it. I was frightened, I took a sedative, I did my breathing exercises as my doctor had taught me'.

Such encounters can affect an entire community of women victims, resulting in distrust and reluctance to access the courts.[81] Although she is 'living for the day when the criminal will be brought to justice', Mirsada cautioned that pressure should not be put on victims of wartime rape to give statements and testify in court.[82] Similar to Mirsada, Lola also found her rapist on Facebook. She spent a few years searching for his profile and recently found him.

While we were talking, Lola fetched her phone from the table to show me Jurić's profile. With her eyes wide open, she pressed her index finger on the screen and said in a hushed voice,

> *Here he is. These are his details. All correct. Look [she scrolled back and forth over his personal data]. The date of birth, correct...everything fits. He even proudly put on his public profile that he was in the HVO unit in Odžak.*

I looked at Jurić's profile on Lola's phone in disbelief. He was smiling at Lola and myself from the screen, seemingly enjoying his freedom, fishing and spending time with his friends. My mouth felt dry. Not only do Jurić and others like him make a mockery of the criminal justice system, but they publicly laugh in their victims' faces. Lola continued, shivering a little.

> *The Croatian government will not arrest him...he crosses the Sava river in the night and comes to Odžak...I am sure he is crossing that river and he is often there...He was coming to one local kafana [pub] in town during the trial. I know that for sure... My neighbour is married to a Croat man. She works in that kafana and he was going there during the trial... and I am*

---

[81] Epstein and Goodman discuss how the "ripple effect" discourages the "broader community of women seeking help they need." Deborah Epstein and Lisa Goodman, 'Discounting Women: Doubting Domestic Violence Survivors' Credibility and Dismissing Their Experiences' (2019) 167 *University of Pennsylvania Law Review* 399, 453.

[82] Husaric (n 80).

> sure he still visits that place... I saw just two days ago that he [Jurić] liked something on her Facebook profile that means he is in touch with her. I was inquiring with her and her husband a bit, indirectly, you know, I cannot ask directly about him... I wanted to find out something about him, where is he and that sort of thing, but they do not want to tell me anything...

She suddenly paused for a moment and looked around as if she feared that some unsuspected presence might be listening in to this conversation, overhearing every word. Her body was on high alert. The air had already been moist, but the humidity had built even more in the past few minutes. We were alone in the house standing close to each other in her living room. Still, the fear was there; the feeling as someone was spying on us. Lola lowered her voice and then continued,

> ...their lips are sealed when it comes to him. They don't want to say anything about him... But they must be in touch with him. They may even talk to him on the phone. Why they would like each other's Facebook posts if they are not in contact with each other? I think that he comes to town when the night falls down, but I have no one to confirm that to me. I am sure one hundred percent that he crosses the river by boat. He has photos on the Facebook of him fishing and one is him posing with a big fish. [she shows me a photo of Jurić holding a fish with his both hands as she said this]

I asked Lola if she informed anyone about her findings and thoughts. She turned to look at me, her eyebrow raised, perhaps surprised by the naivety of my question.

> Whom to show? No one is interested in it. Only you are interested so I am showing it to you. Who else wants to know about this? No one. I did not show it to anyone. What is the point in telling anyone... no one will do anything.

Lola slumped in her chair, her face drained. I said nothing for a long time because there was not much to contradict her. Some of the judiciary, lawyers and activists I talked to who work on the war crimes have been aware of the war criminals' Facebook profiles but there is little or nothing they can do about it. Most of them won't be extradited by their destination states. I am not arguing that telling the truth is unimportant and that testimonies do not play an important role in preserving the memory and changing hearts and minds. The listening or reading of victims' testimonies is important in changing people's perspectives to side with the victims rather than the perpetrators.[83] Acting as a witness is important since testimonies contained in legal documents and transcripts can offer 'an invaluable and unique source of data about sexual violence and everyday experiences of conflict'.[84]

However, the risks and benefits of telling these stories have to be balanced. Sometimes decisions by survivors not to testify may be a life-saving exercise. Silence, as Jelke Boesten notes, 'may not only be a way of individual coping with past experiences, but also an act of mitigating the sequels of such violence'.[85] It is well-known that victims and witnesses may be reluctant to come forward and testify because of societal and other barriers. They also face a continuum of violence in the form of 'institutional abuse' once they do decide to speak up.[86] The BiH institutional system is the opposite of friendly, it is full of hurdles and obstacles that obstruct justice.

Gorana Mlinarević, a researcher and lawyer from BiH, summarised well the paradoxical situation in which many women victims of wartime rape found themselves in:

> The short-term imprisonment is a disappointing fact. The problem is that war criminals are celebrated as heroes in their communities. Their families are economically safe contrary to the families of victims. While they are in prison, they do not have to worry about having a roof over their head which is for many victims a huge concern. Once they serve their sentence, they return to the society without any repercussions and can

---

[83] Luis Moreno Ocampo, 'Stopping the Crimes While Repairing the Victims: Personal Reflections of a Global Prosecutor' in Jacqueline Bhabha, Margareta Matache and Caroline Elkins (eds), *Time for Reparations: A Global Perspective* (University of Pennsylvania Press, 2021) 291.

[84] Kirsten Campbell, Elma Demir and Maria O'Reilly, 'Understanding Conflict-Related Sexual Violence and the "Everyday" Experience of Conflict through Witness Testimonies' (2019) 54(2) *Cooperation and Conflict* 254, 258.

[85] Jelke Boesten, *Sexual Violence During War and Peace: Gender, Power, and Post-Conflict Justice in Peru* (Macmillan, 2014) 87.

[86] Kristina Ljevak, 'Život u miru nakon silovanja u ratu', *Diskriminacija* (online, 24 October 2016) <https://www.diskriminacija.ba/teme/život-u-miru-nakon-silovanja-u-ratu>.

continue to stir hatred and threaten their witnesses. Many women fight for their survival because of the poverty in which they found themselves. Often they are the sole breadwinner in their families and due to the abuse they survived in war they are often sick. If they receive any compensation as a civilian victim of war, they spend it mostly on medications.[87]

The detrimental impact that disclosure of sexual violence may have on a victim's family exacerbates security concerns victims may have, thus some are reluctant to even report the crime, let alone testify in court.[88] Many women victims are afraid of acting as witnesses due to a lack of witness protection and community support. At least one woman who testified at the same time as Lola, moved overseas with her family after the case was over. She emigrated due to the social stigma that she felt would follow her and her family if she stayed in her village. Despite being a 'protected witness', everyone in the village knew about her case and that she was raped as a young girl during the war. Her full name was cited in the court's documents so anyone who followed the trial or read documents could easily identify her. The court has not retracted from the judgement her full name and even the country where she moved to during the proceedings. It stated that 'the case had affected her marriage, so once she told her husband that she was raped, they left Bosnia and Herzegovina'.[89]

However, not all women can or want to leave their village or country. Lola and other women silence-breakers decided to stay and come forward to testify, despite the witness protection system being weak. As Lola told me,

> *I went to the court to give evidence about what happened not only to me but to Serb people so it never happens again.. And then what did I get from it all... I am afraid, I sometimes panic because of the situation I found myself in... What if something happens to my children or my grandchildren?*

---

[87] Ibid.

[88] Serge Brammertz and Michelle Jarvis (eds), *Prosecuting Conflict-Related Sexual Violence at the ICTY* (Oxford University Press, 2016) 42.

[89] This case is held on file by the author.

Lola told her story but the cost of doing so may have been too high. While some women migrated to other countries in fear of their security, Lola remains living in the same village she lived in before, during and after the trial. The perpetrator can easily find her if he wishes to do so.

CHAPTER 6

Women Living in 'Not-War Not-Peace' Time

Women's stories of wartime violence have been shifted from the margins to the centre and thus have made a vital contribution to the field of transitional justice. However, in the aftermath of war there remains a dearth of women's stories about their encounters with the local justice bureaucracies. Women victims' everyday experiences with the different transitional justice mechanisms on the ground remain under-researched. There is an assumption that if transitional justice mechanisms were successful in delivering some form of justice, such as prosecuting perpetrators, it could help women victims regain their dignity. While 'closure' cannot simply be achieved by delivering some form of justice, there is a hope that victims may at least experience a small degree of satisfaction by being beneficiaries of justice.

There is very little discussion in the literature about the harm failed justice can inflict; about women such as Lola and how they can live with this failure as they exit their trials empty handed, with no justice in sight. This 'missing history'[1] demands our attention when understanding the implications of key transitional justice mechanisms in post-conflict contexts. This is important since such mechanisms and processes are intrinsically involved in 'memory making' through documenting the abuses of the past in various ways and to various degrees. Law is central

---

[1] Svetlana Alexievich, *Chernobyl Prayer* (Penguin, 2016) 24.

© The Author(s), under exclusive license to Springer Nature Singapore Pte Ltd. 2023
O. Simic, *Lola's War*,
https://doi.org/10.1007/978-981-99-1942-0_6

to 'memory making'. Law renders certain harms, victims and victimisers either 'seen' or 'unseen', and categorizes certain actors...into binary groupings to be either victims or perpetrators and judges particular actors and actions to be either morally good or morally bad.[2] The stories of the 'unseen' have rarely been documented because, as Hearty argues,

> law['s] functioning through prescription ... makes certain events, victims, and interpretations visible and then asks society to duly remember them. Other events, victims, and interpretations are, by contrast, hidden and forgotten.[3]

This book has revealed how one woman found a way of moving on amidst the wreckage of broken trust, surrounded by individuals and communities still suffering from the wounds inflicted on them by terrible violence. By paying close attention to women's silences and narratives, feminist studies in transitional justice can offer a fuller understanding of how agency emerges in (post) war contexts.[4] Lola's case offers a deeper engagement with everyday experiences of survival and endurance in the omnipresent constraints and losses of the post-war milieu in Bosnia and Herzegovina (BiH).[5] It gives us a glimpse into how some women may adapt and live with their trauma in an environment where ethnically divided politics, poor governance, economic stagnation, corruption and ineffective post-war reconstruction efforts have been endemic.

No doubt armed conflicts contribute to a toxic environment for human health and well-being, but there are multiple actors and environments that also play disturbing roles in post-war reconstruction.[6] These can reproduce various forms of violence and neglect that, albeit in different

---

[2] Kevin Hearty, 'Law, "Presentist" Agendas and the Making of "Official" Memory after Collective Violence', (2022) 49 *Journal of Law and Society* 495.

[3] Ibid 503.

[4] See Elisabeth Porter, 'Gendered Narratives: Stories and Silences in Transitional Justice' (2016) 17(1) *Human Rights Review* 35; Johanna Mannergren Selimovic, 'Gendered Silences in Post-conflict Societies: A Typology' (2020) 8(1) *Peacebuilding* 1.

[5] Peter Locke in his study uses the term of 'getting by' in exploring everyday experiences of survival in the post-war Sarajevo. See Peter Locke, 'City of Survivors: Trauma, Grief, and Getting by in Post-war Sarajevo' (Ph.D. Dissertation, Princeton University, 2009).

[6] Kimberly Theidon, *Legacies of War: Violence, Ecologies, and Kin* (Duke Uni Press, 2022) 6.

forms, continue during transitional justice times. Structural and bureaucratic violence play a prominent role. While they may be invisible and intangible, their effects can be devastating for women survivors' sense of self and citizenship. Women survivors, such as Lola, may live in the post-conflict environment—a so-called 'peace'—but as Cynthia Enloe has more accurately described, it is 'the war in its ongoing aftermath'.[7]

The aftermath can still feel like a war for many: victims now have to wage war with the state institutions to get justice for the harm they suffered. Many like Lola live in the charged social landscape in which rape survivors, war veterans, war criminals, witnesses, orphans, children born of wartime rape and the beneficiaries of war live side by side, each navigating their own existence and trauma.[8] They inhabit, what Primo Levi calls the grey zone of 'half tints and moral complexity'.[9] It is now crucial to understand the roles of victims, perpetrators and bystanders before and during the war, and how these roles fluctuate in the post-war environment.[10] This is an environment in which 'social repair' and 'social reconstruction' are bound to happen: reconstructing the social ruins that are 'among the most enduring legacies of war'.[11]

The problems that are 'essentially political, social, or economic', cannot be 'medicalized', nor can 'the people affected by them' be 'pathologized as victims without agency, sufferers that can be cured through psychological counselling'.[12] The people that live in the aftermath of war live in ongoing violence, not necessarily physical violence, but 'the violence that lives on in bureaucracies of justice and in the social stigmatisation of those who have to navigate them'.[13] Such violence, while not necessarily

---

[7] Cynthia Enloe, *Nimo's War, Ema's War: Making Feminist Sense of the Iraq War* (University of California Press, 2010) 17.

[8] See Kimberly Theidon, *Intimate Enemies: Violence and Reconciliation in Peru* (University of Pennsylvania Press, 2012) xiii.

[9] Primo Levi, *The Drowned and The Saved* (Abacus, 2013).

[10] Alette Smeulers, 'Concluding Thoughts' in Alette Smeulers, Martje Weerdesteijn and Barbora Hola (eds) *Perpetrators of International Crimes* (Oxford University Press, 2019) 321.

[11] Theidon (n 8).

[12] Stef Craps, *Postcolonial Witnessing: Trauma Out of Bounds* (Palgrave Macmillan, 2013) 28.

[13] Roxani C Krystalli, 'Narrating Victimhood: Dilemmas and (in)dignities' (2021) 23(1) *International Feminist Journal of Politics* 125, 139.

life threatening, can damage victims mental health that in the long run can affect their physical well-being. Many survivors, such as Lola, have burnt out mentally and physically from years of struggle with the state apparatus.

Despite the many failures of retributive justice, the belief that the punishment of offenders is a vital component of transitional justice is still prevailing. As Elena Maculan and Alicia Gil Gil argue, retributive justice has come to be understood as a mechanism for giving satisfaction to the victim, indeed even a victim's right.[14] Lola and other women victims are still expected and encouraged to pursue with trials, to testify and bring charges against their alleged perpetrators. In fact, if they don't, they may not receive reparations or the important status of victim that would enable them to get some social welfare benefits.

Much of the literature in the transitional justice field focuses on whether material reparations or criminal justice has been enforced or not, but there is little written about the direct impact of their unsuccessful implementation on lived experiences of victims. Even less is written about women who have gone through criminal trials and ended up in Lola's position. To provide a more socio-legal analysis of the experience of trials for wartime rape, beyond the normative basis of criminal justice, and to unpack victims' agency in practice, this book has examined these issues through a one-woman case study on how victims who did not receive justice manage their harm.

'*Why did this had to happen to me? Why me?*' Lola questioned her role in victimisation multiple times in our conversations.

These are the universal questions commonly asked by survivors searching for causes of their victimisation; why them and not someone else. Survivors make sense of the traumatic event by understanding what happened, how it happened and why it happened. The search for answers includes not only the search for a causal explanation, but also for 'understanding of [the] place that these experiences have in one's life story'.[15]

---

[14] Elena Maculan and Alicia Gil Gil, 'The Rationale and Purposes of Criminal Law and Punishment in Transitional Contexts' (2020) 40(1) *Oxford Journal of Legal Studies* 132.

[15] Vladan Beara, 'The Contribution of REBT in Addressing the Givens of Existence' (2015) 33(2) *Journal of Rational—Emotive and Cognitive—Behaviour Therapy* 179, 195.

Lola never received answers to her questions or a glimpse of remorse, let alone an apology from her perpetrator. It is well-known that a perpetrator's explicit expression of remorse has enormous value in victims' healing.[16] Obviously such healing and closure has not taken place for Lola and her children. As Peter Locke argues, some wounds in war's aftermath 'simply cannot be healed' and an act of mourning 'for what can never be recovered' is an open-ended business.[17] Rather than sitting deep inside like ticking bombs, these untold stories can be invited and heard. Lola's story sheds light on the ways in which survivors have been constrained in pursuing and receiving some form of justice. While women survivors use their resilience to go through the slow and painful bureaucracy of criminal and administrative justice systems, the patchwork of the rule of law and absence of any institutional or state-led support systems have been systematic barriers that survivors alone cannot resolve.

All women survivors of wartime rape in BiH bear a triple burden: of being physically and mentally scarred, of community stigma and of being politically invisible. Thirty years after these crimes were committed, their suffering has not yet been acknowledged by the state. Women wartime rape survivors in Republika Srpska have been marginalised even further: they received scant attention for their plight either from international or their own local community or financial aid programmes, unlike their counterparts in the Federation of BiH. As Michael Potter and Hedley Abernethy argue, the formation of ethno-national identity during the war has had a significant influence on 'who is present and who is absent in post-conflict power relations'.[18]

Over the last three decades, little has been done by the BiH state institutions to assist women survivors recover and heal from the crimes committed against them. In the face of flawed and problematic-to-implement transitional justice mechanisms available, women are disillusioned; they worry that they will never receive any form of justice in

---

[16] Joseph V Montville, 'Psychoanalytical Enlightenment and the Greening of Diplomacy' (1989) 37(2) *Journal of American Psychoanalytic Association* 297.

[17] Locke (n 5) 31.

[18] Michael Potter and Hedley Abernethy, 'What About the Women: Transitional Justice and Gender in Bosnia and Herzegovina and Northern Island' in Olivera Simic and Zala Volčič (eds), *Transitional Justice and Civil Society in the Balkans* (Springer, 2013) 163, 164.

their lifetime. They have been left feeling betrayed by the state institutions, especially after they have put their bodies and minds on the line, and thrown themselves into the courtrooms, yet they have either received very little or nothing in return.

Transcending the feeling of her dignity being robbed and having to reconcile with the prospect of no justice in sight is what Lola need to make peace with. Her decades-long encounters with the legal justice system have resulted only in disappointment and frustration. The experiences that Lola have had with the justice system unsurprisingly make other women survivors sceptical and unwilling to pursue retributive justice. It also makes them feel hopeless and they become prone to transmitting their depression onto their children and grandchildren.[19]

Such experiences can also make them even more fearful; Lola's rapist was prosecuted and sentenced, but he fled the country and remains free. By testifying in the court, Lola put her and her children's lives in danger. Since then, Lola has been fearful for her family's safety, in particular the safety of her daughters and now her granddaughters.

> *My granddaughters are no bigger than my children were back then when it all happened ... I am not alone, now I have all of them to fear for.*

She has good reason to be fearful and on guard: any day Jurić could find her and take his revenge on her and her family. With Jurić still at large Lola's future remains uncertain. She lives without witness protection and is not reassured by the police advice to simply call them if she receives any threats or sees any suspicious behaviour. Nonetheless, she does phone them if she notices anything out of the ordinary.

> *Now out of nothing I can see something...because of the fear inside of me. A few weeks ago, an unknown car approached to me to ask if I was waiting for a lift. I was standing at the curb of the street. I have never seen that man or the car. I froze. I blurted 'no'. He pressed the gas and left. I called police to tell them about this incident. I understand that this may have been mistake but it was weird and I think because of my experience I see things differently and react with fear on anything that may be even a little bit suspicious.*

---

[19] 'Loza Foundations Speaks Up For the Women That Survived the Rape Camps', *Loza Foundation* (Web Page, 29 October 2018) <https://lozafoundation.org/en/2018/10/29/loza-foundation-speaks-women-survived-rape-camps/>.

Lola's everyday encounters are a chilling realisation that for women like her there is no 'endgame', no escape from that 'wartime rape' location; from the status of victim and witness. There is a feeling of powerlessness and the ultimate realisation that all legal avenues have been exhausted; avenues that Lola walked through with her last bits of strength and hope. When I asked her if she would go through this process again knowing what the end result would be, Lola said her voice raising,

> *I would go again to the court, I would say everything what I said again. I am not afraid, I am telling the truth always. I would repeat the same. I did this for my people. I was inquiring if it is possible to raise another indictment for the perpetrators who were acquitted but they told me that it is not. It could be possible only if some new victims show up. I did not have experience, I did not know how to do these things. I should have pursue with this...but no one supported me...and then they wonder why people do not want to testify. They don't want because they hear about our experiences. They see what is going on... People are afraid. They were congratulating me when I decided to go to court. They were telling me how brave I was that I should get a medal for courage. But I did it not just for me but for everyone, for our children, our future, so it never happens again. It is important to tell our stories so they are documented, they stay somewhere written...How great it would be if everyone wanted to tell their story...but people don't want, they are afraid...*

Lola's experience questions the utility of criminal trials in post-conflict states. Her and other women's experiences[20] restore and redeem the importance of other transitional justice mechanisms available. These women are not powerless or passive, but exhausted by the constant obstacles they face in pursuing any form of justice, be it administrative, reparative or retributive. They are on their own when justice goes wrong; their lives are potentially endangered as their perpetrators are free to roam. While transitioning from a post-war and post-genocide country to a democratic one, BiH remains structurally unjust and unequal. The argument that criminal trials should neither be the only nor the most important mechanism, is not new, however the focus on criminal trials still holds currency with many survivors of mass atrocities in BiH. For

---

[20] There are other women victims who are not satisfied with trials and sentences to perpetrators: See Azra Husarić, 'Bosnian War Rape Survivors "Still Afraid to Speak Out"', *Recom Reconciliation Network* (Web Page, 5 March 2021) <https://www.recom.link/en/bosnian-war-rape-survivors-still-afraid-to-speak-out/>.

them 'justice is done' only once their perpetrators are punished and incarcerated. In Lola's case, justice remains an unfinished business.

The Truth-Telling

Lola decided to go through the criminal proceedings armed only with her inner resilience and hope to see her perpetrators sentenced. Her story raises dilemma of where to go from here: Where is the justice for the harm that Lola suffered, for the trauma that she experienced? What remedy is she entitled to after all of her legal avenues have been exhausted? What rights is she entitled to as a citizen? Has telling the truth brought any benefits to Lola or any of the other women victims in their pursuits of justice?

Truth-telling must be affirmed, validated and served as a warning for future generations. The healing power of truth-telling was been promoted in the work of the South African Truth and Reconciliation Commission which, in its final report, noted that the 'healing potential of storytelling [lies in] revealing the truth before a respectful audience and to an official body'.[21] However, scholars such as Eric Stover have been sceptical about the 'cathartic effect'[22] of testifying. Stover asserts that:

> Human rights activists often valorise the 'therapeutic value' of war crimes trials for victims and witnesses. They argue that victims who are able to recount horrific events in a context of acknowledgment and support will often find closure and be able to move on with their lives. The findings...however, suggest that such claims so far as war crimes trials are concerned reflect more wishful thinking than fact. The few participants who experienced cathartic feelings immediately or soon after testifying...- found that the glow quickly faded once they returned to their shattered villages and towns. This was especially true for witnesses who faced uncertainties in their lives.[23]

---

[21] *Truth and Reconciliation Commission of South Africa, Report* (1998) vol 5, ch 9.

[22] Jeremy Sarkin, 'Enhancing the Legitimacy, Status and Role of the International Criminal Court by Using Transitional Justice or Restorative Justice Strategies' (2012) 6(1) *Interdisciplinary Journal of Human Rights Law* 83, 93.

[23] Eric Stover, 'Witnesses and the promise of justice in The Hague' in Eric Stover and Harvey M Weinstein (eds), *My Neighbour, My Enemy: Justice and Community in the Aftermath of Mass Atrocity* (Cambridge University Press, 2005) 104, 107.

Lola told the truth at the trial but *was not heard*. She does not see herself as a beneficiary of truth-telling. Through her impenetrable blue eyes and jagged breath, she leaned forward towards me and whispered,

> *I am afraid he will never serve his sentence. I don't know why no one is looking for him, why Bosnia is not asking for his extradition. I heard that after five years, his case can be subject to a statute of limitations...I got nothing from it all. I have no money to start civil proceedings to get financial compensation from him. Anyhow I would not get any since he is inaccessible to the courts... I testified so it never happens again, and it never happens to my kids. What did I get? Nothing...nothing at all. On the contrary, I put us all in a danger...*

Lola frowned and leaned back in her chair. Her face looked tight and worried. She seemed at a loss to understand what the point of it all was; of her conflicting feelings. Preoccupied with her thoughts, her eyes darted around. I could see the agitation that comes from the uncertainty of her everyday life. It was not enough that Lola had a desire to testify; the ability for the local and international community to hear her was necessary, as was the sentencing of her rapist. As Tanya Serisier argues with a reference to 'speaking out' about rape, 'narrative requires both an individual to speak and a collective to listen'.[24] If there is no 'community of listeners'[25] then stories will not be heard, received or verified in a meaningful way. How Lola feels now is perhaps best described by what Jill Stauffer termed 'ethical loneliness'. Stauffer defines it as:

> The isolation one feels when one, as a violated person...has been abandoned by humanity or by those who have power over one's life's possibilities. It is a condition undergone by persons who have been unjustly treated and dehumanized by human beings and political structures, who emerge from that injustice only to find that the surrounding world will not listen to or cannot properly hear their testimony — their claims about

---

[24] Tanya Serisier, *Speaking Out: Feminism, Rape and Narrative Politics* (Palgrave Macmillan, 2018) 6.

[25] See Andrew Benjamin, 'Tradition and Experience: Walter Benjamin's "On Some Motifs in Baudelaire"' in Andrew Benjamin (ed), *The Problems of Modernity: Adorno and Benjamin* (Routledge, 1989) 121.

what they suffered and about what is now owned them — on their own terms.²⁶

Lola talks about wanting incarceration for the perpetrator: Jurić's punishment would thus become a matter of deterrence which is in the interests of the public, and her and her children's safety. Lola told me many times,

> He has to be brought to justice; he has to not only be tried but punished so that the crimes do not happen again.

The UN Security Council Resolutions 2467 and 2106 appeals to the deterrent effects of criminal prosecutions and convictions, noting that 'the consistent and rigorous prosecution of sexual violence crimes… [is] central to deterrence and prevention'.²⁷ If legal and penal institutions are supposed to express the values of society and the whole state, rather than a subgroup of victimised persons,²⁸ failure to enforce sentences and convict perpetrators is even more dramatic. What message does the state and its courts send if the law is not a remedy for the wrongs committed, but a tool that is complicit in them?—That there is a lack of political will to condemn perpetrators' behaviour, enforce basic human rights principles and guarantee that individuals cannot get away with committing terrible crimes.

Women survivors have borne the brunt of local transitional justice processes. They live with the physical and psychological bruises of wartime abuse that have not healed in post-conflict transitional times. They remain the open wounds that the state and its justice system rub salt in. Investing time in speaking and listening to women about their needs and wants and creating a strategy to bring them some form of justice and rehabilitation should be prioritised. However, for women to speak up in the legal theatre and then risk being denied compassion and compensation may feel worse than saying nothing at all. Women victims who do not wish to speak,

---

[26] Jill Stauffer, *Ethical Loneliness: The Injustice of Not Being Heard* (Columbia University Press, 2015) 1.

[27] See SC Res 2467, UN SCOR, 8514th mtg, UN Doc S/RES/2467 (23 April 2019) [14]; SC Res 2106, UN SCOR, 6984th mtg, UN Doc S/RES/2106 (24 June 2013) [4].

[28] Trudy Govier, *Victims and Victimhood* (Broadview Press, 2015) 148.

and women victims who are not from the majority victim group which resulted from the war, have had their voices muffled. As Serisier writes,

> Entrenching the law's status as a location for women's speech further marginalises the voices of those who do not or cannot mobilise the grammar of the criminal justice system to be heard. It entrenches a situation in which being heard relies on dominant narratives of race and class rather than an acceptance of women's right to be free of sexual violence and to be heard when they speak of it.[29]

Further conversations about the meanings of justice are necessary; not as a theoretical concept but as a real-life moment when there is no one to be punished for the crimes committed. To identify as a victim carries both positive and negative consequences for the person or group who has experienced a crime. As Stephanie Fohring argues, with the label comes numerous social and psychological burdens as the stereotypical qualities of a victim such as weakness, vulnerability, frailty and fear, are less than alluring.[30] Erving Goffman was the first to describe such stereotypes and the resultant stigma as 'the situation of the individual who is disqualified from full social acceptance'.[31] Fohring notes that such social construction, combined with the perpetual politicisation of victim's rights and victimhood, 'has reinforced the dichotomy not only between victim and offender but also between victims and survivors, and deserving and undeserving victims'.[32] Lola, by a virtue of her ethnic origin, belongs to a group of 'undeserving' victims, the label of which has made her journey even more troublesome.

Still, Lola and other women survivors are not *just* disadvantaged and vulnerable, they are also agents in their own lives. Lola's transitional justice journey has been peppered with acts of resistance that speak to her agency and power rather than her weakness, victimhood and vulnerability. Yet, transitional justice institutions, such as courts, 'require'

---

[29] Serisier (n 24) 90.

[30] Stephanie Fohring, 'Introduction to the Special Issue: Victim identities and hierarchies' (2018) 24(2) *International Review of Victimology* 147.

[31] Erving Goffman, *Stigma: Notes on the Management of a Spoiled Identity* (Simon and Shuster Inc, 1986) 9.

[32] Fohring (n 30).

women such as Lola to 'act vulnerable'.[33] 'Victim' as a category hinges on the experience of disadvantage and injury.[34] The concept of agency is vital to Lola and many other survivors as it speaks to individuals who, despite their horrendous experiences 'do make creative, courageous choices to overcome terrible traumas suffered in war or develop resilience to cope with the ongoing suffering'.[35] After so much struggle, instead of being awarded for their persistence, most feel betrayed. With no sense of justice, they don't feel as though their country can ever truly heal. Some, including Lola, do not consider their country as their homeland anymore. Their sense of belonging to their community and trust in the state institutions is diminished.[36] Lola is left vulnerable to the same people who harmed her 30 years ago during the war. Today, in times of peace, these same men can harm her again.

TRACES OF PAIN

Three decades ago, the Dayton Peace Agreement ended one of the most brutal civil wars in Europe after World War Two. However, the Peace Agreement has been in tatters for years and now peace and reconciliation seem more elusive than ever.[37] The BiH authorities have never implemented the draft transitional justice strategy, and instead have focused solely on criminal trials as a way of dealing with the brutal past. This is despite it being widely acknowledged that criminal trials alone cannot bring justice and closure to victims, nor can they guarantee political stability. There is a consensus among transitional justice scholars that

[33] Julieta Lemaitre, 'After the War: Displaced Women, Ordinary Ethics, and Grassroots Reconstruction in Colombia' (2016) 25(5) *Social & Legal Studies* 545, 460.

[34] Kieran McEvoy and Kirsten McConnachie (2013) 'Victims and Transitional Justice: Voice, Agency and Blame' (2013) 22(4), *Social and Legal Studies* 489; Kristin Bumiller, *The Civil Rights Society: The Social Construction of Victims* (John Hopkins University Press, 1988).

[35] Elisabeth Porter, *Connecting Peace, Justice and Reconciliation* (Lynne Rienner, 2015) 49.

[36] Emina Dizdarevic, 'Bosnian Wartime Sexual Violence Survivors "Feel Betrayed by System"', *Balkan Insight* (online, 4 November 2021) <https://balkaninsight.com/2021/11/04/bosnian-wartime-sexual-violence-survivors-feel-betrayed-by-system/>.

[37] Julian Borger, 'Bosnia Is in Danger of Breaking up, Warns Top International Official', *The Guardian* (online, 2 November 2021) <https://www.theguardian.com/world/2021/nov/02/bosnia-is-in-danger-of-breaking-up-warns-eus-top-official-in-the-state>.

criminal accountability is required, but it is not sufficient in itself to achieve sustainable change.[38]

Despite this common knowledge, criminal prosecutions as a mechanism of transitional justice persists as the principal means of accountability for individuals who have committed international crimes.[39] Yet, the fact that national courts in BiH, similar to other post-conflict societies, face a backlog of cases, raises the need for alternative and complementary transitional justice responses.[40] Prescribing exclusively criminal prosecutions for wartime crimes 'prevents the exploration of new or underutilised alternative mechanisms of justice' such as restorative justice and symbolic reparations.[41] For this reason, the field of transitional justice has shifted its dominant focus from retribution to a more holistic approach that combines both retributive and restorative transitional justice mechanisms.[42] It has become clear that in order to achieve a renewal of human rights and democracy, further steps and actions are required beyond merely the prosecution of offenders.[43]

Still, a patchwork of criminal trials remains the flagship tool of transitional justice processes in BiH. Given their stronghold, all other mechanisms have been dismissed by the government as premature, fraught with perils or naïve. For Lola and other women, their experiences with criminal justice demonstrate that trials themselves can bring little satisfaction to survivors of atrocities and the broader community. While disappointment with this transitional justice tool has been articulated by many survivors,

---

[38] Olivera Simic, 'Arts and Transitional Justice' in Olivera Simic (ed), *An Introduction to Transitional Justice* (Routledge, 2nd ed, 2020) 241, 242.

[39] Kathryn Sikkink and Hun Joon Kim, 'The Justice Cascade: The Origins and Effectiveness of Prosecutions of Human Rights Violations' (2013) 9 *Annual Review of Law and Social Science* 269, 270.

[40] Aleksandar Marsavelski and John Braithwaite, 'Transitional Justice Cascades' (2020) 53(2) *Cornell International Law Journal* 207.

[41] Elizabeth B Ludwin King, 'Does Justice Always Require Prosecution: The International Criminal Court and Transitional Justice Measures' (2013) 45(1) *The George Washington International Law Review* 85, 90–91.

[42] Renee Jeffery, 'The Role of the Arts in Cambodia's Transitional Justice Process' (2021) 34(3) *International Journal of Politics, Culture, and Society* 335, 338–339; Alexander L Boraine, 'Transitional Justice: A Holistic Interpretation' (2006) 60(1) *Journal of International Affairs* 17, 19.

[43] Jeffery (n 42) 339; Peter Manning, *Transitional Justice and Memory in Cambodia: Beyond the Extraordinary Chambers* (Routledge, 2017) 26.

what has been left out of the analysis is that some women have lost a lot more than what they have gained from participating in these criminal trials. This may be considered unsurprising given 'the notorious failure of the criminal legal system to address, let alone prevent, acts of sexual violence'.[44]

The wartime sexual violence cases that have ended in the sentencing of the perpetrator need to be scrutinised and questioned. We should be asking: Where is the offender and is he serving his sentence? Although he was 'successfully' prosecuted, Jurić denied any responsibility, did not atone for his crimes, and now lives his life in freedom. The case may have been closed with the handing down of the judgement but an actual 'closing [of] the books'[45] may never happen. For Lola it seems impossible to find 'closure', not only because her perpetrator is still at large, but also because she cannot escape from her everyday life which offers too many reminders of the harm she suffered.

Lola's pre-war family home, the ruins of which are still standing, is a constant physical and metaphorical reminder of her past life which abruptly vanished. As Edith Eger said, 'when we grieve, it's not just over what happened—we grieve for what didn't happen... a vacant, empty place, the vast dark of the life that would never be'.[46] The shattered house marks Lola's shattered life; it remains in the same spot where it was originally built. Lola's trauma also remains there. Lola's pre-war home represents the impotency of the court's actions. It shows that even if those perpetrators were punished, there are constant reminders in society that intrude into victims' lives, and most likely contribute, to the inability of closing cases such as Lola's. There may never be finality, for no other reason than the surrounding environmental clues which constitute the permanent reminders of what happened. These clues are more personal and subjective than the inability of the courts to deal with cases such as Lola's. Regardless of the court's outcome, they are permanent and continuing. The ongoing trauma, as Antony Pemberton and Rianne Letschert

---

[44] Karen Crawley, 'Tanya Serisier: Speaking Out: Feminism, Rape and Narrative Politics' (2021) 29 *Feminist Legal Studies* 423, 425.

[45] Jon Elster, *Closing the Books: Transitional Justice in Historical Perspective* (Cambridge University Press, 2004).

[46] Edith Eger, *The Choice* (Penguin, 2017) 251.

argue, 'begs the question, what, if anything, can meaningfully be understood as justice in the face of the enormity of such evil?'[47] Villagers' homes were destroyed and they were forcibly expelled from their land. Lola and her neighbours were subjected to a method of 'ethnic cleansing' during the war. Around thirty-seven per cent of pre-war housing in BiH was partially or totally destroyed during the war.[48] With the destruction of houses, 'the multi-ethnic and diverse society that existed prior to the conflict has all but disappeared'.[49]

I went with Lola and her neighbour, a man in his late sixties, who was also expelled and detained on the same day as Lola in 1992, to see her pre-war house and visit the local cemetery where her husband was buried. Since Lola does not have a car or drive her neighbour sometimes gives her a lift (charging her less than a taxi fare). Lola negotiated the price for a ride with her neighbour. She confirmed the price with me before we took off. Lola wanted to make sure I could pay for the ride. The house she lives in today is around fourteen kilometres from her pre-war home.

> *I don't go there often. I would like to go more often to visit my husband's grave, but I am afraid. I have a fear... after everything that happened. I heard lots of stories. I don't feel well going there...it's not anymore fear for myself as much as for my children, for my grandchildren. Before I had only three children with me and now I have them and five grandchildren. I have a daughter in law, sons in law. I am afraid for all of them...that something may happen to them. I don't know where he is hiding...*

The distance between her two houses is geographically short but for Lola it is an emotionally and physically impenetrable distance. The thought that she might be recognised or ambushed haunts her. For Lola, going back to Odžak County feels like travelling to a foreign country, a country not of her own. If she goes there she needs to be on guard the whole time. The thought of passing a Jurić in the street and having them stare at each other in horror is real to her. Once we entered the

---

[47] Antony Pemberton and Rianne Letschert, 'Victimology of Atrocity Crimes' in Barbora Holá, Hollie Nyseth Nzitatira and Maartje Weerdesteijn (eds), *The Oxford Handbook of Atrocity Crimes* (Oxford University Press, 2022) 461.

[48] Ana Povrženic, 'Housing Reconstruction in Bosnia: Field Realities', *Forced Migration Review* (online, undated) <https://www.fmreview.org/house/povrzenic>; https://www.fmreview.org/sites/fmr/files/FMRdownloads/en/house/povrzenic.pdf.

[49] Ibid.

municipality Odžak I could feel the rising tension in the car. There was a silence as we passed by the sign that inscribed the name of the town. As we moved forward, both, Lola and her neighbour were pointing to different directions and locations remembering those wartime days when they were forcibly expelled and detained. *'This is a 'Strolit', a factory they turned into detention centre'*. Lola said, clearing her throat, *'and it works as a factory today too'*. 'Strolit' was a foundry where Serb civilians were detained during the months of May–July 1992. Serb men were beaten, tortured and abused while there.[50]

Just a few hundred metres down the road was the primary school called 'Brotherhood and Unity' which had served as a detention centre for mainly women and children.[51] After the war these two places regained their original purpose of a primary school and foundry. There are many spaces such as these two in BiH which were used as detention centres and then after the war reverted to their previous use.[52] I figured that Lola and her neighbour must have thought it weird to watch the children run around happily in the school yard. They fell silent for a few moments as we passed, perhaps the images and flashbacks to scenes of torture were playing back in their minds. What must it be like for the victims who now go to such places to pick up their grandchildren; to visit the schools which had been used as torture chambers? I cannot fathom what that must feel like. Such is the reality of living in the aftermath of war and violence, of the impossibility of running away from the past that haunts women like Lola at every turn.

When Lola's neighbour slowed down his car and finally stopped I was confused because I did not see any houses around us. I did not even notice the ruins of what was once a house to the right side of where we had stopped. The grass was long and tall.

---

[50] 'Strolit Foundry', *onms.nenasilje.org* (Web Page, updated 4 July 2021) <https://onms.nenasilje.org/2021/strolit-foundry-odzak/?lang=en>; Lamija Grebo, 'Bosnian Activists Mark Wartime Detention Camp Sites', *Balkan Insight* (online, 16 March 2021) <https://balkaninsight.com/2021/03/16/bosnian-activists-mark-wartime-detention-camp-sites/>.

[51] Grebo (n 50).

[52] See, for example, Olivera Simic and Zala Volcic, 'In the Land of Wartime Rape, Bosnia, Cinema and Reparation' (2014) 2(2) *Griffith Journal of Law and Human Dignity* 377.

I asked Lola 'did we arrive?' When she confirmed, I was confused. I waited a moment and then clumsily asked, 'Where is the house?'.

She pointed towards the tall grass in front of us and said, '*Here*'.

Only then did I notice the frames of the destroyed house with only a roof and chimney poking through the wild grass that had been growing around it for the past 30 years. I felt a single bead of perspiration run from the base of my neck down the centre of my back. Lola had a dark look on her face and shook her head as we watched it from the safe distance. We got out of the car and stood on the local unpaved road that passes by her ruined family house. The legacy of war has left its footprints not just on the lives of individuals but on nature too.

It was impossible to get closer to the house, to enter into its dilapidated structures. The long grass and also the real possibility of landmines planted around the house prevents anyone from wanting to move towards it.[53]

'*This is it. It has been standing here for all these years*', she waved a hand.

A shiver ran through my body. I waited a moment and then asked, 'What do you want to do with it. Can you sell the plot at least?'.

Lola glanced at me sideways. She did not speak right away.

> *Yes, I can for 200 euros. It is what I had been offered. It's a blackmail...I am not going to sell it for nothing... Let it stand here as long as I am alive. My house is the first house in the row of houses destroyed in the village.*

As we freely moved through the village, we observed eighty per cent of the houses which looked similar to Lola's: broken, with the grass and flowers growing through their shattered window frames and what was once the roof and ceilings. Nature had found its way through the destruction, nurturing overgrown grass and other plants. The plants grow on the sites of destroyed properties and where so many human lives were lost—murdered. The plants growing on the sites of wartime mass graves have

---

[53] Matthew Clayfield, 'Bosnia and Herzegovina May Never Be Clear of Landmines', *ABC News* (online, 15 October 2017) <https://www.abc.net.au/news/2017-10-15/bosnia-may-never-be-clear-of-land-mines/9029692>.

recently been exhibited in BiH showing how 'a deceased human body takes on another life as it nurtures grass and another plants'.[54]

As we slowly drove through the village and I observed one house after another, there was something beautiful, surreal and frightening all at the same time. The residents of these houses were expelled from them back in May 1992 and sent to detention camps. It was October 2022 when we visited the village, but after more than 30 years almost no one had returned. It is a ghost village now; a space where there is no armed conflict, but the local violent sentiment is very much present and alive. The material traces of destruction vary in durability, but they shape the BiH post-war national ambience. These traces are 'text-like in the sense that they are (partial and fragmental) representations of previous semiotic acts'[55] and still dependent on 'semiotic regimes'. However, these 'material, ephemeral and non-contextualized' meanings and practices have still been neglected in the literature.[56]

Only a handful of families have dared to return and they have been trying to rebuild their lives. But, housing reconstruction is not just about rebuilding homes; it is about return and restoring the right to return to those who lost this right during the war.[57] *'See this house?'* Lola was pointing to the house on the left. *'They returned from abroad so they had funds to rebuild their property'*, Lola told me casually from the front passenger seat, shaking her head slowly. She continued after a moment. *'No one ever offered me funds to rebuild my house so I never did anything with it'*. Although BiH received multiple billions of dollars for reconstruction[58] which prioritised the reconstruction of houses, it looks like the war is still raging in Lola's house and village, and symbolically it does. The war

---

[54] Azem Kurtic, 'Plants Found at Bosnian War Graves Exhibited in Sarajevo', *Balkan Insight* (online, 14 November 2022) <https://balkaninsight.com/2022/11/14/plants-found-at-bosnian-war-graves-exhibited-in-sarajevo/>.

[55] Anders Bjorkwall and Arlene Archer, 'Semiotics of Destruction: Traces on the Environment' (2021) 21(2) *Visual Communication*, 218.

[56] Crispin Thurlow, 'Queering Critical Discourse Studies or/and Performing "Post-class" Ideologies' (2016) 13(5) *Critical Discourse Studies* 485.

[57] Povrzenic (n 48).

[58] John Pomfret, 'Rivalries Stall Reconstruction of Bosnia', *Washington Post* (online, 13 October 1996) <https://www.washingtonpost.com/archive/politics/1996/10/13/rivalries-stall-reconstruction-of-bosnia/e33b7d9e-543d-4dc1-9256-ece7b88e8a4a/>; Patrice C McMahon, 'Rebuilding Bosnia: A Model to Emulate or to Avoid?' (2004) 119(4) *Political Science Quarterly* 569.

was over 30 years ago but not for Lola. Standing in disrepair since 1992, Lola's house is an inherent part of the BiH war semiotic landscape. Along with her fellow neighbours and former residents of the village, Lola only goes back there after the war to visit dead relatives and their 'dead' homes. There are no living relatives, family or friends to visit. They are all gone. Only the dead meshed with the ground will remain.

On our way to the graveyard, Lola pointed to various houses and told me the names of the people, her former neighbours and friends that had once lived there with her. Then, as she pointed her finger through the front window shield she said, '*This is Jurić's house, I passed by it often before the war*'. I felt heat rise in my chest. She averted her eyes for a moment and then as she looked back at me she said, '*I would regularly see and greet his family in their front yard*'. The house was a short distance from the road and I could only see its construction frames. My heart skipped a beat as I struggled to imagine Lola's daily encounters with Jurić. It seemed so fantastic and incomprehensible. After driving for ten minutes we stopped the car at the gates of the local cemetery. As we approached the graveyard, Lola squinted her eyes against the sun and then paused. I stood next to her and she pointed with her right index finger to a few houses down the road,

> *You see that yellow house? I was detained with other women in it. They would take us to that house [she pointed to the house nearby] to rape us.*

I felt a knot in my stomach. Every time Lola comes to pay her respects to the dead she must endure the reminder of the abuse and crimes made against her.

She studied my face for a moment and then turned around and walked into the cemetery. I could not feel my legs but I followed her until we reached the far end of the graveyard. She started to whisper a prayer while making the sign of the cross across her chest. I stood in front of four large cement gravestones, one next to the other. I had expected only to see one. While she was lighting the candles, Lola told me about her parents-in-law who were detained alongside her. This was the first time she had mentioned this to me. Both had died and were buried next to their son, her husband. His younger brother who died before the war was there too. Looking from their headstones to Lola's face contorted with pain, I reflected on how in the grave, all the pain is over. It is the pain of the alive ones that lives on. There is no escape from it.

With a paper tissue in her hand, Lola bent down to clean the headstones of the dust and dirt that had settled upon them. Lola stopped near the grey vase with a few dried flowers. The vase was made of cement and attached to the right side of her husband's headstone.

You see, they have broken the vase again? We fix it, they break it. Why? Why someone cannot leave even dead in peace?

Lola slapped her hands together and seemed at a loss for words. She glanced at me without expecting an answer. She then bowed her head, muttered something under her breath and continued cleaning what was left from the broken vase. I winced, but stayed quiet, feeling the coldness seeping into my body from the stone below. We both knew that the broken vase on her husband's grave was not an isolated incident but that it was an ongoing war waged by another means. Destroying and disrespecting monuments, cemeteries and other religious sites was widespread during the war[59] and it has continued in this 'not-war not-peace' time.

Several graveyards in BiH have recently been vandalised by extreme nationalists.[60] These acts of disturbing the dead serve as warnings to the living that they should not return as they will never find peace. I thought it but did not let the words out. As we were leaving the graveyard a few crows were circling in the late afternoon sky. The daylight was fading fast, and there was a cool mist among the graves. There were no other visitors

---

[59] Tadeusz Mazowiecki, *Report on the Situation of Human Rights in the Territory of The Former Yugoslavia/Submitted By Tadeusz Mazowiecki, Special Rapporteur Of The Commission On Human Rights, Pursuant to Paragraph 15 of Commission Resolution 1992/S-1/1 of 14 August 1992* [26]; also see *Committee of Culture and Education, War Damage to the Cultural Heritage in Croatia and Bosnia-Herzegovina*, 8th Information Report, Doc 7341, 28 June 1995 <https://assembly.coe.int/nw/xml/XRef/X2H-Xref-ViewHTML.asp?FileID=6989&lang=EN>.

[60] 'Orthodox Cemetery Desecrated in Bosnia and Herzegovina', *Orthodox Christianity* (Web Page, 12 July 2022) <https://orthochristian.com/147169.html>; Jasmine Liu, 'Partisan Cemetery in Bosnia Destroyed in "Neo-Fascist Rampage"', *Hyperallergic* (Web Page, 20 June 2022) <https://hyperallergic.com/741542/partisan-cemetery-in-bosnia-destroyed-in-neo-fascist-rampage>.

for the dead except for the crows and us. '*Let's go home. I don't like to wait for a night time here*', Lola mumbled and lost in her thoughts she hurried towards the car.

Epilogue

Elizabeth Wolgast points out that in the aftermath of rape or torture, 'the punishment and suffering of the offender might provide some satisfaction, but it cannot … restore the situation to the way it was before the offense. The victims … have [not] become un-raped or un-tortured'.[1] However, if there is no justice for victims who remain suffering, forgiveness and vengeance remain two 'competing conceptions' before justice arrives.[2] Lola cannot forgive but wants no vengeance either. She wants justice. She wants Jurić arrested and jailed.

> *I live for the day to see him in jail. It is a high time they arrest him.*

Survivors live in mutual 'ecosystems'[3] and often take different routes beyond the court system, to achieve some kind of closure. Transitional justice is not an event but a journey and dealing with past trauma is a life-long process. How can society mobilise the necessary resources to mitigate the trauma-triggers, given it is not possible to eradicate them?

---

[1] Ibid, citing Elizabeth H Wolgast, *The Grammar of Justice* (Cornell University Press, 1987).

[2] Robert Meister, *After Evil: A Politics of Human Rights* (Columbia University Press, 2011) 8.

[3] Janine Natalya Clark, 'Beyond a "survivor-centred approach" to conflict-related sexual violence' (2021) 97(4) *International Affairs* 1067.

The legacy of Lola's trial may be similar to the legacy of her past wretched life: the trial and judgement brought enduring and prolonged suffering with no resolution. This legacy sends the message that systemic violence, including rape and torture is a permissible form of treatment towards members of certain groups.[4] The state's inaction and unwillingness to punish the perpetrators is 'a form of *communication*' which conveys to society what the offender '*could do* to the victim and get away with'.[5]

As discussed in this book, victims of wartime sexual violence suffer from anxiety, nightmares, depression and other types of mental health issues which have lingering emotional and physical scars. The wounds remain even if their harm is acknowledged and their perpetrator punished. In Lola's case, her perpetrator has never been punished although she publicly testified about his crimes making her wounds feel even more deep and raw. Susan Herman and Cressida Wasserman argue that victims' trauma, heightened tensions, fears and threats to their safety are often revived once their perpetrators are released from prison.[6] Since Lola's perpetrator has never been arrested, she has lived in a perpetual state of trepidation ever since the war began.

For Lola the consequences of sexual abuse are still present every day. She must take daily medications to maintain her well-being. She is not 'dealing with the past' but with a lifetime of traumatic, fragmented memories that are encroaching on her everyday life. She is 'dealing with the present'.[7] Lola will probably spend the rest of her life trying to chase away those memories, to push them to the margins. In her everyday life the past and the present merge. Yet, Lola is trying to create a sphere that is free from trauma '*for the sake of her children*', as she tells me. Medications help her in trying to do so: they numb her raw emotions and suppress them when they threaten to boil over.

Lola moves on with her life saturated with fears and anxieties, but she also has glimpses of joy. Although she suffers from multiple medical

---

[4] Colleen Murphy, *A Moral Theory of Political Reconciliation* (Cambridge, 2010) 106.

[5] David Alm, 'Crime Victims and the Right to Punishment' (2019) 13 *Criminal Law and Philosophy* 63.

[6] Susan Herman and Cressida Wasserman, 'A Role for Victims in Offender Reentry' (2001) 47(3) *Crime and Delinquency* 428.

[7] See Janine Natalya Clark, 'The living past in the lives of victims-/survivors of conflict-related sexual violence: Temporal implications for transitional justice' (2022) *Memory Studies* 1.

conditions, Lola works in her garden and in the summer she wakes up early to harvest potatoes, onions, tomatoes and other vegetables. She has two pigs, three dogs, two cats and dozens of chickens to be fed. I observed Lola as both she and her daughter-in-law were busy feeding the animals, talking to them and cleaning their pots. There is joy and laughter in these daily rituals. Lola bakes at least two loaves of bread each day. Bread is almost sacred in Bosnia and Herzegovina (BiH) as are all types of pies.

> *I make my own bread. We cannot afford to buy it. It is cheaper to make it. My grandchildren love my bread and my pastries.*

She turned her face towards me with her eyes laughing. There is pain, but there is love too in Lola's *everydayness*. The joy is coupled with the devastation of loss. The two are blended. '*They tell me that I make the best uštipci* [fried dough balls] *in the world*'. A flush rose in her cheeks, her eyes twinkled.

The last time I visited Lola she made a feast for me. She put enough food on the table to feed at least five people. She cooked chicken soup, *sarma* [stuffed cabbage leaves], homemade bread, baked potatoes and chicken. '*I was cooking whole morning for you. I hope you will like it*', she said, her face lit up and lips widened into a smile. I knew that she would cook, and I knew that I could do nothing to prevent her from over-catering for my visit. Food is an extremely important part of the culture in BiH, to prepare and share food is part of the social fabric. Food is meant to be shared. It is more than a sensory experience; food is a comfort and a joy to be shared with loved ones.[8]

Lola has learnt to raise her children alone and provide for them with her own hands. As a mother survivor of wartime rape, Lola navigates life between her own process of healing and her role as a mother. For rural women such as Lola taking care of herself is as important as taking care of her children and grandchildren, of producing food, cooking, gardening,

---

[8] See, Aleksander Hemon, '"Bread is practically sacred": How the taste of home sustained my refugee parents', The Guardian (online, 13 June 2019) <https://www.theguardian.com/food/2019/jun/13/bread-is-practically-sacred-how-the-taste-of-home-sustained-my-refugee-parents> .

tending to animals. Her role as a mother, albeit hard, may have helped Lola to return to normal, to move on and heal.[9]

Lola's real-life account of living through transitional justice and using its mechanisms, tells us how she *practised* them, and how such practice rubbed salt into her open wounds not allowing them to heal. Survivors such as Lola have found themselves in a perpetual struggle for justice; a journey that many of them imagined was to be reached at the end of their legal voyage marked by the conviction of their perpetrators. Lola's existence has been bound up by the belief that one day injustice will be over. Still, the arrival of such a day rests upon hope in the state institutions and their justice mechanisms. Despite being suspicious of state institutions responses to her cries for justice, she depends on them. Lola's rapist's conviction that ended in impunity epitomises systemic failure. Her pain epitomises the pain of all women victims of wartime rape.

The war interrupted—and still intrudes in—Lola's life. It is impossible to undo it. Thirty years after the war, Lola is still hounded by loss. The loss of her husband, of their young marriage, of love. The loss of their future, the vision they shared of marriage and family life together. Victims such as Lola, demand fair treatment and deserve recognition. Stories such as Lola's need to be imprinted in the histories of male wars. The courts did not resolve or validate the sequelae of Lola's past injuries or allow her wounds to heal. However, her truths are documented and will serve as a reminder of the injustices that live on without punishment or resolution. Despite many hurdles she encountered, Lola did not allow darkness to swallow her but made a choice to continue fighting for justice. She maintains some hope that justice can be resurrected; that her broken trust in the state can be redeemed. Lola holds on to this hope and finds her own sense of purpose in helping her children and grandchildren to survive the aftermath of war that brought poverty and trauma to the fore. It is not just her own loss that hurts; it ripples out and perpetuates into the future generations. Lola, rather than 'moving on with her life', is coping with life unfolding before her. As J Scott Kenney stated, 'coping is not recovering completely, returning to "normality" or going back to

---

[9] See, Nena Mocnik, *Trauma Transmission and Sexual Violence* (Routledge, 2021).

the way they were before [...] instead subjects referred to the ability to live their lives "around it" and "go on"'.[10]

Lola constantly worries about her children and grandchildren. She is terrified something might happen to them. The fact that they live in the same household with Lola exacerbates her anxiety. *'I worry something may happen to them. I worry when they go out...I worry when they fight'*. One day I met with Lola and her granddaughter in the city shopping centre. We had not seen each other for some time. Her black hair was pulled back in a low bun. She had on a neutral-coloured shirt buttoned up to her neck. She wore dark blue pants and black sandals. Somewhat clumsily but with the aim of relaxing the atmosphere and opening up a conversation, I complemented her gold necklace and matching earrings. A dim light sparked in her blue eyes. Lola smiled up at me shyly, *'they are very old'*, she whispered. The two pieces of jewellery indeed looked old and could have been a gift received a long time ago, before the war started. She tucked her hair behind her small ears. She seemed shy and pleased at the same time by my small compliment.

It was three in the afternoon and the sun was piercing through the glass roof of the shopping centre. Her 13-year-old granddaughter wanted to go for a walk around it while we had a coffee in one of the restaurants. Lola was not happy with this proposal. She was terrified her granddaughter would get lost and never return. Her face was lost in despair as Lola kept repeating, *'You will get lost. I worry'*. Lola's overwhelming fear for the well-being of her children is now transmitted to her grandchildren. As a young, widowed mother who survived rape and torture and who had to raise her young children by herself she was excessively concerned about them. In one of the 'Duga's' organisational documents Lola was described as 'keeping her children pathologically next to her since she was afraid of revenge ... behaviour which affects children's behaviour and health since they are overwhelmed with their mother's overwhelming concern'.[11] As I watched Lola nervously arguing with her granddaughter, I remembered this passage from the file the organisation documented about Lola in 1992. Thirty years later I observed the same fear overwhelming her.

---

[10] J Scott Kenney, 'Human Agency Revisited: The Paradoxical Experiences of Victims of Crime' (2004) 11(2–3) *International Review of Victimology* 225.

[11] Document on file with author.

Together with her granddaughter, I reassured Lola nothing would happen to her; she had a cell phone so we could easily find out where she was at any time. Perhaps Lola's fear was not that her granddaughter would be 'lost' in the shopping centre, rather she would become victim to the predator awaiting his revenge. The research on survivor parents has found that they are overly anxious about their children and often over-protective, to the point of suffocation.[12] It has been suggested that the reason for this over-protection and over-involvement in their children's lives, is due to the survivors' overwhelming feeling that their children exist in order to replace everything that was so traumatically lost.[13]

The enduring after-effects of sentences not executed in BiH have been seldom studied. This book thus contributes to the discourse surrounding it. Lola's story epitomises the lofty goals of criminal accountability that the international community had for BiH; a country where victims and their executioners remain neighbours.[14] Some perpetrators, like Jurić were never arrested, some were apprehended, many were prosecuted, served their sentences and returned to their pre-war communities where they encounter their victims on the local streets.[15] Some were prosecuted and sentenced but have never served their time.[16] As Nyla Ali Khan notes, 'the project of repairing a damaged and "broken" society is work in progress'.[17] The war in BiH is over but in the hearts and minds of its people, it lives on. The country remains in a de facto frozen conflict, where political leaders pursue wartime goals, generate divisions and push

---

[12] SM Sonnenberg, 'Workshop Report: Children of survivors' (1974) 22(1) *Journal of American Psychoanalytical Association* 200; H A Barocas and C B Barocas, 'Manifestation of Concentration Camp Effects on the Second Generation' (1974) 130(7) *American Journal of Psychiatry* 820.

[13] Dan Bar-On and Julia Chaitin, *Parenthood and the Holocaust* (Yad Vashem, 2001) 5.

[14] Bjorn Krondorfer, *Unsettling Empath: Working with groups in conflict* (Rowman and Littlefield Publishers, 2020) 7.

[15] Some victims reported to me that they meet those they testified against on the streets of their pre-war residence once they had been released from the prison.

[16] Meliha Kešmer, 'U BiH 30 odsto optuzenih za zlocine nedostupo sudovima', *Radio Slobodna Evropa* (online, 3 June 2022) <https://www.slobodnaevropa.org/a/ratni-zlocin-bih-sud-savcic-rat-genocid/31881819.html> .

[17] Nyla Ali Khan, *Educational Strategies for Youth Empowerment in Conflict Zones* (Palgrave MacMillan, 2021) 6.

nationalistic agendas.[18] It is a divided country, ravaged by ethnic conflict in which the past still breathes, taking away oxygen from its citizens. It is a land where cumulated grief, untold stories and wounds unhealed cut through ethnic partitions.

BiH is a country in which one regime was dissolved and yet another one hasn't been born. Bosnian people are caught in the middle of this messy transition, they have waited three decades for their homeland rebirth, for its new beginning. The pain from not being able to forge a new democratic state affects its vulnerable people like Lola the most. The legacies of the past mayhem are often intangible and invisible, but are ingrained in the minds and hearts of survivors and their descendants. They are the victims of structural violence and poverty 'as these have emerged as stubborn legacies from an oppressive or war-torn past in many parts of the world'.[19] As I am finishing this book, another case of alleged war crimes has been under investigation and Lola has been informed by the police that she should prepare herself to receive a call from the local courts to act as a witness. The police officers came in person to her house to deliver the news.

> *Apparently me, my male neighbour and my deceased sister had been witnesses of crimes committed by someone they want us to testify against...I don't want to go to the Odžak County to testify. There is no way I will go there alone... I am terrified of going there...The police officers told me they were ordered to find me and tell me I should be prepared to go as a witness...They just use us, victims for their businesss and we get nothing from it...I get only stress and fear. I have to recall all the horrors again and again...I am not going there alone...*

I could hear a strain in Lola's voice. She sighed and shook her head with dismay. She gazed into my eyes, waiting for a reaction. I had no words. We both knew that she would have to go to the court or if unwilling be summoned to do so. For Lola there is no escape from dealing with the past in the present. Lola raised a hand and pursed her lips as if there was something important she wanted to say, but could not get the

---

[18] *Security Council, Bosnia and Herzegovina Remains in Effect 'a Frozen Conflict' as Political Leaders Push Nationalistic Agendas, High Representative Tells Security Council* SC/14511, (4 May 2021).

[19] Paul Gready, *The Era of Transitional Justice: The aftermath of the Truth and Reconciliation Commission in South Africa and Beyond* (Routledge, 2011), 3.

words out. Tears began to well up in her eyes; her eyelids became heavy reflecting her thoughts. We sat in silence for a while, listening to the ticking clock on the wall. Lola's narrative is open-ended and unfolding, moving beyond the events following her victimisation and the criminal trial, disrupted by the non-execution of her perpetrator's sentence and her enduring identity of being a victim, survivor and witness of the horrific yet unpunished crimes. She lives in limbo as the scales of justice remain imbalanced and out of her control.

Bibliography

Articles/Books/Reports

Adams, William C., 'Conducting Semi-Structured Interviews' in Kathryn E Newcomer, Harry P Hatry and Joseph S Wholey (eds), *Handbook of Practical Program Evaluation* (Jossey-Bass, 4th ed, 2015) 492

Alayarian, Aida, 'Children, torture and psychological consequences' (2009) 19(2) *Torture* 145

Alcalá, Pilar Riaño, and Erin Baines, 'Editorial Note' (2012) 6 *International Journal of Transitional Justice* 385

Alexievich, Svetlana, *Chernobyl Prayer* (Penguin, 2016)

Alm, David, 'Crime Victims and the Right to Punishment' (2019) 13 *Criminal Law and Philosophy* 63

American Psychiatric Association, *Diagnostic and Statistical Manual of Mental Disorders: DSM-5-TR* (American Psychiatric Association Publishing, 5th ed, 2022)

Anderson, Claire, and Susan Kirkpatrick 'Narrative interviewing' (2016) 38 *International Journal of Clinical Pharmacy* 631..

Apuuli, Kasaija Phillip, 'The Prospect of Establishing a Truth-Telling and Reconciliation Commission in Uganda' (2013) 10 *US-China Law Review* 596

Arendt, Hannah, 'Collective Responsibility' in SJJW Bernauer (ed), *Amor Mundi:Explorations in the Faith and Thought of Hannah Arendt* (Martinus Nijhoff Publishers, 1987) 43

Arendt, Hannah, 'Organized Guilt and Universal Responsibility' in Hannah Arendt (ed), *Essays in Understanding: 1930–1945* (Harcourt Brace, 1994) 121

Bami, Xhorxhina, 'Rape Used as Weapon During Kosovo War, Says NGO', *Balkan Insight* (online, 26 October 2022) <https://balkaninsight.com/2022/10/26/rape-used-as-weapon-during-kosovo-war-says-ngo/>

Barbora, Hola and Olivera Simic, 'ICTY Celebrities: War Criminals Coming Home' (2018) 28(4) *International Criminal Justice Review* 285

Barocas, H A, and C B Barocas, 'Manifestation of Concentration Camp Effects on the Second Generation' (1974) 130(7) *American Journal of Psychiatry* 820

Bar-On, Dan, and Julia Chaitin, *Parenthood and the Holocaust* (Yad Vashem, 2001)

Basic, Goran, 'Conditions for Reconciliation: Narratives of Survivors from the War in Bosnia and Herzegovina', (2015) 17(2) *Journal of Criminal Justice and Security* 107

Beara, Vladan, 'The Contribution of REBT in Addressing the Givens of Existence' (2015) 33(2) *Journal of Rational - Emotive and Cognitive – Behaviour Therapy* 179

Becirevic, Edina, *Genocide on the River Drina* (Yale University Press, 2014)

Benjamin, Andrew, 'Tradition and Experience: Walter Benjamin's "On Some Motifs in Baudelaire"' in Andrew Benjamin (ed), *The Problems of Modernity: Adorno and Benjamin* (Routledge, 1989) 121Bergsmo, Morten, Alf Butenschøn Skre and Elisabeth J Wood (eds), *Understanding and Proving International Sex Crimes* (Torkel Opsahl Academic EPublisher, 2012).

Bieber, Florian, 'Nationalist Mobilization and Stories of Serb Suffering', (2002) 6(1) *Rethinking History* 95

Bieneck, Steffen, and Barbara Krahé, 'Blaming the Victim and Exonerating the Perpetrator in Cases of Rape and Robbery: Is there a double standard?' (2011) 26(9) *Journal of Interpersonal Violence* 26, 1785

Björkdahl, Annika, and Susanne Buckley-Zistel, *Spacialising Peace and Conflict: Mapping the Production of Places, Sites and Scales of Violence* (Palgrave Macmillan, 2016)

Bjorkwall, Anders, and Arlene Archer, 'Semiotics of Destruction: Traces on the Environment' (2021) 21(2) *Visual Communication* 218

Boesten, Jelke, and Marsha Henry, 'Between Fatigue and Silence: The Challenges of Conducting Research on Sexual Violence in Conflict' (2018) 25(4) *Social Politics: International Studies in Gender, State & Society,* 568

Boesten, Jelke, *Sexual Violence During War and Peace: Gender, Power and Post-Conflict Justice in Peru* (Palgrave Macmillan, 2014) 87

Boraine, Alex, *A Country Unmasked* (Oxford University Press, 2000)

Boraine, Alexander L, 'Transitional Justice: A Holistic Interpretation' (2006) 60(1) *Journal of International Affairs* 17

Bougarel, Xavier, 'Twenty Years Later: Was ethnic war just a myth? (2013) 61(4) *Südosteuropa* 573, 574.

Bouris, Erica, *Complex Political Victims* (Kumarian Press, 2007)
Brammertz, Serge and Michelle Jarvis (eds), *Prosecuting Conflict-Related Sexual Violence at the ICTY* (Oxford University Press, 2016)
Bringa, Tone, *Being Muslim the Bosnian Way: Identity and Community in a Central Bosnian Village* (Princeton University Press, 1995)
Bringedal Houge, Anette, 'Narrative Expressivism: A Criminological Approach to the Expressive Function of International Criminal Justice' (2019) 19(3) *Criminology & Criminal Justice* 297
Brison, Susan, *Aftermath: Violence and the Remaking of a Self* (Princeton University Press, 2002)
Brkanić, Džana, 'Prijetnje svjedocima bez istraga', *Justice Report* (online, 6 November 2014) <https://www.justice-report.com/bh/sadržaj-članci/prijetnje-svjedocima-bez-istraga>
Bumiller, Kristin, *The Civil Rights Society: The Social Construction of Victims* (John Hopkins University Press, 1988)
Burnett, Simon, and Annemaree Lloyd, 'Hidden and Forbidden: Conceptualising Dark Knowledge' (2020) 76(6) *Journal of Documentation* 1341
Buss, Doris E, 'Rethinking "Rape as a Weapon of War"' (2009) 17(2) *Feminist Legal Studies* 145
Butler, Judith, 'Rethinking Vulnerability and Resistance', in Judith Butler, Zeynep Gambetti and Letitia Sabsay (eds), *Vulnerability and Resistance* (Duke University Press, 2016)
Butler, Judith, *Precarious Life: The Powers of Mourning and Violence* (Verso, 2004)
Campbell, Kirsten, 'Reassembling International Justice: The Making of "the Social"' in International Criminal Law and Transitional Justice' (2014) 8(1) *International Journal of Transitional Justice* 53
Campbell, Kirsten, Elma Demir and Maria O'Reilly, 'Understanding Conflict-Related Sexual Violence and the "Everyday" Experience of Conflict Through Witness Testimonies' (2019) 54(2) *Cooperation and Conflict* 254
Campbell, Rebecca, 'What Really Happened: A Validation Study of Rape Survivors' Help-Seeking Experiences with the Legal and Medical Systems' (2005) 20(1) *Violence & Victims* 55
Campbell, Rebecca, et al, 'Longitudinal Research with Sexual Assault Survivors: A Methodological Review' (2011) 26(3) *Journal of Interpersonal Violence* 433
Chemaly, Soraya, *Rage Becomes Her: Power of Women's Anger* (Atria Books, 2018)
Cherif Bassiouni, M, and Peter Manikas, *The Law of the International Criminal Tribunal for the Former Yugoslavia* (Transnational Publishers, 1996)
Cherry, Myisha, *The Case for Rage: Why Anger is Essential to Anti-Racist Struggle* (Oxford University Press, 2021)

Chinkin, Christine, 'Rape and Sexual Abuse of Women in International Law' (1994) 5(3) *European Journal of International Law* 326

Clark, Janine Natalya 'Beyond a "Survivor-Centred Approach" to Conflict-Related Sexual Violence?' (2021) 97(4) *International Affairs* 1067

Clark, Janine Natalya, 'Helping or Harming: NGOs and Victims/Survivors of Conflict-Related Sexual Violence in Bosnia-Herzegovina' (2019) 18(2) *Journal of Human Rights* 246

Clark, Janine Natalya, 'Social Ecologies of Health and Conflict-Related Sexual Violence: Translating "Healthworlds" into Transitional Justice' (2022) *Journal of Human Rights* 9

Clark, Janine Natalya, 'Storytelling, resilience and transitional justice: Reversing narrative social bulimia' (2022) 3(2) *Theoretical Criminology* 131

Clark, Janine Natalya, 'The living past in the lives of victims-/survivors of conflict-related sexual violence: Temporal implications for transitional justice' (2022) *Memory Studies* 1

Clark, Janine Natalya, *Rape, Sexual Violence and Transitional Justice Challenges: Lessons from Bosnia Herzegovina* (Routledge, 2017)

Clark, Janine Natalya, *Resilience, Conflict-Related Sexual Violence and Transitional Justice: A Social-Ecological Framing* (Routledge, 2022)

Clark, Janine Natayla, 'Working with Survivors of War Rape and Sexual Violence: Fieldwork Reflections from Bosnia-Herzegovina' (2017) 17(4) *Qualitative Research* 424

Clark, John, 'Northern Ireland: A Balanced Approach to Amnesty, Reconciliation and Reintegration' [2008] (January-February) *Military Review* 37

Clark, Kate, The Nuhanovic Foundation, *War Reparations and Litigation: The Case of Bosnia*, (Report, 2014) <http://www.nuhanovicfoundation.org/user/file/war_reparation_and_litigation_-_bosnia-report_version_5_march_2015.pdf>

Clark, Tom, '"We're Over-Researched Here!": Exploring Accounts of Research Fatigue within Qualitative Research Engagements' (2008) 42(5) *Sociology* 953, 955

Cobb, Sara B. *Speaking of Violence: The politics and poetics of narrative in conflict resolution* (Oxford University Press, 2013)

Cockburn, Cynthia, 'The Continuum of Violence: A Gender Perspective on War and Peace' in Wenona Giles and Jennifer Hyndman (eds), *Sites of Violence: Gender and Conflict Zones* (University of California Press, 2004) 24

Cockburn, Cynthia, 'The Gendered Dynamics of Armed Conflict and Political Violence' in Caroline Moser and Fiona C Clark (eds), *Victims, Perpetrators or Actors: Gender, Armed Conflict and Political Violence* (Zed Books, 2001) 13

Coles Stewart M., and Josh Pasek, 'Intersectional Invisibility Revisited: How Group Prototypes Lead to the Erasure and Exclusion of Black Women' 2020 6(4) *Translational Issues in Psychological Science* 314

Combs, Nancy Amoury, *Guilty Pleas in International Criminal Law: Constructing a Restorative Justice Approach* (Stanford University Press, 2007)

Coulter, Chris '*Being a Bush Wife: Women's lives through war and peace in Northern Sierra Leone*' (PhD Thesis, Uppsala University, 2006) 22, 4

Craps, Stef, *Postcolonial Witnessing: Trauma Out of Bounds* (Palgrave Macmillan, 2013)

Crawley, Karen, 'Tanya Serisier: Speaking Out: Feminism, Rape and Narrative Politics' (2021) 29 *Feminist Legal Studies* 423

Crossley, Michele L, 'Narrative Psychology, Trauma and the Study of Self/Identity' (2000) 10(4) *Theory & Psychology* 527

Čvoro, Uroš, *Post-Conflict Monuments in Bosnia and Herzegovina: Unfinished Histories* (Routledge, 2020)

Dahlman, Carl T, and Gerard Toal, *Bosnia Remade: Ethnic Cleansing and its Reversal* (Oxford University Press, 2011)

Daianu, Daniel, and Thanos Veremis (eds), *Balkan Reconstruction* (Routledge, 2001)

Danieli, Yael, 'Conclusion and Future Directions' in *International Handbook of Multigenerational Legacies of Trauma* (Spring, 1998) 669

Danieli, Yael, 'Preface' in Yael Denieli (ed), *International Handbook of Multigenerational Legacies of Trauma* (Springer, 1998) xvi.

Das, Veena, 'Violence, Crisis, and the Everyday' (2013) 45(4) *International Journal of Middle East Studies* 798

David, Lea, 'Policing Memory in Bosnia: Ontological Security and International Administration of Memorialization Policies' (2019) 32(2) *International Journal of Politics, Culture and Society* 211

David, Roman, 'International Criminal Tribunals and the Perception of Justice: The Effect of the ICTY in Croatia' (2014) 8(3) *The International Journal of Transitional Justice* 476

Davies, Thom, 'Slow Violence and Toxic Geographies: "Out of sight" to Whom?' (2022) 40(2) *Environment and Planning: Politics and Space* 409

De Grieff, Pablo, 'Theorizing Transitional Justice' in Melissa S Williams, Rosemary Nagy and Jon Elster (eds), *Transitional Justice: NOMOS LI* (New York University Press, 2012) 31

DeJonckheere, Melissa, and Lisa M Vaughn, 'Semistructured Interviewing in Primary Care Research: A balance of relationship and rigour' (2019) 7(2) *Family Medicine and Community Health* 1

Delpla, Isabelle, 'In the Midst of Injustice: The ICTY from the Perspective of some Victim Associations' in Xavier Bougarel, Elissa Helms and Gerlachlus Duijzings (eds), *The New Bosnian Mosaic: Identities, Memories and Moral Claims in a Post-War Society* (Routledge, 2007)

Dizdarevic, Emina, 'Bosnian Wartime Sexual Violence Survivors "Feel Betrayed by System"', *Balkan Insight* (online, 4 November 2021) <https://balkaninsight.com/2021/11/04/bosnian-wartime-sexual-violence-survivors-feel-betrayed-by-system/>

Doak, Jonathan, 'The Therapeutic Dimension of Transitional Justice: Emotional Repair and Victim Satisfaction in International Trials and Truth Commissions' (2011) 11(2) *International Criminal Law Review* 263.

Doe, A., 'Brnjicu potvrdjena kazna za silovanje Srpkinja', Nezavisne.com (Report, 8 June 2017) <https://www.nezavisne.com/novosti/hronika/Brnjicu-potvrdjena-kazna-za-silovanje-Srpkinja/429785>

Doubt, Keith, *Through the Window: Kinship and Elopement in Bosnia-Herzegovina* (Central European University Press, 2014)

Douglas, Heather, *Women, Intimate Partner Violence, and the Law* (Oxford University Press, 2021)

Douglas, Lawrence, *The Memory of Judgment: Making Law and History in the Trials of the Holocaust* (Yale University Press, 2001)

Dragović-Soso, Jasna, 'History of a Failure: Attempts to Create a National Truth and Reconciliation Commission in Bosnia and Herzegovina, 1997–2006' (2016) 10(2) *International Journal of Transitional Justice* 292

Drumbl, Mark A, *Atrocity, Punishment, and International Law* (Cambridge University Press, 2007) 149

Dube, Siphiwe Ignatius 'Transitional Justice Beyond the Normative: Towards a Literary Theory of Political Transitions' (2011) 5 *The International Journal of Transitional Justice* 177

Edelman, Lucila, Diana Kordon and Dario Lagos, 'Transmission of Trauma: The Argentine Case' in Yael Danieli (ed), *International Handbook of Multigenerational Legacies of Trauma* (Springer, 1998) 447

'Editorial Note' (2014) 8(1) *International Journal of Transitional Justice* 1

Edkins, Jenny, *Trauma and the Memory of Politics* (Cambridge University Press, 2003)

Eger, Edith, *The Choice* (Penguin, 2017)

Elster, Jon, *Closing the Books: Transitional Justice in Historical Perspective* (Cambridge University Press, 2004)

Engle Merry, Sally, *Getting Justice and Getting Even: Legal Consciousness Among Working-Class Americans* (University of Chicago Press, 1990)

Engle, Karen, *The Grip of Sexual Violence in Conflict* (Stanford University Press, 2020)

Enloe, Cynthia, *Nimo's War, Ema's War: Making Feminist Sense of the Iraq War* (University of California Press, 2010)

Enloe, Cynthia, *The Big Push: Exposing and Challenging the Persistence of Patriarchy* (Myriad Editions, 2017)

Enloe, Cynthia, *The Curious Feminist: Searching for Women in a New Age of Empire* (University of California Press, 2004)

Epstein, Deborah, and Lisa Goodman, 'Discounting Women: Doubting Domestic Violence Survivors' Credibility and Dismissing Their Experiences' (2019) 167 *University of Pennsylvania Law Review* 399

Felman, Shoshana, 'Forms of Judicial Blindness: Traumatic Narratives and Legal Repetitions' in Austin Sarat and Thomas R Kearns (eds), *History, Memory and the Law* (University of Michigan Press, 2002)

Ferguson, James, *The Anti-Politics Machine: Development, Depoliticization, and Bureaucratic Power in Lesotho* (University of Minnesota Press, 2nd ed, 1994) xiv

Fletcher, Laurel E, and Harvey M Weinstein, 'Transitional Justice and the "Plight" of Victimhood' in Cheryl Lawther, Luke Moffett and Dov Jacobs (eds), *Research Handbook on Transitional Justice* (Edward Elgar Publishing, 2017)

Fohring, Stephanie, 'Introduction to the Special Issue: Victim Identities and Hierarchies' (2018) 24(2) *International Journal of Victimology* 147

Frankl, Viktor E., *Man's Search for Meaning* (Beacon Press, 1946)

Friedman, Hershey H., 'The Power of Remorse and Apology' (2006) 7(1) *Journal of College and Character* 1.

Friedman, Rebekka, and Andrew Jillions, 'The Pitfalls and Politics of Holistic Justice' (2015) 6(2) *Global Policy* 141

Galtung, Johan, 'Violence, Peace and Peace Research' (1969) 6(3) *Journal of Peace Research* 167

Gebhardt, Miriam, *Crimes Unspoken: The Rape of German Women at the End of the Second World War* (Polity, 2016)

Genn, Hazel, 'Understanding Civil Justice' 1997 50(1) *Current Legal Problems* 155

Genn, Hazel, *Paths to Justice: What People Do and Think About Going to Law* (Hart Publishing, 1999)

Gilligan, James, *Violence: Reflections on Our Deadliest Epidemic* (Jessica Kingsley, 1996)

Gilmore, Sunneva, and Luke Moffett, 'Finding a way to live with the past: 'Self-Repair', 'Informal Repair', and Reparations in Transitional Justice' (2021) 48(3) *Journal of Law and Society* 455

Goffman, Erving, *Stigma: Notes on the Management of a Spoiled Identity* (Simon and Shuster Inc, 1986)

Goldstein Bolocan, Maya, 'Rwandan Gacaca: An Experiment in Transitional Justice' [2004] (2) *Journal of Dispute Resolution* 355

Govier, Trudy, *Victims and Victimhood* (Broadview Press, 2015)

Gravelin, Claire R., Monica Baldwin, and Matthew Biernat, 'The Impact of Power and Powerlessness on Blaming the Victim of Sexual Assault' (2017) 22(1) *Group Processes & Intergroup Relations* 98–115

Gready, Paul *Writing as Resistance: Life Stories of Imprisonment, Exile, and Homecoming From Apartheid South Africa* (Lexington Books, 2003)

Gready, Paul, *The Era of Transitional Justice: The Aftermath of the Truth and Reconciliation Commission in South Africa and Beyond* (Routledge, 2011)

Groenhuijsen, Marc S, 'Victims' Rights in the Criminal Justice System: A Call for More Comprehensive Implementation Theory' in Jan JM van Dijk, Ron GH van Kaam, and Jo-Anne Wemmers (eds), *Caring for Crime Victims: Selected Proceedings of the Ninth International Symposium on Victimology* (Criminal Justice Press, 1999) 85

Hadžić, A., 'Pokušaj zastrašivanja svjedoka zločina u Zvorniku', *Politika* (online, 28 April 2022) <https://politicki.ba/vijesti/pokusaj-zastrasivanja-svjedoka-zlocina-u-zvorniku/22916>

Halilovich, Hariz, 'Behind the Emic Lines: Ethics and Politics of Insiders' Ethnography' in Lejla Voloder and Liudmila Kirpitchenko, *Insider Research on Migration and Mobility: International Perspectives on Researcher Positioning* (Ashgate, 2014) 87

Halilovich, Hariz, 'Etika, ljudska prava i istraživanje: Etnografija u posljeratnoj Bosni i Hercegovin Ethics' (2008) 45(2) *Narodna Umjetnost: Hrvatski Časopis za Etnologiju i Folkloristiku* [*Croatian Journal of Ethnology and Folklore*] 165

Halilovich, Hariz, 'Missing people and missing stories in the aftermath of genocide: Reclaiming local memories at the place of suffering' in Mina Rauschenbach, Julia Viebach and Stephan Parmentier (eds), *Localising Memory in Transitional Justice: The Dynamics and Informal Practices of Memorialisation after Mass Violence and Dictatorship* (Routledge, 2022) 209

Halliday, Simon, and Patrick Schmidt, *Conducting Law and Society Research: Reflections of Methods and Practices* (Cambridge University Press, 2009)

Hayner, Priscilla B., *Unspeakable Truths: Confronting State Terror and Atrocity* (Routledge, 2000)

Hearty, Kevin, '"Victims of" Human Rights Abuses in Transitional Justice: Hierarchies, Perpetrators and the Struggle for Peace' (2018) 22(7) *The International Journal of Human Rights* 888

Hearty, Kevin, 'Law, "Presentist" Agendas and the Making of "Official" Memory after Collective Violence', (2022) 49 *Journal of Law and Society* 495.

Hearty, Kevin, 'Truth Beyond the "Trigger Puller": Moral Accountability, Transitional (In)Justice and the Limitations of Legal Truth' (2021) 15(3) *International Journal of Transitional Justice* 658

Helms, Elissa, 2010, 'The Gender of Coffee: Woman and reconciliation initiatives in Bosnia and Herzegovina' (2010) 57 *Focal—Journal of Global and Historical Anthropology* 17, 17–23

Helms, Elissa, *Innocence and Victimhood: Gender, Nation, and Women's Activism in Postwar Bosnia-Herzegovina* (University of Wisconsin Press, 2013)

Henig, David '"Knocking on My Neighbour's Door": On metamorphoses of sociality in rural Bosnia', (2012) 32(1) *Critique of Anthropology* 3.

Henry, Nicola, 'Witness to Rape: The Limits and Potential of International War Crimes Trials for Victims of Wartime Sexual Violence' (2009) 3(1) *International Journal of Transitional Justice* 114

Henry, Nicola, *War and Rape: Law, Memory and Justice* (Routledge, 2011)

Herman, Judith, 'The Mental Health of Crime Victims: Impact of Legal Intervention' (2003) 16(2) *Journal of Traumatic Stress* 159

Herman, Susan, and Cressida Wasserman, 'A Role for Victims in Offender Reentry' (2001) 47(3) *Crime and Delinquency* 428

Hirstov, Petko, 'Imaginary Historical Pattern of Family and a Model for Construction of Political and Social Organizations — Extended Family (Zadruga) in Bulgaria' (2022) 6(3) *Genealogy* 59

Holmes, Andrew Gary Darwin, 'Researcher Positionality: A Consideration of its Influence and Place in Qualitative Research' (2020) 8(4) *Shanlax International Journal of Education* 1

Horne, Cynthia M, 'Trust and Transitional Justice' in Lavinia Stan and Nedelsky (eds), *Encyclopaedia of Transitional Justice* (Cambridge University Press, 2nd ed, forthcoming)

Houge, Anette Bringedal and Inger Skjelsbæk, 'Securitising Sexual Violence: Transitions from War to Peace' in Kate Fitz-Gibbon et al (eds), *Intimate Partner Violence, Risk and Security: Securing Women's Lives in a Global World* (Routledge, 2018)

Houge, Anette Bringedal, 'Narrative Expressivism: A criminological approach to the expressive function of International Criminal Justice' (2019) 19(3) *Criminology & Criminal Justice* 297

Houge, Anette Bringedal, 'Violent Re-Presentations: Reflections on the Ethics of re-presentation in violence research' (2022) *Qualitative Research*, 13

Hydén, Margareta, '"I Must have Been an Idiot to Let it Go On": Agency and Positioning in Battered Women's Narratives of Leaving' (2005) 15(2) *Feminism and Psychology* 169

Igreja, Victor, 'Negotiating Relationships in Transition: War, Famine, and Embodied Accountability in Mozambique' (2019) 61(4) *Comparative Studies in Society and History* 774, 789

Igreja, Victor, 'Negotiating the Legacies of Intragroup Violence in Timor Leste' (2021) 15 (2) *International Journal of Transitional Justice* 309

Isser, Deborah H., 'Conclusion: Understanding and Engaging Customary Justice Systems' in Deborah H Isser (ed), *Customary Justice and the Rule of Law in War-Torn Societies* (United States Institute of Peace Press, 2011) 325, 327

Jacobs, Janet Liebman, 'Women, Genocide, and Memory: The Ethics of Feminist Ethnography in Holocaust Research' (2004) 18(2) *Gender and Society* 223

Jaffe, Peter, et al, 'Similarities in Behavioural and Social Maladjustment Among Child Victims and Witnesses to Family Violence' (1986) 56(1) *American Journal of Orthopsychiatry* 142

Janoff-Bulman, Ronni, *Shattered Assumptions: Towards a New Psychology of Trauma* (The Free Press, 1992)

Jaspers, Karl, *The Question of German Guilt* tr EB Ashton (Fordham University Press, 1965)

Jeffery, Renee, 'The Role of the Arts in Cambodia's Transitional Justice Process' (2021) 34(3) *International Journal of Politics, Culture, and Society* 335

Jones, Nicola, et al, 'The Fallout of Rape as a Weapon of War: The Life-Long and Intergenerational Impacts of Sexual Violence in Conflict' (Research Report, Overseas Development Institute, 8 June 2014)

Kaldor, Mary, 'In Defence of New Wars' (2013) 2(1) *Stability: International Journal of Security and Development* 4

Kaldor, Mary, *New and Old Wars: Organised Violence in a Global Era* (Polity Press, 1st ed, 1999)

Kane, Odia 'The Denial of Victimhood: Exploring the Attitudes Surrounding Collegiate Black Women and Rape' (Conference Paper, *National Conference of Black Political Scientists Annual Meeting*, 13 November 2018)

Kapur, Ratna, 'The Tragedy of Victimization Rhetoric: Resurrecting the "Native" Subject in International/Post-Colonial Feminist Legal Politics' (2002) 15 *Harvard Human Rights Journal* 1

Kaser, Karl, 'The Balkan Joint Family Household: Seeking its Origins' in Karl Kaser (ed), *Household and Family in the Balkans: Two Decades of Historical Family Research at University of Graz* (Lit, 2012) 109

Kelly, Liz, 'The Continuum of Sexual Violence' in Jalna Hanmer and Mary Maynard (eds), *Women, Violence and Social Control* (Macmillan, 1987)

Kelly, Liz, *Surviving Sexual Violence* (Polity Press, 1988)

Kenney, J Scott, 'Human Agency Revisited: The Paradoxical Experiences of Victims of Crime' (2004) 11(2–3) *International Review of Victimology* 225

Kerr, Rachel, 'International Criminal Justice' in Olivera Simic (ed), *An Introduction to Transitional Justice* (Taylor & Francis Group, 2016) 47

Khan, Nyla Ali, *Educational Strategies for Youth Empowerment in Conflict Zones* (Palgrave MacMillan, 2021)

Kinzie, J David, J Boehnlein and William H Sack, 'The Effects of Massive Trauma on Cambodian Parents and Children' in Yael Danieli (ed), *International Handbook of Multigenerational Legacies of Trauma* (Plenum Press, 1998) 211

Korner, Her Honour Judge Joanna, *Improving War Crimes Processing at the State Level in Bosnia and Herzegovina* (Report, 16 September 2020)

Kritz, Neil J., (ed), *Transitional Justice: How Emerging Democracies Reckon with Former Regimes* (United States Institute of Peace Press, 1995)

Krondorfer, Bjorn, *Unsettling Empathy: Working with Groups in Conflict* (Rowman and Littlefield Publishers, 2020)

Krystallii, Roxani, 'Narrating Victimhood: Dilemmas and (In)Dignities' (2021) 23(1) *International Feminist Journal of Politics* 125

Kuradusenge, Claudine, 'Denied Victimhood and Contested Narratives: The case of Hutu Diaspora' (2016) 10(2) *Genocide Studies and Prevention: An International Journal* 59.

Lawther, Cheryl, '"Let Me tell You": Transitional Justice, Victimhood and Dealing with a Contested Past' (2021) 30(6) *Social & Legal Studies* 890

Lemaitre, Julieta, 'After the War: Displaced Women, Ordinary Ethics, and Grassroots Reconstruction in Colombia' (2016) 25(5) *Social & Legal Studies* 545

Levi, Primo, *The Drowned and the Saved* (Abacus, 2013)

Locke, Peter, 'City of Survivors: Trauma, Grief, and Getting-By in Post-War Sarajevo' (PhD Dissertation, Princeton University, 2009)

Lockwood, William G, 'Coverts and Consanguinity: The Social Organization of Moslem Slavs in Western Bosnia' (1972) 11(1) *Ethnology* 55

Lockwood, William G, *European Moslems: Economy and Ethnicity in Western Bosnia* (Academic Press, 1975)

Ludwin King, Elizabeth B, 'Does Justice always Require Prosecution: The International Criminal Court and Transitional Justice Measures' (2013) 45(1) *The George Washington International Law Review* 85

Lundy, Patricia, and Mark McGovern, 'Whose Justice: Rethinking Transitional Justice from the Bottom Up' (2008) 35(2) *Journal of Law and Society* 265

Maček, Ivana, *Sarajevo Under Siege: Anthropology in Wartime* (University of Pennsylvania Press, 2011)

Maculan, Elena, and Alicia Gil Gil, 'The Rationale and Purposes of Criminal Law and Punishment in Transitional Contexts' (2020) 40(1) *Oxford Journal of Legal Studies* 132

Madlingozi, Tshepo, 'Good Victim, Bad Victim: Apartheid's Beneficiaries, Victims and the Struggle for Social Justice' in Wessel le Roux and Karin van Marle (eds), *Law, Memory and the Legacy of Apartheid: Ten Years After AZAPO v President of South Africa* (Pretoria University Law Press, 2007)

Madlingozi, Tshepo, 'On Transitional Justice Entrepreneurs and the Production of Victims' (2010) 13(2) *Journal of Human Rights Practice* 212

Mallinder, Louise, 'Metaconflict and international human rights law in dealing with Northern Ireland's past' (2019) 8(1) *Cambridge International Law Journal* 5.

Manning, Peter, *Transitional Justice and Memory in Cambodia: Beyond the Extraordinary Chambers* (Routledge, 2017)

Marin, Paul A, 'Bosnia is Beginning to Recover After Four Years of War, and is Offering the First Signs of Legitimate Business Opportunities', *Business of America: The Magazine of International Trade* (Washington DC, September 1997)

Marsavelski, Aleksandar, and John Braithwaite, 'Transitional Justice Cascades' (2020) 53(2) *Cornell International Law Journal* 207

Maynard, Mary, 'Methods, Practice and Epistemology: The Debate about Feminism and Research' in Mary Maynard and June Purvis, *Researching Women's Lives from a Feminist Perspective* (Routledge, 1994) 17

Mazowiecki, Tadeusz, *Report on the Situation of Human Rights in the Territory of The Former Yugoslavia / Submitted By Tadeusz Mazowiecki,Special Rapporteur Of The Commission On Human Rights, Pursuant to Paragraph 15 of Commission Resolution 1992/S-1/1 of 14 August 1992*

McEvoy, Kieran and McConnachie, Kirsten, 'Victims and Transitional Justice: Voice, Agency and Blame', (2013) 22(4): *Social and Legal Studies* 489

McMahon, Patrice C, 'Rebuilding Bosnia: A Model to Emulate or to Avoid?', (2004) 119(4) *Political Science Quarterly* 569

McWilliam, Kelly, 'Digital storytelling and the "problem" of sentimentality' (2017) 165(1) *Media International Australia* 77

Medic, Nevena, 'Helpers Across the Ethnic Divide: The role of komšiluk in rescuing during the Bosnian conflict' (2021) 2(2) *Historia Moderna* 86, 95.

Medica Zenica and Medica Mondiale, *'We are Still Alive': Research on the Long-Term Consequences of War Rape and Coping Strategies of Survivors in Bosnia and Herzegovina* (Report, November 2014)

Meister, Robert, *After Evil: A Politics of Human Rights* (Columbia University Press, 2011)

Mendeloff, David 'Trauma and Vengeance: Assessing the Psychological and Emotional Effects of Post-Conflict Justice' (2009) 31(3) *Human Rights Quarterly* 592

Minow, Martha, *Between Vengeance and Forgiveness: Facing History after Genocide and Mass Violence* (Beacon Press, 1998)

Mocnik, Nena, *Trauma Transmission and Sexual Violence* (Routledge, 2021).

Mojzes, Paul, *Balkan Genocides: Holocaust and Ethnic Cleansing in the Twentieth Century* (Rowman & Littlefield, 2015)

Montville, Joseph V., 'Psychoanalytical Enlightenment and the Greening of Diplomacy' (1989) 37(2) *Journal of American Psychoanalytic Association* 297

Morris, Heather, *Stories of Hope: Finding Inspiration in Everyday Lives* (Manilla Press, 2020) 165

Mosley, Philip E, 'The Peasant Family: The Zadruga, or Communal Joint Family in the Balkans and Its Recent Evolution' in Robert F Byrnes (ed), *Communal Families in the Balkans: The Zadruga* (University of Notre Dame Press, 1976) 19

Mulaj, Klejda, *Politics of Ethnic Cleansing* (Lexington Books, 2008)

Murphy, Colleen, *A Moral Theory of Political Reconciliation* (Cambridge, 2010)

Neuffer, Elizabeth, *The Key to My Neighbour's House: Seeking Justice in Bosnia and Rwanda* (Bloomsbury, 2003)

Nino, Carlos Santiago, *Radical Evil on Trial* (Yale University Press, 1998)

Nixon, Rob, *Slow Violence and the Environmentalism of the Poor* (Harvard University Press, 2011)

Nordstrom, Carolyn, *Shadows of War: Violence, Power, and International Profiteering in the Twenty-First Century* (University of California Press, 2004)

O'Neill, Siobhan, et al, 'Associations Between DSM-IV Mental Disorders and Subsequent Self-Reported Diagnosis of Cancer' (2014) 76(3) *Journal of Psychosomatic Research* 207

O'Rourke, Catherine, *Gender Politics in Transitional Justice* (Routledge, 2013)

Obradovic, Nikolina, Mirna Jusic and Nermin Oruc, *In-Work Poverty in Bosnia and Herzegovina* (European Social Policy Network Report, 2019)

Ocampo, Luis Moreno, 'Stopping the Crimes While Repairing the Victims: Personal Reflections of a Global Prosecutor' in Jacqueline Bhabha, Margareta Matache and Caroline Elkins (eds), *Time for Reparations: A Global Perspective* (University of Pennsylvania Press, 2021) 291

Orentclicher, Diane, *Some Kind of Justice: Bosnian Expectations of the ICTY* (Oxford University Press, 2018)

Orth, Uli, 'Secondary Victimization of Crime Victims by Criminal Proceedings' (2002) 15(4) *Social Justice Research* 313

Peel, Michael (ed), *Rape as a Method of Torture* (Medical Foundation for the Care of Victims of Torture, 2004)

Pemberton, Antony, and Rianne Letschert, 'Victimology of Atrocity Crimes' in Barbora Holá, Hollie Nyseth Nzitatira and Maartje Weerdesteijn (eds), *The Oxford Handbook of Atrocity Crimes* (Oxford University Press, 2022) 461

Pemberton, Antony, et al, 'Coherence in International Criminal Justice: A Victimological Perspective' (2015) 25(2) *International Criminal Law Review* 339

Pemberton, Antony, Eva Mulder and Pauline GM Aarten, 'Stories of Injustice: Towards a narrative of victimology' (2019) 16(4) *European Journal of Criminology* 391

Pemberton, Antony, Pauline GM Aarten and Eva Mulder, 'Stories as property: Narrative ownership as a key concept in victims' experiences with criminal justice' (2019) 19(4) *Criminology and Criminal Justice* 204.

Petryna, Adriana, *Life Exposed: Biological Citizens after Chernobyl* (Princeton University Press, 2003)

Pickering, Michael and Emily Keightley, 'Communities of Memory and the Problem of Transmission' (2013) 16 (1) *European Journal of Cultural Studies* 115

Porter, Elisabeth, 'Gendered Narratives: Stories and Silences in Transitional Justice' (2016) 17(1) *Human Rights Review* 35

Porter, Elisabeth, *Connecting Peace, Justice and Reconciliation* (Lynne Rienne, 2015)

Posner, Eric A, *The Perils of Global Legalism* (University of Chicago Press, 2009)

Potter, Michael, and Hedley Abernethy, 'What About the Women: Transitional Justice and Gender in Bosnia and Herzegovina and Northern Island' in Olivera Simic and Zala Volčič (eds), *Transitional Justice and Civil Society in the Balkans* (Springer, 2013) 163

Preston, Valerie, and Madeleine Wong, 'Geographies of Violence: Women and Conflict in Ghana' in Wenona Giles and Jennifer Hyndman (eds), *Sites of Violence: Gender and Conflict Zones* (University of California Press, 2004) 152

Regodic, Grozda, *U zagrljaju Duge* (Grafid, Banjaluka, 2021)

Rezun, Miron, *Europe's Nightmare: The Struggle for Kosovo* (Praeger, 2001) 16

Riessman, Catherine Kohler, *Narrative Methods for the Human Sciences* (Sage Publications, 2008)

Rivera, Echo A, Cris M Sullivan and April M Zeoli, 'Secondary Victimization of Abused Mothers by Family Court Mediators' (2012) 7(3) *Feminist Criminology* 234

Robins, Simon, 'Failing Victims: The Limits of Transitional Justice in Addressing the Needs of Victims of Violations' (2017) 11(1) *Human Rights and International Legal Discourse* 41

Rock, Paul, 'On Becoming a Victim' in Carolyn Hoyle and Richard Young (eds), *New Visions of Crime Victims* (Hart, 2002) 1

Roehrig, Terence, 'Executive Leadership and the Continuing Quest for Justice in Argentina' (2009) 31(1) *Human Rights Quarterly* 721

Rosental et al (eds.) *Gender in International Criminal Law* (Oxford University Press, 2022) 110

Rothberg, Michael, *Multidirectional Memory: Remembering the Holocaust in the Age of Decolonization* (Stanford University Press, 2009)

Ruffer, Galya, 'Testimony of Sexual Violence in the Democratic Republic of Congo and the Injustice of Rape: Moral Outrage, Epistemic Injustice, and the Failures of Bearing Witness' (2013) 15(2) *Oregon Review of International Law* 225

Sarkin, Jeremy, 'Enhancing the Legitimacy, Status and Role of the International Criminal Court by Using Transitional Justice or Restorative Justice Strategies' (2012) 6(1) *Interdisciplinary Journal of Human Rights Law* 83

Savelsberg, Joachim J, and Ryan D King, *American Memories: Atrocities and the Law* (Russell Sage Foundation, 2011)

Scanlon, Christopher, and John Adlam, *Psycho-Social Explorations of Trauma, Exclusion and Violence: Un-Housed Minds and Inhospitable Environments* (Routledge, 2022)

Schaffer, Kay, and Sidonie Smith, *Human Rights and Narrated Lives: The Ethics of Recognition* (Palgrave Macmillan, 2004)

Schok, Michaela, *Meaning as a Mission: Making Sense of War and Peacekeeping* (Eburon Academic Publishing 2009)

Selimovic, Johanna Mannergren, 'Gendered silences in post-conflict societies: a typology' (2020) 8(1) *Peacebuilding* 1

Selimovic, Johanna Mannergren, 'Perpetrators and Victims: Local Responses to the International Criminal Tribunal for the former Yugoslavia' [2010] (57) *Focaal: Journal of Global and Historical Anthropology* 50

Selimovic, Johanna Mannergren, 'The Stuff from the Siege: Transitional Justice and the Power of Everyday Objects in Museums' (2022) 16(2) *International Journal of Transitional Justice* 220.

Serisier, Tanya, *Speaking Out: Feminism, Rape and Narrative Politics* (Palgrave Macmillan, 2018)

Shaw, Rosalind, 'Linking justice with reintegration engagement? Ex combatants and Sierra Leone Experiments' in Rosalind Shaw, Lars Waldorf and Pierre Hazan (eds), *Localizing Transitional Justice: Interventions and priorities after mass violence* (Stanford University Press, 2010) 111

Shaw, Rosalind, 'Memory Frictions: Localizing the Truth and Reconciliation Commission in Sierra Leone' (2007) 1(2) *International Journal of Transitional Justice* 183, 203

Shillinglaw, Stephanie, *Sexual Violence in Conflict: Delivering Justice for Survivors and Holding Perpetrators to Account* (Report, September 2019) 2 <https://www.wiltonpark.org.uk/wp-content/uploads/WP1651-Report-1-1.pdf>

Shklar, Judith N, *The Faces of Injustice* (Yale University Press, 1990)

Sikkink, Kathryn, and Hun Joon Kim, 'The Justice Cascade: The Origins and Effectiveness of Prosecutions of Human Rights Violations' (2013) 9 *Annual Review of Law and Social Science* 269

Sikkink, Kathryn, *The Justice Cascade: How Human Rights Prosecutions Are Changing World Politics* (W W Norton & Company, 2011)

Simic, Olivera 'Drinking coffee in Bosnia: Listening to stories of wartime violence and rape' (2017) 18(4) *Journal of International Women's Studies* 321.

Simic, Olivera, 'Arts and Transitional Justice' in Olivera Simic (ed), *An Introduction to Transitional Justice* (Routledge, 2nd ed, 2020) 241

Simic, Olivera, 'Breathing Sense into Women's Lives Shattered by War: Dah Theatre Belgrade' (2010) 14 *Law Text Culture* 117

Simic, Olivera, *An Introduction to Transitional Justice* (Taylor & Francis Group, 2nd ed, 2020)

Simic, Olivera, and Dijana Milošević, 'Enacting Justice: The Role of Dah Theatre Company in Transitional Justice Processes in Serbia and Beyond' in Peter D Rush and Olivera Simic (eds), *The Arts of Transitional Justice: Culture, Activism, and Memory after Atrocity* (Springer, 2014)

Simic, Olivera, and Zala Volcic, 'In the Land of Wartime Rape: Bosnia, Cinema and Reparation' (2014) 2(2) *Griffith Journal of Law & Human Dignity* 377

Simic, Olivera, *Silenced Victims of Wartime Sexual Violence* (Routledge, 2018)

Skilbeck, Rupert, 'Funding Justice: The Price of War Crimes Trials' (2008) 15(3) *Human Rights Brief* 6

Skjelsbæk, Inger, *The Political Psychology of War Rape: Studies from Bosnia and Herzegovina* (Routledge, 2012)

Smeulers, Alette, 'Concluding Thoughts' in Alette Smeulers, Martje Weerdesteijn and Barbora Hola (eds.) *Perpetrators of International Crimes* (Oxford University Press, 2019) 321

Smith, Linda Tuhiwai, *Decolonizing Methodologies: Research and Indigenous Peoples* (University of Otago Press, 1999

Sonnenberg, S M, 'Workshop Report: Children of Survivors' (1974) 22(1) *Journal of American Psychoanalytical Association* 200

Stack Sullivan, Harry, *The Interpersonal Theory of Psychiatry* (W.W. Norton & Company,1953)

Stauffer, Jill, *Ethical Loneliness: The Injustice of Not Being Heard* (Columbia University Press, 2015)

Stiglemayer, Alexandra, (ed), *Mass Rape: The War Against Women in Bosnia-Herzegovina*, tr Marion Faber (University of Nebraska Press, 1994)

Stiles, Melissa M 'Witnessing Domestic Violence: The Effect on Children' (2002) 66(11) *American Family Physician* 2052

Stover, Eric, 'Witnesses and the Promise of Justice in The Hague' in Eric Stover and Harvey M Weinstein (eds), *My Neighbour, My Enemy: Justice and Community in the Aftermath of Mass Atrocity* (Cambridge University Press, 2005) 104

Stover, Eric, *The Witnesses: War Crimes and the Promise of Justice in The Hague* (University of Pennsylvania Press, 2005) 11

Suleiman, Susan R., 'The 1.5 generation: Thinking about Child Survivors and the Holocaust' (2002) 59 (3) *American Imago* 277

Sveaass and Nils Johan Lavik, 'Psychological Aspects of Human Rights Violations: The Importance of Justice and Reconciliation' (2000) 69(1) *Nordic Journal of International Law* 35

Taussig, Michael, *The Nervous System* (Routledge, 1992)

Teitel, Ruti G, 'Transitional Justice Genealogy' (2003) 16 *Harvard Human Rights Journal* 69

Teitel, Ruti G, 'Transitional Justice in a New Era' (2002) 26(4) *Fordham International Law Journal* 893, 896.

Theidon, Kimberly, *Intimate Enemies: Violence and Reconciliation in Peru* (University of Pennsylvania Press, 2013)

Theidon, Kimberly, *Legacies of War: Violence, Ecologies, and Kin* (Duke University Press, 2022)

Thumim, Nancy, 'Exploring Self-Representations in Wales and London: Tension in the Text' in John Hartley and Kelly McWilliam (eds), *Story Circle: Digital Storytelling Around the World* (Wiley, 2009) 205, 216

Thurlow, Crispin, 'Queering Critical Discourse Studies or/and Performing "Post-Class" Ideologies', (2016) 13(5) *Critical Discourse Studies* 485

Tompkins, Tamara L, 'Prosecuting Rape as a War Crime: Speaking the Unspeakable' (1995) 70(4) *Notre Dame Law Review* 845

TRIAL International, *Bosnia and Herzegovina Study on Opportunities for Reparations for Survivors of Conflict-Related Sexual Violence: We raise our voices* (Report, March 2022) <https://trialinternational.org/wp-content/uploads/2022/03/GSFReportBiH_ENG_Web.pdf>

TRIAL International, *Punishing Conflict-Related Sexual Violence: Guidelines for Combatting Inconsistencies in Sentencing* (Report, 2018) <https://trial.ba/wp-content/uploads/2019/05/01_publication__en_page_by_page_WEB.pdf>

TRIAL International, *Rape Myths in Wartime Sexual Violence Trials: Transferring the Burden from Survivor to Perpetrator* (Report, 2017)

Tribunal' (2002) 5 *Yale Human Rights and Development Law Journal* 217

Truth and Reconciliation Commission of South Africa, *Report* (1998) Vol 5

Tsavoussis, Areti, et al, 'Child-Witnessed Domestic Violence and its Adverse Effects on Brain Development: A Call for Societal Self-Examination and Awareness' (2014) 2 *Frontiers in Public Health* 175:1

Tsirigotis, Konstantinos, and Joanna Łuczak, 'Resilience in Women Who Experience Domestic Violence' (2018) 89(1) *Psychiatric Quarterly* 201

Ungar, Michael, 'Resilience, Trauma, Context, and Culture' (2013) 14(3) *Trauma, Violence and Abuse* 255

United Nations Development Programme, *Needs Assessment in the Field of Support to Witnesses/Victims in BiH* (Report, 25 July 2013)

United Nations Security Council, *Final Report of the United Nations Commission of Experts Established Pursuant to Security Council Resolution 780 (1992)*, annex ('Annex III.A Special Forces') (28 December 1994)

Van der Auweraert, Peter, 'Reparations for Wartime Victims in the Former Yugoslavia: In Search of the Way Forward', *International Organization for Migration* (Internet Publication, June 2013) <https://www.iom.int/sites/g/files/tmzbdl486/files/migrated_files/What-We-Do/docs/Reparations-for-Wartime-Victims-in-the-Former-Yugoslavia-In-Search-of-the-Way-Forward.pdf>

Van der Kolk, Bessel, *The Body Keeps The Score: Mind, and Body in the Healing of Trauma* (Viking, 2014).

Veena Das, 'Language and Body: Transactions in the Construction of Pain' (1996) 125(1) *Daedalus* 67

Vele, Faruk, 'Ratni zlocinac Marko Maka Radic pusten na slobodu', *Tacno* (online, 25 February 2019) <https://www.tacno.net/mostar/ratni-zlocinac-marko-maka-radic-pusten-na-slobodu/>

Vidojković, Dario, 'Ne dozvolimo da se ugasi, Udruženje žena žrtava rata Republike Srpske"!' *Basta Balkana* (online, 3 September 2017) <https://www.bastabalkana.com/2017/02/ne-dozvolimo-da-se-ugasi-udruzenje-zena-zrtava-rata-republike-srpske/>

Wald, Patricia M, 'Dealing with Witnesses in War Crimes Trials: Lessons from the Yugoslav

Wentholt, Niké, and Europa Südost, 'Mirroring Transitional Justice: Construction and Impact of European Union ICTY-Conditionality' (2017) 65(1) *Regensburg* 77

West, Rebecca, *Black Lamb and Grey Falcon: A Journey through* Yugoslavia (A&U Canongate, 2021)

West, Richard, *Tito and the Rise and Fall of Yugoslavia* (Faber and Faber, 2012).

Wibben, Annick, *Feminist Security Studies: A Narrative Approach* (Taylor & Francis, 2010)

Williams, J E., 'Secondary victimization: confronting public attitudes about rape' (1984) 9(1) *Victimology* 66.

Wolgast, Elizabeth H, *The Grammar of Justice* (Cornell University Press, 1987)

Zarkov, Dubravka, 'Sexual Violence Against Men in Contemporary Warfare" in Indira

Židek , Nikolina '"Nobody asked me how I felt". Childhood Memories of Exile among the Croatian post-WW2 Diaspora in Argentina' (2021) 8 (1) *Contemporary Southeastern Europe* 3–5

Žižek, Slavoj, *Violenc*e (Profile Books, 2008)

Cases

Application of the Convention on the Prevention and Punishment of the Crime of Genocide (Bosnia and Herzegovina v. Serbia and Montenegro) (Judgment) [2007] ICJ Rep 43

Decision concerning Communication No 854/2017

Prosecutor v Branke Šekaric, S1 3 K 021481 17 K, Court of Bosnia and Herzegovina, 17 May 2017

Prosecutor v Ilija Jurić, Appeals Division of the Court of Bosnia and Herzegovina, S1 1 K 018179 16 Kžž, 21 March 2017 (third degree verdict) [tr author]

Prosecutor v Ilija Jurić, Appeals Division of the Court of Bosnia and Herzegovina, No S1 1 K 018179 16 Kžž, 17 March 2016 (second degree verdict)

Prosecutor v Ilija Jurić, Court of Bosnia and Herzegovina, S1 1 K 018179 16 Kžž, 9 November 2015

Prosecutor v Kunarac, Kovac, and Vukovic (Judgment) (International Tribunal for the Former Yugoslavia, Trial Chamber, Case No. IT-96–23/I-T (22 February 2001) [464] ('Kunarac')

Prosecutor v Marijan Brnjić Appeals Division of the Court of Bosnia and Herzegovina, S1 1 K 019816 17 Krž, 18 May 2017 (second degree verdict)

Prosecutor v Marijan Brnjić et al, Appeals Division of the Court of Bosnia and Herzegovina, S1 1 K 016706 16 Krž, 22 April 2016

Prosecutor v Marko Samardžija, Court of Bosnia and Herzegovina, X-KRŽ-05/07, 3 November 2006, 39.

The Decision of the Association of Former Camp Inmates 'Odžak 92', no 01–43/07, 12 December 2007

Legislation

Constitution of the Republic of Croatia, The (Croatia) (consolidated text, Official Gazette Nos 56/90, 135/97, 113/00, 28/01, 76/10 and 5/14).

Criminal Code of Bosnia and Herzegovina (Bosnia and Herzegovina) art 240

Law of Civil Obligations, (Republic of Yugoslavia) Official Gazette of Socialist Federal Republic of Yugoslavia, No 29/78, 39/85, 45/89 and 57/89

Law on Amending and Supplementing the Law No.04/L-054 on the Status and the Rights of the Martyrs, Invalids, Veterans, Members of Kosovo Liberation Army, Sexual Violence Victims of the War, Civilian Victims and their Families (Republic of Kosovo) Law No. 04/L-172

Law on the Rights of Victims of Sexual Violence during the Armed Aggression against the Republic of Croatia in the Homeland War (Croatia)

The Municipal Court of Sarajevo, No 65 O P 108160 09 P, 18 June 2015

Zakon o Zaštiti Civilnih Žrtava Rata [Law on the Protection of Civilian Victims of War], Official Gazette of the Republika Srpska, No 24/10

Zakon o Zaštiti Žrtava Ratne Torture Republike Srpske [Law on the Protection of Victims of War Torture], *Official Gazette of the Republika Srpska*, No 90/18

Treaties

Constitution of the Federation of Bosnia and Herzegovina (Annex 4 of the General Framework Agreement for Peace in Bosnia and Herzegovina) *Dayton Peace Agreement 'Dayton Peace Accords'* (signed 14 December 1995)

Convention (II) with Respect to the Laws and Customs of War on Land and its Annex: Regulations concerning the Laws and Customs of War on Land, The Hague, adopted 29 July 1899 (entered into force 4 September 1900)

Convention (IV) Respecting the Laws and Customs of War on Land and its Annex: Regulations Concerning the Laws and Customs of War on Land, The Hague, adopted 18 October 1907 (entered into force 26 January 1910) ('*Hague Convention 1907*')

Convention on the Prevention and Punishment of the Crime of Genocide, opened for signature 9 December 1948, UN DOC A/RES/3/260 (entered into force 12 January 1951)

Convention on the Transfer of Sentenced Persons, opened for signature 21 March 1983, ETS 112 (entered into force 1 July 1985)

Geneva Convention (I) for the Amelioration of the Condition of the Wounded and Sick in Armed Forces in the Field of 12 August 1949 (entered into force 21 October 1950)

Protocol Additional to the Geneva Conventions of 12 August 1949, and relating to the Protection of Victims of International Armed Conflicts (Protocol I) (8 June 1977) (entered into force 7 December 1978)

Protocol Additional to the Geneva Conventions of 12 August 1949, and relating to the Protection of Victims of Non-International Armed Conflicts (Protocol II) (8 June 1977) (entered into force 7 December 1978)

Rome Statute for the International Criminal Court, opened for signature 17 July 1998, 2187 UNTS 90 (entered into force 1 July 2002)

Security Council, SC Res 798, UN SCOR, 3150th mtg, UN Doc S/Res/798 (18 December 1992)

Other Sources

'About the ICTY', *United Nations International Criminal Tribunal for the former Yugoslavia*, (Web Page) <https://www.icty.org/en/about>

Amnesty International, '*We Need Support, not Pity': Last Chance for Justice for Bosnia's Wartime Rape Survivors* (Report, 12 September 2017) <https://www.amnesty.org/en/documents/eur63/6679/2017/en/>

Anderson, Alec, and Chiara Zardoni, 'An Investment in Bosnia and Herzegovina's Future: Compensating Survivors of Wartime Sexual Violence', *Global Voices* (online, 23 September 2021) <https://globalvoices.org/2021/09/23/an-investment-in-bosnias-future-compensating-survivors-of-wartime-sexual-violence/amp/>

Arbutina, Zoran 'The Legacy of the ICTY Tribunal in the Hague', *Deutsche Welle* (online, 29 November 2017) [9] <https://beta.dw.com/en/icty-hague-tribunal-ends-prosecutions-of-yugoslav-war-crimes-but-legacy-lingers/a-41587892>

ATV TV, 'Deset godina Udruženje žena žrtava rata: "Uradili smo mnogo" - Gost vijesti Bozica Zivkovic Rajilic', (Rutube, 7 December 2022) <https://rutube.ru/video/8bc1697c1adab38228a2b414e0f6e0a8/>

Augustinović, Marija, 'Hiljade silovanih u ratu u BiH žive krijući traume' *Radio Slobodna Evropa* (online, 25 November 2021) <https://www.slobodnaevropa.org/amp/bih-zrtve-ratno-silovanje-stigma-diskriminacija/31578526.html>

Begic, Jasmin 'Bosnian Army Ex-Commander Retried in 'El Mujahideen' Fighters Case', Balkan Insight (online, 1 December 2021) <https://balkaninsight.com/2021/12/01/bosnian-army-ex-commander-retried-in-el-mujahidee>

Blagojević, Vid '60 Women Raped, Serbs Tortured in 132 Ways: 29 Years have Passed since the Persecution of the Serbian People in Posavina, 42 Camp Inmates have been Killed', Hoboctn (online, 5 August 2021) <https://www.novosti.rs/Republika-srpska/vesti/995196/silovali-60-zena-mucili-srbe-132-nacina-progona-srpskog-naroda-posavini-proslo-29-godina-ubijena-42-logorasa-foto>

Bode, Maling, et al, 'Response to the Draft of the "Global Code of Conduct for Investigating and Documenting Conflict-Related Sexual Violence"', *Response to Draft Mura Code* (Web Page, January 2021) [6] <https://responsetodraftmuradcode.wordpress.com>

Borger, Julian, 'Bosnia is in Danger of Breaking Up, Warns Top International Official', *The Guardian* (online, 2 November 2021) <https://www.theguardian.com/world/2021/nov/02/bosnia-is-in-danger-of-breaking-up-warns-eus-top-official-in-the-state>

'Bosnia and Herzegovina Must Uphold the Rights of a War Rape Survivor', *TRIAL International* (Web Page, 12 July 2017) <https://trialinternational.org/latest-post/bosnia-and-herzegovina-must-uphold-the-rights-of-a-war-rape-survivor/>

'Bosnia and Herzegovina: Submission to the United Nations Committee Against Torture', *Amnesty International* (Internet Publication, 2017) <https://tbinternet.ohchr.org/Treaties/CAT/Shared%20Documents/BIH/INT_CAT_CSS_BIH_29189_E.pdf> ('Amnesty International Submission')

'Bosnia Arrests Five More War Crimes Suspects As Sweep Continues', *RadioFreeEurope/RadioLiberty* (online, 7 December 2013) <https://www.rferl.org/a/bosnia-war-crimes-suspects-arrests/31597717.html>

'Bosnia Arrests Four Croat War Crimes Suspects', *Balkan Insight* (online, 22 April 2014) <https://balkaninsight.com/2014/04/22/bosnia-arrests-four-new-war-crimes-suspects/>

'Bosnia-Herzegovina: Rape and Sexual Abuse by Armed Forces', *Amnesty International* (Web Document, 21 January 1993) <https://www.amnesty.org/en/documents/eur63/001/1993/en/>

'Bosnia-Herzegovina: 25 Years After the End of the Conflict COVID-19 Brings Additional Uncertainty for the Families of the Missing', *International Committee of the Red Cross* (Web Page, 18 January 2021) <https://www.icrc.org/en/document/missing-persons-bosnia-herzegovina-25-years-after>

Brkanić, Džana, 'Requested Extension of Banning Measures Against Jurić', *Detektor* (online, 23 February 2015) <https://detektor.ba/2015/02/23/zatrazeno-produzenje-mjera-zabrane-Juriću/>

Centre for Gender Equality and Equality, 'Information on the Findings and Recommendations of the Study on the Position of Serbian Women Victims of the War Crime of Sexual Violence in Bosnia and Herzegovina' (Gender Centre of the Government of the Republic Serbia, March 2015) <https://www.vladars.net/sr-SP-Cyrl/Vlada/centri/gendercentarrs/Documents/Informacija%20%20latinica_204855676.pdf>

Clayfield, Matthew, 'Bosnia and Herzegovina May Never Be Clear of Landmines', *ABC News* (online, 15 October 2017) <https://www.abc.net.au/news/2017-10-15/bosnia-may-never-be-clear-of-land-mines/9029692>

'Changing the Narrative: The Role of Communications in Transitional Justice', *Institute for Integrated Transitions* (Internet Publication, 2019) <https://ifit-transitions.org/wp-content/uploads/2021/03/Changing-the-Narrative-The-Role-of-Communications-in-Transitional-Justice.pdf>

Committee of Culture and Education, *War Damage to the Cultural Heritage in Croatia and Bosnia-Herzegovina*, 8th Information Report, Doc 7341, 28 June 1995 <https://assembly.coe.int/nw/xml/XRef/X2H-XrefViewHTML.asp?FileID=6989&lang=EN>

Committee on the Elimination of Discrimination against Women, *Concluding Observations on the Combined Fourth and Fifth Periodic Reports of Bosnia and Herzegovina*, 55th sess, UN Doc CEDAW/C/BIH/CO/4–5 (30 July 2013)

Committee on the Elimination of Discrimination against Women, 'Views adopted by the Committee under article 7 (3) of the Optional Protocol, concerning communication' No. 116/2017, (26 August 2020)

Committee Against Torture, *Consideration of Reports Submitted by States Parties under Article 19 of the Convention: Concluding Observations of the Committee*

Against Torture, 45th sess, UN Doc CAT/C/BIH/CO/2–5 (20 January 2011)

Committee Against Torture, *Decision adopted by the Committee under article 22 of the Convention, concerning Communication No. 854/2017*, UN Doc CAT/C/67/D/854/2017 (22 August 2019)

'Compensation to War Crimes Victims in BIH a Matter of Willingness', *TRIAL International* (Internet Publication, 2 June 2021) <https://trialinternational.org/wp-content/uploads/2021/06/News_BiH_Compensation_20210506.pdf>

'Crimes of Sexual Violence: In Numbers', *United Nations International Criminal Tribunal for the former Yugoslavia* (Web Page, September 2016) <https://www.icty.org/en/features/crimes-sexual-violence/in-numbers>

'Da li se primjenjuje Zakon o zastititi zrtava ratne torture', *ATV BL* (online, 30 April 2019) <https://www.atvbl.rs/vijesti/Republika-srpska/da-li-se-primjenjuje-zakon-o-zastiti-zrtava-ratne-torture-30-4-2019>

Daalder, Ivo H, 'Decision to Intervene: How the War in Bosnia Ended', *Brookings.edu* (Article, 1 December 1998) <https://www.brookings.edu/articles/decision-to-intervene-how-the-war-in-bosnia-ended/>

Delauney, Guy, 'Bosnian leader stokes fears of Balkan breakup', *BBC News* (online, 3 November 2021) <https://www.bbc.com/news/world-europe-59130945>

Dizdarević, Emina 'Another Bosnian Croat Defendant in Stolac Crimes Case Dies', *Balkan Insight* (online, 16 January 2020) <https://www.balkaninsight.com/2020/01/16/another-bosnian-croat-defendant-in-stolac-crimes-case-dies/>

D M, 'Zastitta zena-zrtava ratnog nasilja' *Novosti* (online, 16 January 2013) https://www.novosti.rs/vesti/planeta.300.html:415221-РС-Заштита-жена-жртава-ратног-насиља

Dzaferagic, Nejra, and Djordje Vujatovic, 'War Criminal's Escape Outrages Bosnian Serb Victims Associations', Balkan Insight (online, 11 August 2022) https://balkaninsight.com/2022/08/11/war-criminals-escape-outrages-bosnian-serb-victims-associations/

Evason, Nina, 'Bosnian Culture', SBS (online, 2017) <https://culturalatlas.sbs.com.au/bosnian-culture/bosnian-culture-family>

Fine, Devon, and Léa Périllat, 'Podrska svjedocima tokom sudjena za ratne zlocine' *Balkan Diskurs*, <https://balkandiskurs.com/2022/06/17/podrska-svjedocima-tokom-sudjenja-za-ratne-zlocine/>

Grbavica: The Land of My Dreams (Tanja Aćimović, 2006)

Grebo, Lamija, 'Bosnian Activists Mark Wartime Detention Camp Sites', *Balkan Insight* (online, 16 March 2021) <https://balkaninsight.com/2021/03/16/bosnian-activists-mark-wartime-detention-camp-sites/>

Hemon, Aleksander, '"Bread is practically sacred": How the taste of home sustained my refugee parents', The Guardian (online, 13 June 2019) <https://www.theguardian.com/food/2019/jun/13/bread-is-practically-sacred-how-the-taste-of-home-sustained-my-refugee-parents>

Husarić, Azra, 'Bosnian War Rape Survivors "Still Afraid to Speak Out"', Balkan Insight (online, 3 March 2021) <https://balkaninsight.com/2021/03/03/bosnian-war-rape-survivors-still-afraid-to-speak-out/?lang=sr>

Husarić, Azra, 'Bosnian War Rape Survivors "Still Afraid to Speak Out"', Recom Reconciliation Network (Web Page, 5 March 2021) <https://www.recom.link/en/bosnian-war-rape-survivors-still-afraid-to-speak-out/>

'In Bosnia and Herzegovina, Stigmatization Persists for Victims Of Wartime Sexual Violence', Trial International (online, 17 April 2020) <https://trialinternational.org/latest-post/in-bosnia-and-herzegovina-stigmatization-persists-for-victims-of-wartime-sexual-violence/>

International Center for Transitional Justice, A Transitioning World (Annual Report, 2008)

International Center for Transitional Justice, 'Unfulfilled Expectations: Victims' perceptions of justice and reparations in Timor-Leste' ICTJ.org (Report, February 2010) <https://www.ictj.org/sites/default/files/ICTJ-TimorLeste-Unfulfilled-Expectations-2010-English.pdf>

International Commission on Missing Persons, Vodič Za Civilne Žrtve Rata: Kako Ostvariti Pravo Na Zaštitu Kao Civilna Žrtva Rata U Republici Srpskoj (Report, 2007) <https://www.icmp.int/wp-content/uploads/2014/08/guidebook-wictim-of-war-rs-bos.pdf>

'Istorijat', Humanitarno udruženje žena "Duga" Banjaluka (Web Page) <https://dugasuvenir.com/istorijat/>

'Jasenovac Extermination Camp, The', Holocaust Education and Archive Research Team, (Web Page, undated) <http://www.holocaustresearchproject.org/othercamps/jasenovac.html>

'Jurić: Konacana presuda 26 Septembra', Ratni Zločini Tranzicijska Pravda (online, 9 September 2016) <https://detektor.ba/2016/09/09/Jurić-konacna-presuda-26-septembra/>

Katana, Erduan, 'RS se zakonski štiti od isplata odštete logorašima', Radio Slobodna Evropa (online, 4 July 2014) <https://www.slobodnaevropa.org/amp/rs-se-zakonski-stiti-od-isplata-odstete-logorasima/25445828.html>

Kerr, Rachel, Centre for International Policy Studies, Lost in Translation: The ICTY and the Legacy of War Crimes in the Western Balkans (Policy Brief no 19, July 2012)

Kešmer, Meliha, 'U BiH 30 odsto optuzenih za zlocine nedostupo sudovima', Radio Slobodna Evropa (online, 3 June 2022) <https://www.slobodnaevropa.org/a/ratni-zlocin-bih-sud-savcic-rat-genocid/31881819.html>

Kremenovic, Mladen, 'Srbe bi da upisu kao zrtve Srpske agresije', *Politika* (online, 17 November 2022) <https://www.politika.rs/scc/clanak/525517/Republika-srpska-zrtve 17 November 2022>

Kurtic, Azem, 'Plants Found at Bosnian War Graves Exhibited in Sarajevo', *Balkan Insight* (online, 14 November 2022) <https://balkaninsight.com/2022/11/14/plants-found-at-bosnian-war-graves-exhibited-in-sarajevo/>

Liu, Jasmine, 'Partisan Cemetery in Bosnia Destroyed in "Neo-Fascist Rampage"', *Hyperallergic* (Web Page, 20 June 2022) <https://hyperallergic.com/741542/partisan-cemetery-in-bosnia-destroyed-in-neo-fascist-rampage/>

Ljevak, Kristina, 'Život u miru nakon silovanja u ratu', *Diskriminacija* (online, 24 October 2016) <https://www.diskriminacija.ba/teme/život-u-miru-nakon-silovanja-u-ratu>

'Loza Foundations Speaks Up For the Women That Survived the Rape Camps', *Loza Foundation* (Web Page, 29 October 2018) <https://lozafoundation.org/en/2018/10/29/loza-foundation-speaks-women-survived-rape-camps/>

Mackic, Erna, 'Poor Cooperation Leaves Balkan War Crime Suspects at Large', Balkan Insight (online, 1 October 2018) <https://balkaninsight.com/2018/10/01/poor-cooperation-leaves-balkan-war-crime-suspects-at-large-09-26-2018/>

Maglajlija, Vedran, 'Udruženja žrtava: Zakon o zaštiti žrtava ratne torture u RS-u diskriminatorski' *Aljazeera* (online, 29 June 2018) <https://balkans.aljazeera.net/teme/2018/6/29/udruzenja-zrtava-zakon-o-zastiti-zrtava-ratne-torture-u-rs-u-diskriminatorski>

McVeigh, Karen, 'Hague hails "tremendous start" to sexual violence scheme set up with Jolie', *The Guardian* (online, 23 November 2018) <https://www.theguardian.com/global-development/2018/nov/23/william-hague-hails-tremendous-start-sexual-violence-scheme-angelina-jolie>

Milekic, Sven, 'Croatia Plans Compensation for Wartime Sexual Violence Victims' *Balkan Insight* (online, 2 April 2015) <https://balkaninsight.com/2015/04/02/croatia-gives-reparations-for-wartime-sexual-violence-victims/>

Milojević, Milorad, 'Žrtve ratne torture traže ukidanje roka za sticanje statusa u Republici Srpskoj', *Radio Slobodna Evropa* (online, 28 October 2022) <https://www.slobodnaevropa.org/a/bih-Republika-srpska-zrtve-ratne-torture-ukidanje-roka-sticanje-statusa/32103819.html>

Milanovic, Marko, 'Understanding the ICTY's Impact in the Former Yugoslavia', *EJIL: Talk! Blog of the European Journal of International Law* 5. 11 April 2016, <https://www.ejiltalk.org/understanding-the-ictys-impact-in-the-former-yugoslavia/>

'Mirsad Repak Found Guilty of Dretelj Crimes', *Balkan Insight* (online, 11 March 2020) <https://balkaninsight.com/2010/03/11/mirsad-repak-found-guilty-of-dretelj-crimes/>

Mission to Bosnia and Herzegovina, Organization for Security and Co-operation in Europe, *Towards Justice for Survivors of Conflict-Related Sexual Violence in Bosnia and Herzegovina: Progress before Courts in BiH 2004–2016* (Report, 20 June 2017) https://www.osce.org/files/f/documents/d/1/494881_0.pdf

Mission to Bosnia and Herzegovina, Organisation for Security and Co-operation in Europe, *War Crimes Case Processing in Bosnia and Herzegovina (2004–2021)* (Report, 30 June 2022) https://www.osce.org/files/f/documents/d/1/494881_0.pdf

Mission to Bosnia and Herzegovina, Organisation for Security and Co-operation in Europe, 'Zaštita i podrška svjedoka u predmetima ratnih zločina u Bosni i Hercegovini: Prepreke i preporuke godinu dana nakon usvajanja Državne strategije za rad na predmetima ratnih zločina' (Report, January 2010) <https://www.osce.org/files/f/documents/e/4/118894.pdf>

Mitrović, Snežana, 'Zrtve ratnih mucenja u RS: logorasi tesko istvaruju svoja prava' *N1* (online, 6 November 2022) <https://ba.n1info.com/vijesti/zrtve-ratnih-mucenja-u-rs-imam-traume-i-teske-posljedice/>

'Moramo zaustaviti prenosenje traume', *Radio Slobodna Evropa* (25 September 2022) <https://www.slobodnaevropa.org/a/perspektiva-mladi-sff/32051214.html>

Moreno Guerrero, Martha, 'Women in Black, Thirty Years of Defying Serbian Nationalism', *Atalayar* (Web Page, 1 November 2021) <https://atalayar.com/en/content/women-black-thirty-years-defying-serbian-nationalism>

'Mujahideen Fighters 'Cut off' Bosnian Serb Soldiers' Heads', Balkan Insight (online, 21 April 2016) <https://balkaninsight.com/2016/04/21/bosnian-serb-soldier-recalls-mujahideen-cutting-off-heads-04-21-2016/>

'My Body, A War Zone: Breaking the silence surrounding sexual violence in conflict', *Peace Insight* (Blog post, 1 September 2015) <https://www.peaceinsight.org/en/articles/my-body-a-war-zone-breaking-the-silence-surrounding-sexual-violence-in-conflict/?location=western-balkans&theme=women-peace-security>

Office of the United Nations High Commissioner for Human Rights, *Rule-of-Law Tools for Post-Conflict States: Reparations Programmes*, UN Doc HR/PUB/08/01 (2008)

OMCT, 'Urgent Interventions: Physical assault against 9 members of the Youth Initiative for Human Rights (YIHR)', *OMCT SOS-Torture Network* (Web Page, 27 January 2017) <https://www.omct.org/en/resources/urgent-interventions/physical-assault-against-9-members-of-the-youth-initiative-for-human-rights-yihr>

Organization for Security and Co-operation in Europe, *Delivering Justice in Bosnia and Herzegovina: An Overview of War Crimes Processing from 2005 to 2010* (Report, 19 May 2011)

Organization for Security and Co-operation in Europe, '*OSCE Mission presents Judge Korner's report on war crimes processing at state level in Bosnia and Herzegovina*' (Press Release, 16 September 2020) <https://www.osce.org/mission-to-bosnia-and-herzegovina/463764>

'Orthodox Cemetery Desecrated in Bosnia and Herzegovina', *Orthodox Christianity* (Web Page, 12 July 2022) <https://orthochristian.com/147169.html>

'Perspektiva sa mladima na SFF-u: 'Moramo zaustaviti prenosenje traume'', Radio Slobodna Evropa (25 September 2022) <https://www.slobodnaevropa.org/a/perspektiva-mladi-sff/32051214.html>

Pomfret, John, 'Rivalries Stall Reconstruction of Bosnia', *Washington Post* (online, 13 October 1996) <https://www.washingtonpost.com/archive/politics/1996/10/13/rivalries-stall-reconstruction-of-bosnia/e33b7d9e-543d-4dc1-9256-ece7b88e8a4a/>

Povrženic, Ana, 'Housing reconstruction in Bosnia: field realities', *Forced Migration Review* (online, undated) <https://www.fmreview.org/sites/fmr/files/FMRdownloads/en/house/povrzenic.pdf>

'Preminula Olga Draško: Borila se za istinu o stradanju Srba, Hrvati je mučili i silovali u logoru', *Telegraf* (online, 20 September 2019) <https://www.telegraf.rs/vesti/jugosfera/3104230-preminula-olga-drasko-borila-se-za-istinu-o-stradanju-srba-hrvati-je-mucili-i-silovali-u-logoru>

Prijedor, Psiholuminis, 'Vladan Beara - Sekundarna traumatizacija i rad sa sekundarno traumatizovanim osobama – predavanje' (YouTube, 21 April 2020) <https://www.youtube.com/watch?v=R9a-IshWrH4>

'Remembering the Past: Recommendations to effectively establish the "National Reparations Programme" and "Public Memory Institute"', *Relief Web* (online, 27 February 2012) <https://reliefweb.int/report/timor-leste/remembering-past-recommendations-effectively-establish-"national-reparations>

'Remorse and Restorative Justice: Is it needed?', *Restorative Justice International* (online, 28 November 2012) <https://www.restorativejusticeinternational.com/remorse-restorative-justice-is-it-needed/>

'Rivalries Stall Reconstruction of Bosnia', *Washington Post* (online, 13 October 1996) <https://www.washingtonpost.com/archive/politics/1996/10/13/rivalries-stall-reconstruction-of-bosnia/e33b7d9e-543d-4dc1-9256-ece7b88e8a4a/>

Rovcanin, Haris, 'Absent War Crime Suspects Pose Problem for Bosnia's New Prosecutor', *Balkan Insight* (online, 5 January 2023) <https://balkaninsight.com/2023/01/05/absent-war-crime-suspects-pose-problem-for-bosnias-new-prosecutor/>

'RS: zastita zena-zrtava ratnog nasilja', *Vecernje Novosti,* (online, 16 January 2013) https://www.novosti.rs/vesti/planeta.300.html:415221-PC-Заштита-жена-жртава-ратног-насиља

Rules of Procedure and Evidence for the International Criminal Tribunal for the Former Yugoslavia, UN Doc IT/32/REV.50 (8 July 2015)

'Sakib Mahmuljin osuđen na osam godina zatvora', *Aljazeera* (online, 28 April 2022) <https://balkans.aljazeera.net/news/balkan/2022/4/28/sakib-mahmuljin-osudjen-na-osam-godina-zatvora>

Security Council, *Bosnia and Herzegovina Remains in Effect 'a Frozen Conflict' as Political Leaders Push Nationalistic Agendas, High Representative Tells Security Council* SC/14511, (4 May 2021) <https://press.un.org/en/2021/sc1 4511.doc.htm>

Security Council, SC Res 1325, UN Doc S/RES/1325 (31 October 2000)

Security Council, SC Res 2106, UN SCOR, 6984th mtg, UN Doc S/RES/2106 (24 June 2013)

Security Council, SC Res 2467, UN SCOR, 8514th mtg, UN Doc S/RES/2467 (23 April 2019)

Security Council, *Women and Peace and Security,* 7938th mtg, UN Doc S/PV.7938 (15 May 2017)

'Security Council Resolutions on Women, Peace and Security: Normative Frameworks', *Peacemaker.UN.org* (Web page, undated)

Special Rapporteur on the Promotion of Truth, Justice, Reparation and Guarantees of Non-Recurrence, '*Preliminary Observations from the Official Visit to Bosnia and Herzegovina*' OHCHR.org (Media Release, United Nations Office of the High Commissioner for Human Rights, 10 December 2021) <https://peacemaker.un.org/wps/normative-frameworks/un-security-council-resolutions>

SRNA, 'NSRS Razamtrano vise informacija', *PTPC* (online, 21 April 2015) <https://lat.rtrs.tv/vijesti/vijest.php?id=146170>

SRNA, 'Rajilic: Perfidna namjera da Srbe proglase zrtvama "Srpske agresije"', *PTPC* (online, 18 November 2022) <https://www.rtrs.tv/vijesti/vijest.php?id=493906>

Stojanovic, Milica, Haris Rovcanin and Anja Vladisavljevic, 'Cases Closed: Deaths of Ageing Balkan War Suspects Thwart Justice', *Balkan Insight* (online, 26 August 2021) <https://balkaninsight.com/2021/08/26/cases-closed-deaths-of-ageing-balkan-war-suspects-thwart-justice/>

'Strolit foundry', *onms.nenasilje.org* (Web Page, updated 4 July 2021) <https://onms.nenasilje.org/2021/strolit-foundry-Odžak/?lang=en>

'Sudije suda BiH od Tuzilastva trazile istragu zbog objave identiteta zasticenog svjedoka' *Faktor* (online, 30 Septemeber 2020) <https://faktor.ba/vijest/ko-je-podstrekivao-medije-sudije-suda-bih-trazile-istragu-zbog-objave-identi teta-zasticenog-svjedoka-/99272>

Tanjug, 'Attack on activists at the headquarters of Women in Black in Belgrade, Serbia', *War Resisters' International* (Web Page, 12 October 2010) <https://wri-irg.org/es/story/2010/attack-activists-headquarters-women-black-belgrade-serbia?language=en>;

Tausan, Marija, 'Bosnia Convicts Serb Ex-Soldier of Wartime Rape', *Balkan Insight* (online, 18 November 2022) <https://balkaninsight.com/2022/11/18/bosnia-convicts-serb-ex-soldier-of-wartime-rape-2/>

UN Security Council, *Letter dated 24 May 1994 from the Secretary-General to the President of the Security Council*, UN SCOR, UN Doc S/1994/674 (27 May 1994) [87] <https://www.icty.org/x/file/About/OTP/un_commission_of_experts_report1994_en.pdf> ('*Letter from the Secretary-General to the President of the Security Council*')

'Udruženje "Žena-žrtva rata" prijavilo tužiteljstvu i SIPA-i prijetnje žrtvama i svjedocima', Klix (online, 12 May 2008) <https://www.klix.ba/vijesti/bih/udruzenje-zena-zrtva-rata-prijavilo-tuziteljstvu-i-sipa-i-prijetnje-zrtvama-i-svjedocima/080512087>

Udružene Žene Banjaluka [United Women Banjaluka], *Primjena Zakona o Zaštiti Žrtava Ratne Torture* (Internet Publication, 2020) <http://unitedwomenbl.org/wp-content/uploads/2020/06/1.pdf>

United Nations Population Fund, *Combating Sexual Violence in Conflict: Because Everyone Counts* (Report, 17 September 2012) <https://ba.unfpa.org/en/publications/combating-sexual-violence-conflict>

'Uskoro zakon na nivou BiH koji bi regulisao pojam ratne štete?', *Nezavisne* (online, 16 November 2013) <https://www.nezavisne.com/novosti/bih/Uskoro-zakon-na-nivou-BiH-koji-bi-regulisao-pojam-ratne-stete/218419>

'Usvojen Zakon o unutrašnjem dugu Republike Srpske', *Ekapija* (online, 27 February 2014) <https://ba.ekapija.com/news/859801/usvojen-zakon-o-unutrasnjem-dugu-republike-srpske>

'Utočište u Srbiji: Objavljujemo spisak i lokacije svih osoba koje traži Sud BiH zbog ratnih zločina', Patria (online, 21 September 2021) <https://nap.ba/news/84253>

'Uzivaju u slobodi i ne kriju se: Objavljen spisak i lokacije svih osoba koje traži Sud BiH zbog ratnih zločina', *Slobodna Bosna* (online, 21 September 2021) <https://www.slobodna-bosna.ba/vijest/216537/uzivaju_u_slobodi_i_ne_kriju_se_objavljen_spisak_i_lokacije_svih_osoba_koje_trazi_sud_bih_zbog_ratnih_zlochina.html>

Velić, Emir, 'Mnogi optuženici za ratne zločine u BiH su još uvijek na slobodi', *Istinomjer* (online, 17 November 2021) <https://istinomjer.ba/mnogi-optuzenici-za-ratne-zlocine-u-bih-su-jos-uvijek-na-slobodi/>

'Victims of the Wars 1992–1995' *adpacem.org* (Web page, undated <https://adpacem.org/en/bosnia-and-herzegovina-our-support/victims-of-the-wars-1992-1995/>

Vidackovic, N, 'Žene žrtve rata: Preživjele zvjerska mučenja', *Nezavisne* (online, 10 February 2016) <https://www.nezavisne.com/zivot-stil/zivot/Prezivjele-zvjerska-mucenja/352972>

Vidojković, Dario, 'Ne dozvolimo da se ugasi "Udruženje žena žrtava rata Republike Srpske"!', *Basta Balakana* (online, 3 February 2017) <https://www.bastabalkana.com/2017/02/ne-dozvolimo-da-se-ugasi-udruzenje-zena-zrtava-rata-republike-srpske/> [tr author]

'Witness confirms rape by Ilija Jurić', *The Srpska Times* (online, 10 June 2015) <https://thesrpskatimes.com/witness-confirms-rape-by-ilija-Jurić/>

'Women's Court – Feminist Approach to Justice' in Sarajevo, 7–10 May 2015 <http://www.zenskisud.org/en/>

'Zakon o Zaštiti Žrtava Ratne Torture: U RS po osnovu Zakona pravo ostvaruje 200 žena', *Paragraph* (Web Page, 2 June 2020) <https://www.paragraf.ba/dnevne-vijesti/02072020/02072020-vijest1.html>

'Zatražene mjere zabrane za Iliju Jurića', *Klix* (online, 10 December 2014) <https://www.klix.ba/vijesti/bih/zatrazene-mjere-zabrane-za-iliju-Jurića/141210121>

'Žiković Rajilić: Stalna borba za ostvarivanje prava žena žrtava rata', *Radio Televizija Gradiška* [Radio Television Gradiška] (online, 26 February 2020) <https://www.radiogradiska.com/Živković-Rajilić-stalna-borba-za-ostvarivanje-prava-zena-zrtava-rata/>

Zorlu, Faruk, 'Over 7000 Victims of Bosnian War Still Missing', *Anadolu Agency* (Web Page, 21 July 2018) <https://www.aa.com.tr/en/europe/over-7-000-victims-of-bosnian-war-still-missing/1210377>

Zunic, Amila, 'Bosnian Wartime Jail Guard Pleads Not Guilty to Rape', *Balkan Insight* (online, 24 August 2022) <https://balkaninsight.com/2022/08/24/bosnian-wartime-jail-guard-pleads-not-guilty-to-rape/>

GPSR Compliance

The European Union's (EU) General Product Safety Regulation (GPSR) is a set of rules that requires consumer products to be safe and our obligations to ensure this.

If you have any concerns about our products, you can contact us on

ProductSafety@springernature.com

In case Publisher is established outside the EU, the EU authorized representative is:

Springer Nature Customer Service Center GmbH
Europaplatz 3
69115 Heidelberg, Germany

www.ingramcontent.com/pod-product-compliance
Lightning Source LLC
LaVergne TN
LVHW011006250326
834688LV00004B/105